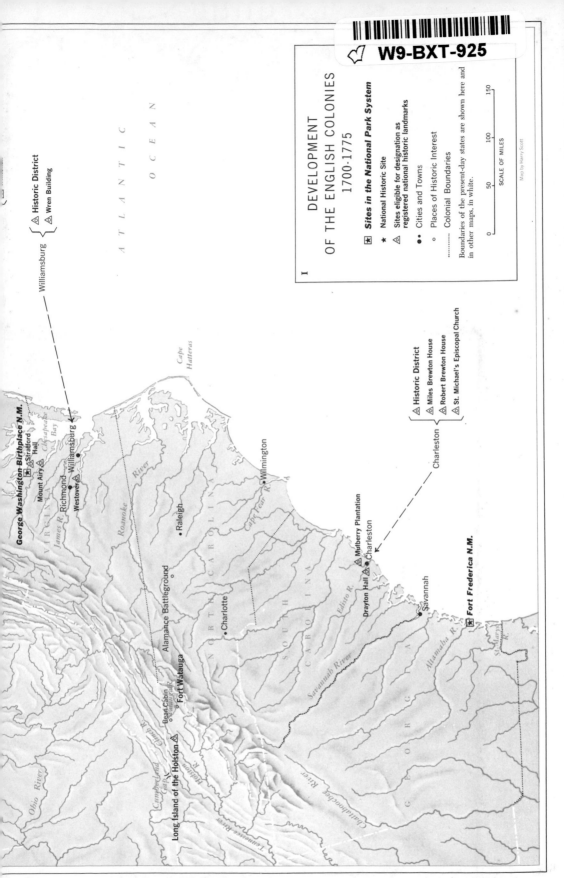

W9-BXT-925

**DEVELOPMENT
OF THE ENGLISH COLONIES
1700-1775**

Sites in the National Park System

⊞ National Historic Site

★ Sites eligible for designation as
 registered national historic landmarks

• Cities and Towns

○ Places of Historic Interest

·········· Colonial Boundaries

Boundaries of the present-day states are shown here and
in other maps, in white.

SCALE OF MILES

0   50   100   150

Map by Harry Scott

ATLANTIC

OCEAN

Williamsburg
⊿ Historic District
⊿ Wren Building

Charleston
⊿ Historic District
⊿ Miles Brewton House
⊿ Robert Brewton House
⊿ St. Michael's Episcopal Church

George Washington Birthplace N.M.
★ Stratford
Hall
Mount Airy ⊿
Chesapeake
Bay
Richmond
James R. Westover ⊿
Williamsburg •

Cape
Hatteras

Roanoke River

VIRGINIA

NORTH CAROLINA

• Raleigh

Cape Fear R.

Wilmington •

Alamance Battleground ○

• Charlotte

SOUTH
CAROLINA

Mulberry Plantation
Drayton Hall ⊿ ⊿ • Charleston

Edisto R.

Savannah River

GEORGIA

• Savannah

Altamaha R.

Fort Frederica N.M.

Savannah R.

Chattahoochee River

Ohio River

Cumberland R.

Cumberland
Gap

Holston
R.

Bean Cabin ○
Fort Watauga

Long Island of the Holston ⊿

Clinch R.

Tennessee River

COLONIALS AND PATRIOTS

COLONIALS

AND PATRIOTS

HISTORIC PLACES
COMMEMORATING OUR FOREBEARS
1700-1783

BY *Frank B. Sarles, Jr.* AND *Charles E. Shedd*

EDITED BY *John Porter Bloom* AND *Robert M. Utley*

Volume VI

THE NATIONAL SURVEY OF HISTORIC SITES AND BUILDINGS

UNITED STATES DEPARTMENT OF THE INTERIOR

NATIONAL PARK SERVICE

WASHINGTON, 1964

This publication is one of a series designed to make available to the public the studies of the National Survey of Historic Sites and Buildings. It is printed at the Government Printing Office and may be purchased from the Superintendent of Documents, Government Printing Office, Washington, D.C. 20402. Price $2.75.

LIBRARY OF CONGRESS CATALOG CARD NUMBER : 64–60050

Contents

[v

Contents

Photographs are by the National Park Service except where specified

MAPS

Foreword

The sources of history are many, involving written documents and physical remains. This volume deals with the great "outdoor archives" of American history as found in historic sites and structures. A visitor at one of these places may stop time at a great moment of history and look with increased understanding into the past. No amount of reading can ever supplant the vivid imagery and feeling of identity with the past which one contact with the site itself will evoke.

Historians and archeologists of the National Park Service, U.S. Department of the Interior, after comprehensive fieldwork, prepared the basic studies from which this volume has been drawn. The studies were reviewed by the Consulting Committee, composed of eminent historians, architects, and archeologists not otherwise connected with the Park Service, and also by the Advisory Board on National Parks, Historic Sites, Buildings, and Monuments. The findings of the National Survey of Historic Sites and Buildings, achieved through this process, are made available to the public by means of this volume.

The Survey's purpose is the evaluation of places important in U.S. history and prehistory. Some sites and buildings may be considered for addition to the National Park System. Others, also of outstanding importance, may be designated Registered National Historic Landmarks, showing that they have exceptional value for commemorating and illustrating America's heritage. The Secretary of the Interior will upon request provide engraved certificates and bronze markers for Registered National Historic Landmark properties, attesting to their value and encouraging the community and the owner to respect their integrity.

Many other places of general interest have been included in the volume, selected from the large number of sites considered by the Survey.

We believe that this book will be of widespread interest, especially to travelers, historians, students, and preservation groups. "The old order changeth, yielding place to new," but, important as this progress is, it should not result in the thoughtless destruction of sites and buildings of great historic value. We hope earnestly that this volume may focus attention on, and stimulate further activities in, the safeguarding and interpretation of an important segment of our heritage.

GEORGE B. HARTZOG, Jr.
Director
National Park Service

Introduction

The conversion of Colonials into American Patriots provides one of the most fascinating and significant chapters of the history of our Nation. The fascination derives in part from the unique circumstances which caused the Colonials to migrate to the "New World," and the forces which molded and shaped their character as a people. The significance of the story is seen in the basic ideals and aspirations of the patriots that produced the independent United States of America, and changed fundamentally the pattern of world relationships.

COLONIALS AND PATRIOTS has two parts. The first offers a brief historical background for the period 1700–83 in American history. The second represents the major contribution made in this work. It consists of classified, carefully evaluated descriptions of historic places that should be visited by one who wishes to become acquainted with American history in its "third dimension." This is the dimension of place. Essential as academic learning is, written history cannot impress upon one's mind and spirit the feeling that comes from standing in the room where a great event transpired or walking the ground where a momentous battle occurred. It has been the privilege of the historians and archeologists of the National Park Service to work primarily in this "third dimension" of history and it is their privilege to communicate their finding to the public now in this form. It will be the reader's privilege and challenge to seek out the experience and inspiration offered by this guidebook into history.

Part II of the Table of Contents gives one a quick notion of the major historic sites which pertain to 18th-century American history.

Fifteen of these areas are units of the National Park System, and represent the Federal Government's major share in the preservation of this particular segment of the national historical heritage. Four National Historic Sites in non-Federal ownership which pertain to this period are listed; and 67 places, including five historic districts, have been classified as being of exceptional value in commemorating and illustrating the history of the United States, and are therefore eligible for Registered National Historic Landmark status. These are preserved mainly by the efforts of historical and patriotic societies, State and local governmental agencies, and in some cases by private individuals. A much longer list of "Other Sites Considered," each described briefly, is included, as well as a list of "Sites Also Noted." Though not all-inclusive, this Table of Contents indicates the wide coverage provided by the Survey.

Turning the pages of descriptions, farther on, one is struck by the rich variety of experience he may capture by visiting the many places described. Units of the National Park System, for example, capture this variety in the differences between the near-tropical rural setting of Fort Frederica, Ga., and the urban surroundings of Federal Hall in New York City. Or compare Salem Maritime National Historic Site, in Massachusetts, with Kings Mountain National Military Park, in South Carolina. One of these places will remind us of the imperial rivalry which required the English Government to make large expenditures for protection against Spaniards in Florida. At the next are reflected the arduous labors in committee and Congress, in urban centers, to form "a more perfect union." In Salem we may think of the magnificent trading ships that braved the seven seas to bring wealth to resolute New Englanders, and at Kings Mountain we do homage to equally resolute southern frontiersmen who contributed a notable victory of arms to the patriot record in the struggle for independence.

Perusing the much longer lists of sites eligible to become Registered National Historic Landmarks, and other non-National Park Service sites, we find equal if not greater opportunities for drawing contrasts. Visiting the sites, one may imagine what life must have been like in a modest house on Elfreth's Alley, Philadelphia; or what suffering must have transpired in the hospital hut at Valley Forge, Pa., in the winter of 1777–78; or what experiences the students encountered in the Wren Building of William and Mary College, Williamsburg, Va.; or where the men came from whose bones were discovered still aboard the Gundelo (small sailing vessel) *Philadelphia* when it was raised from the bottom of Lake Champlain, where it had lain since the Battle of Valcour Bay.

Pursuing avenues of speculation or reverie, such as these sites may stimulate in one's imagination, it is easy to see that this book contains heady materials. Do not read it if you cannot cope with the possibility of arousing in yourself an irresistible urge to get out, to travel, to set your feet onto the ground trod by famous men of our country's earliest days—and trod also by anonymous men of humble birth who contributed their much or their little in the manner of people of all ages.

This volume represents the work of several National Park Service historians. Frank B. Sarles, Jr., and Charles E. Shedd, Jr., prepared the major portion, as Survey historians for their respective Regional Offices in Richmond and Philadelphia. They did the original work in library research and study, the preparation of the inventory, and the major part of the on-site investigation of all sites that could be reached during a limited available time. Editorial labors were shared by Historian Robert M. Utley of the Santa Fe Regional Office and Historian John Porter Bloom of the Washington Office. Dr. Bloom was responsible for the final stages of preparation of the manuscript and related work of production. The Service's Branch of Publications also gave valuable assistance.

As indicated in the acknowledgments at the back of the book, credit for collaboration on the finished product is shared widely by persons both in and out of the Service. This book and the work of the National Park Service in the general field of historic preservation have benefited inestimably from the assistance provided by the National Trust for Historic Preservation in the United States, which is a co-sponsor of the Survey.

JOHN O. LITTLETON, *Chief*
National Survey of Historic Sites and Buildings
National Park Service

Washington, D.C.

COLONIALS AND PATRIOTS

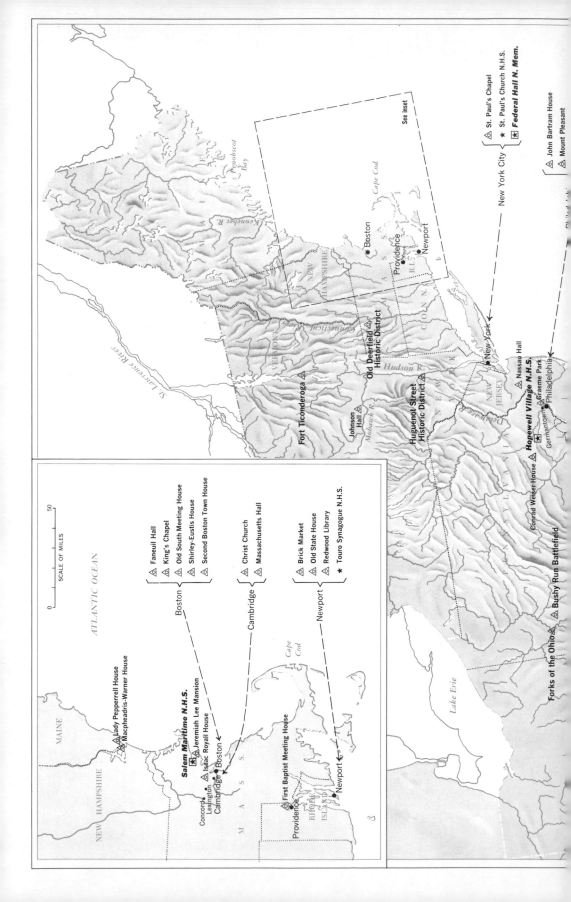

ATLANTIC OCEAN

SCALE OF MILES

0   50

MAINE

NEW HAMPSHIRE

△ Lady Pepperrell House
△ Macpheadris-Warner House

★ Salem Maritime N.H.S.

△ Jeremiah Lee Mansion
△ Isaac Royall House

MASS.

Concord
Lexington
Cambridge → Boston

Cape Cod

★ First Baptist Meeting House

Providence

RHODE ISLAND

→ Newport

Boston
{
△ Faneuil Hall
△ King's Chapel
△ Old South Meeting House
△ Shirley-Eustis House
△ Second Boston Town House
}

Cambridge
{
△ Christ Church
△ Massachusetts Hall
}

Newport
{
△ Brick Market
△ Old State House
△ Redwood Library
★ Touro Synagogue N.H.S.
}

St. Lawrence River

MAINE

Penobscot Bay

Kennebec R.

VERMONT

NEW HAMPSHIRE

Boston ●
Providence ●
R.I.
Newport ●

Cape Cod

MASS.

See Inset

△ Fort Ticonderoga

△ Old Deerfield Historic District

Connecticut R.

CONN.

Hudson R.

△ Johnson Hall

Mohawk R.

NEW YORK

△ Huguenot Street Historic District

New York ●

△ Nassau Hall

NEW JERSEY

Delaware R.

★ Hopewell Village N.H.S.
● Graeme Park
Germantown
★
Philadelphia

△ Conrad Weiser House

PENNSYLVANIA

Forks of the Ohio △

△ Bushy Run Battlefield

Lake Erie

New York City
{
△ St. Paul's Chapel
★ St. Paul's Church N.H.S.
★ Federal Hall N. Mem.
}

△ John Bartram House
△ Mount Pleasant

Philadelphia

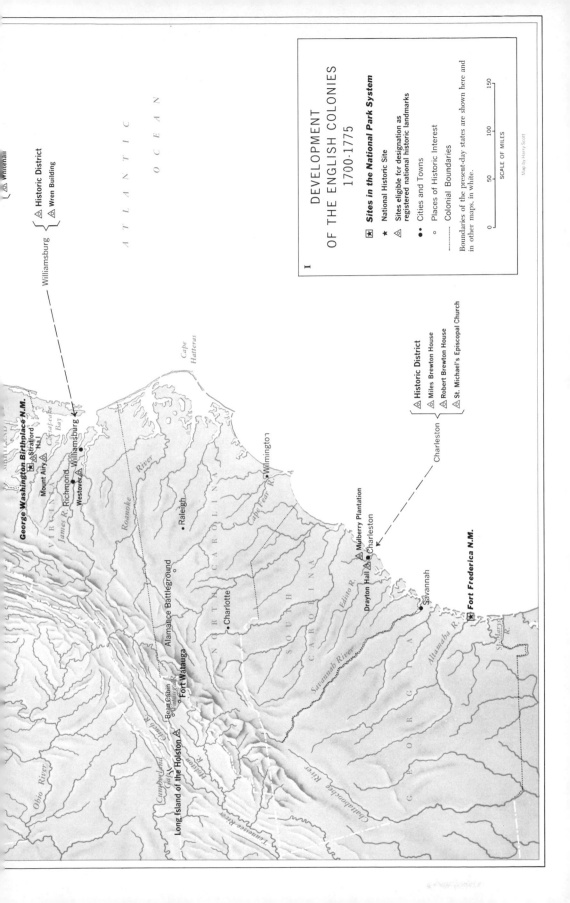

I DEVELOPMENT
OF THE ENGLISH COLONIES
1700-1775

Sites in the National Park System

★ National Historic Site

△ Sites eligible for designation as
registered national historic landmarks

● Cities and Towns

○ Places of Historic Interest

········· Colonial Boundaries

Boundaries of the present-day states are shown here and
in other maps, in white.

SCALE OF MILES

0   50   100   150

Map by Harry Scott

ATLANTIC

OCEAN

Williamsburg { △ Historic District
△ Wren Building

△ Whitehall

George Washington Birthplace N.M.
△ Stratford
Hall

Mount Airy △

Chesapeake Bay

VIRGINIA

James R. Richmond ●
Westover △ Williamsburg ●

Cape
Hatteras

Roanoke River

● Raleigh

NORTH CAROLINA

● Charlotte

Alamance Battleground ○

Cape Fear R.

Wilmington ●

Long Island of the Holston △

Fort Watauga ●
Bean Cabin

Clinch R.

Cumberland Gap

Ohio River

Holston R.

Tennessee River

Charleston { △ Historic District
△ Miles Brewton House
◇ Robert Brewton House
△ St. Michael's Episcopal Church

Mulberry Plantation △

Drayton Hall △ ● Charleston

SOUTH CAROLINA

Edisto R.

Savannah River

GEORGIA

Savannah ●

Altamaha R.

Fort Frederica N.M. ★

Chattahoochee River

Satilla R.

PART I

Colonials and Patriots:

The Historical Background

T HE YEARS SKETCHED out here, 1700–1783, were very momentous ones in the history of our land. From shaky beginnings, and often through great travail, the English Colonies on the mainland of North America had for the most part passed through their infancy by 1700. Some were still quite young, and the 13th colony had not yet been established, but the point of no return had long since been passed for many Englishmen-turned-Americans. Long before 1775 the colonials had drifted away from dependence upon the mother country. Along with independent thought came independent actions, which in time produced political maturity. The English colonials became American patriots, and a new nation emerged. The transition was not sudden, as it is sometimes represented. Max Savelle observed that the War for Independence was "not so much for independence, as for the recognition of a maturity and a *de facto* nationhood that already existed." [1]

Population Growth and Territorial Expansion

Although firmly established by 1700, the Colonies exhibited few portents of the phenomenal growth that lay ahead. Fewer than 300,000 colonists occupied the scattered settlements along the Atlantic coast.

In the middle and southern Colonies, where the coastal plain extended far inland, settlement had just begun to spill beyond the fall line (head of navigation by seagoing vessels) toward the foothills of the Appa-

Ten to twelve soldiers were billeted in huts like this, when Washington's army spent the winter of 1779–80 in Jockey Hollow, near Morristown, N.J. This log hut, chinked with clay and held together by nails and wooden pegs, was reconstructed on the site of one of the original structures at Morristown National Historical Park.

lachians. Seventy-five years later, 2½ million Americans blanketed the eastern seaboard and, here and there, had pushed even beyond the mountain barrier.

A high birth rate explained part of the population increase, for strong sons and healthy daughters were an obvious answer to the problem of the scanty labor supply. Vastly more important was a flood of immigration, part voluntary and part involuntary, that attained its greatest volume after the Peace of Utrecht in 1713. Rhineland Germans, Scotch-Irish, French Huguenots, Swiss, Irish, Scots, and Spanish and Portuguese Jews—all sought new lives in a new world.

The French Huguenots achieved disproportionate importance among the newcomers, even though few in number, because of their comparatively high level of culture and wealth. Essentially urban dwellers, they were attracted to the more thickly settled areas. Almost every colonial city had its Huguenot contingent, but the real stronghold of the Huguenots was Charleston, S.C. By the middle of the 18th century, French influence had stamped itself upon the dress, manners, and architecture of Charleston.

The Germans settled largely in the middle and southern Colonies, and were far more numerous. Attempts were made to guide some of them into industry, but the vast majority preferred to push on to the frontier and become small farmers. Large numbers moved to the Pennsylvania frontier, where they acted as a valuable buffer for the older Colonies to the east. "It has been said that Quaker blood was never shed by the North American Indian," remarked a noted historian; "to this the historians of the German migration reply that the Indians sheathed their knives in the bodies of the German frontiersmen." [2]

Charleston, S.C.: Aerial view of the historic district, looking north from The Battery. St. Michael's Episcopal Church is visible in the right background. Courtesy, Ronald Reilly Photo Shop.

The Scotch-Irish were the most aggressive of the frontiersmen.   They, too, found their way to the back country of the middle and southern Colonies, chiefly Pennsylvania.   Famed as Indian fighters, they helped to protect the older Colonies and, at the same time, because of their fiery temperament and frontiersman's contempt for authority, they made infinite trouble for the governments nearer the coast.

Of the other immigrant groups, the Swiss settled mainly in the Carolinas; the Irish Catholics in Maryland and Pennsylvania; the Scots in Virginia, South Carolina, and Massachusetts; and the Jews in such metropolitan centers as Charleston, Philadelphia, New York, and Newport, R.I.[3]

Elfreth's Alley, a few blocks from Independence Hall, preserves today much of the genuine atmosphere of the Philadelphia of Benjamin Franklin's time. Courtesy, Philadelphia Historical Commission.

These people came of their own free will, but the largest non-English element in the Colonies came involuntarily. By 1775, perhaps a fifth of the colonial population consisted of Negro slaves. The spread of the plantation system in the southern Colonies created a demand for slave labor, and by the close of the colonial period approximately six out of seven slaves resided south of the Mason-Dixon line. Slaves made up 40 percent of the population in Virginia, 60 percent in South Carolina.

Cities and towns reflected the population boom. In 1700, Boston was the colonial metropolis with 7,000 people, and only Philadelphia came close, with 5,000. By 1775, however, Philadelphia's population had risen to 34,000, making her the largest city, and 11 other cities had passed the 5,000 mark. During the same period, colonial towns increased in number by 3½. But the urban centers could accommodate only a fraction of the mushrooming population. The rest turned to the west and pushed beyond the 17-century colonial borders.

In 1700, settlements dotted the seaboard from Penobscot Bay, in present Maine, southward to the Edisto River in South Carolina. They were not continuous, and only in the valley of the Hudson River had they penetrated inland more than 100 miles. Seventy years later, however, settlement had spread down the coast another 150 miles, to the St. Marys River, and inland 200 miles and more, to the crest of the Appalachians. At intervals the restless frontier had swept beyond the Appalachian crest: in the south, to the headwaters of the Clinch and Holston (see pp. 166–168, 228, 229); in the north, up the eastern shore of Lake Champlain and west along the Mohawk Valley, with the lonely outpost of Fort Ontario, on Lake Ontario (see pp. 212–213); in the center—most significantly—past the former French post of Fort Duquesne (see pp. 145–148), and thence 150 miles down the Ohio River.

The westward movement flowed continuously but not evenly. Before 1754 it was slowed by the hostility of Indian tribes angered by the English invasion and incited by French and Spanish agents. In western Pennsylvania, where Indian resistance was weaker than elsewhere, settlement had crossed the mountains before the outbreak of the French and Indian War. But during the next 9 years the frontier line receded to the east side of the Appalachians, and in 1763, with French power crushed, England sought to reserve the trans-Appalachian country to the Indians. The colonists were not to be stopped. Before the outbreak of the Revolution they were firmly established in the upper Ohio Valley.

689–192 O–64—3

A National Park Service archeologist works with potsherds excavated in the course of the continuing effort to illuminate all aspects of the early history of both Europeans and Indians in North America.

Economic Development

The expansiveness that marked all phases of colonial development characterized the colonial economy of the 18th century. Established production, with the added stimulus of a rapidly growing population, made for a generally healthy economy. The expanding frontier brought opportunities for profitable speculation in western lands, which were of particular importance to the "debtor" Colonies. These Colonies were underdeveloped and dependent upon investment and speculation from abroad, which had an inflationary effect that encouraged rapid economic development.

On the other hand, mercantilist dogma ruled the minds of 18th-century economists, and the mother country assigned the Colonies such passive roles as supplying raw materials and providing markets for English manufactures. Mercantilism actively discouraged the growth of American industries, except extractive industries. Economic depend-

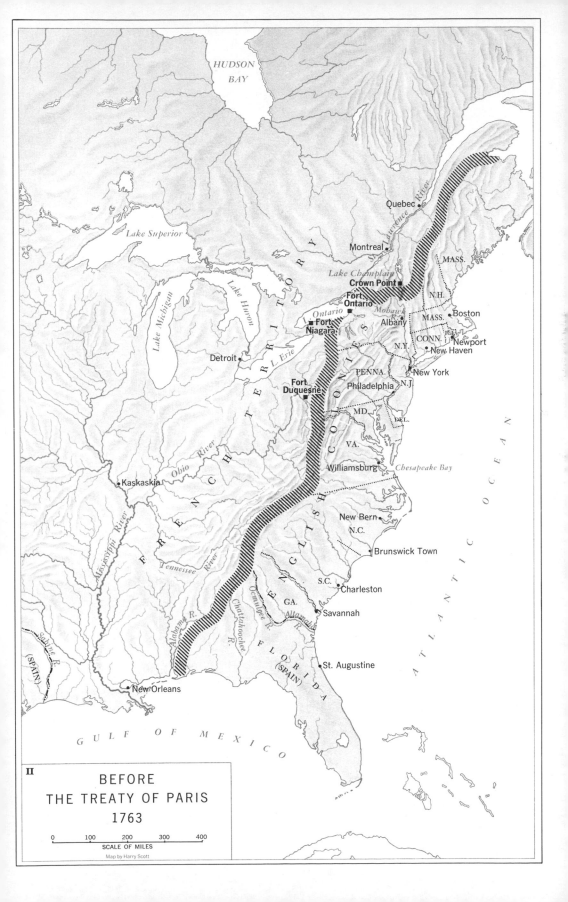

HUDSON
BAY

Lake Superior

Lake Michigan

Lake Huron

Quebec

Montreal

Lake Champlain

Crown Point

**Fort
Ontario**

Ontario

**Fort
Niagara**

L. Erie

Mohawk R.

Albany

MASS.

N.H.

MASS.

CONN.

R.I.

Boston

Newport

New Haven

N.Y.

Detroit

**Fort
Duquesne**

PENNA.

Philadelphia

N.J.

New York

Ohio River

MD.

DEL.

Mississippi River

Kaskaskia

Tennessee River

VA.

Williamsburg

Chesapeake Bay

New Bern

N.C.

Brunswick Town

S.C.

Charleston

GA.

Ocmulgee R.

Altamaha R.

Savannah

Alabama R.

Chattahoochee R.

FLORIDA
(SPAIN)

St. Augustine

Sabine R.
(SPAIN)

New Orleans

GULF   OF   MEXICO

F R E N C H   T E R R I T O R Y

E N G L I S H   C O L O N I E S

A T L A N T I C   O C E A N

St. Lawrence River

II

BEFORE
THE TREATY OF PARIS
1763

0   100   200   300   400
SCALE OF MILES

Map by Harry Scott

ence upon England produced a chronically unfavorable balance of trade
that kept the Colonies drained of hard money. Expedients to relieve
this condition, such as land banks and paper money, roused the British
Parliament to enact prohibitions. The colonists ultimately found relief
in building a favorable balance of trade with the West Indies, and
Spanish coins softened the monetary impact of English mercantilism.

With land cheap and plentiful, agriculture dominated the colonial
economy. The various crops supplied local needs and provided also an
exportable surplus of foodstuffs, indigo, and tobacco. Commerce
ranked next in the colonial economy. Overseas and coastal shipping,
fur trade, and land speculation made prominent contributions to economic welfare. And finally, despite the role assigned to colonies under
mercantilist doctrine, manufacturing secured a foothold during the 18th
century. Among the more important industries were fishing, lumbering,
manufacture of naval stores, shipbuilding, and the mining and the
limited manufacture of iron. (See Hopewell Village National Historic
Site, pp. 66–68.)

Economic differentiation among the Colonies, already clearly evident
by 1700, grew much more pronounced during the 18th century. Each
geographical grouping developed its own set of specialties.

New England made its living from the sea, as illustrated by Salem
Maritime National Historic Site (pp. 57–58). Fishing had been of
major importance from the beginning, but shipping soon surpassed it.
By the middle of the 18th century, New England vessels covered the
globe. The "triangular trade" evolved between New England, Africa,
and the West Indies. Rum made in New England was carried to Africa
and exchanged for slaves, who were taken to the West Indies and traded
for molasses, which in turn was taken home and converted into rum.
New England ships also conducted a brisk trade in agricultural products
with the West Indies and southern Europe, as well as a coastal commerce
among the Colonies. England tried vainly by legislation to channel all
colonial trade through her own ports, but throughout the 18th century
the continental Colonies could not be restrained effectively from trading
in any world market that would admit them. New England industry
logically served the maritime interests, with ships, lumber products, iron,
and rum comprising the leading items of manufacture. Preoccupied
with commerce and industry, hampered by poor soil and climate, New
Englanders came to rely on agriculture very little on the whole. (See
Old Deerfield Village, pp. 177–180.)

The middle Colonies were aptly styled the "food" or "bread" Colonies. They exported large amounts of grain and livestock and smaller quantities of foodstuffs, furs, and other products. Their agricultural units tended to be much larger than those in New England because their economy was based on surplus production. The surplus went to the other continental colonies, to the West Indies, and to southern Europe.

Maryland, geographically associated with the plantation Colonies to the south, grew more and more diversified as small farmers moved into the "back country" west of Baltimore. By midcentury, though still ranking as a debtor colony, Maryland supplemented tobacco exports with small quantities of foodstuffs.

Virginia depended on a single crop, tobacco, and in the 18th century the plight of the tobacco planter steadily worsened. The plantation, though it was a large agricultural unit, was still not self-sufficient. The planter depended upon exporting tobacco to obtain virtually all necessities of life, and the declining tobacco market threw him deeper into debt. But for the presence of vast tracts of western land suitable for large-scale speculation, many tobacco planters would have faced ruin. One among many existing illustrations of Virginia plantation life may be seen at George Washington Birthplace National Monument, pp. 72–73.

Ladies posing in colonial costumes, in front of "Wakefield," George Washington Birthplace National Monument, Va.

Unlike Virginia, North Carolina relied on several crops. Naval stores provided the economic base but tobacco and, in the back country, cattle and other foodstuffs also ranked as significant.   North Carolina remained a debtor colony throughout the colonial period, nevertheless.

South Carolina enjoyed a thriving prosperity, in conspicuous contrast to the other southern Colonies.   Based at first on a lucrative fur trade, profits were bolstered soon by the cultivation of rice and indigo.   By midcentury, rice had become the staple and a source of wealth to a small group of planters.   The typical rice plantation was considerably smaller than the Virginia tobacco plantation.   Back-country South Carolinians found cattle raising the most profitable occupation and produced a surplus for export.

The fur trade, particularly important in South Carolina, Pennsylvania, and New York, was an economic factor in almost every colony at one time or another.   It was significant politically as well as economically.   It was the fur traders, to cite one example, who brought back the first information about the Ohio Valley, and the fur traders together with the land speculators played a large part in bringing on the French and Indian War.

In all of the Colonies land speculation was a continuing phenomenon, and the fever reached its height in the last three decades before the Revolution.   Attention centered on the Ohio River Valley, principally because of the pressure of population in Pennsylvania and the Valley of Virginia.   After the Peace of Paris in 1763, English capitalists became deeply interested in the financial possibilities.   Their attempts to participate helped to build up resentment in influential colonial circles.

Contrasting sharply with the generally healthy condition of the continental Colonies, the "sugar island" colonies of the British West Indies suffered real ills.   Shackled by a one-crop economy, the island planters had to import even the smallest necessities.   The collapse of their American and European markets in the face of French competition forced them into fatal dependence upon the English home market.   In the West Indies the economic trend strengthened the economic rule of the mother country.   In the continental Colonies, on the other hand, the direction of growth weakened the economic rule of Great Britain and at the same time kindled colonial resentment of attempts to enforce the rule.

While the continental Colonies diverged economically from England and from their sister colonies in the Caribbean, they underwent a significant internal economic schism.   The conditions of frontier life created a new society, sharply differentiated from that of the seaboard. The frontier people, although of mixed racial origins, were drawn together by common economic interests. As small hunters and farmers, their standard of living remained chronically depressed compared to that of the "East." They formed a debtor class, deeply suspicious of the eastern merchants they owed and increasingly bitter over their own political impotence. As a class, these people were either indifferent or hostile to Europe and things European, but these feelings ran a poor second in intensity of their feelings against their seaboard compatriots.

Common to all Colonies, this sectional cleavage was most pronounced in the Carolinas where it expressed itself in the "Regulator" movement of the 1760's. The dramatic climax came near the Alamance River in western North Carolina. In a pitched battle on May 16, 1771, the North Carolina Regulators were defeated and dispersed (see p. 217). The Regulator movement coincided with the first rumblings of the American Revolution, and has been misinterpreted often as a manifestation of colonial resentment toward the mother country. In fact, it was caused chiefly by frontier resentment toward the ruling economic classes of the seaboard.

Society and Culture

The colonists brought with them to the New World the rigid caste attitudes of Europe, and colonial society divided itself into distinct stratifications. The aristocrats—wealthy planters and merchants, clergymen, and top public officials—tended to erect social barriers that insulated them from the artisans, farmers, and tradesmen of the middle class, and from the laborers of the lower class.   Still, the manifold economic opportunities of America prevented the barriers from rising as high as in Europe. These obstacles were often scaled by the talented and ambitious, and became less intimidating as the intellectual climate grew less congenial to the alien system.

Even for the great majority who had to be content with their assigned class, life was far less onerous than in the Old World. Because of plentiful land and scarce labor, the dissatisfied worker had only to move on, to find other opportunities. All that he needed was willingness to work. As a result, the lower classes enjoyed a personal freedom rarely found in Europe.

The 18th-century colonists found progressively more time for leisure pursuits, although they were usually preoccupied mainly with making a living—except, perhaps, some of the aristocracy. The sternness of religious belief that characterized the 17th century broke down to a significant degree following the "Great Awakening" in the 1740's. Colonial minds, freed of overpowering religious concern, turned increasingly to politics, art, and literature. Although cultural manifestations were almost exclusively European imports, the very awakening of interest in such matters revealed a broadening intellectual horizon.

The spread of both local and intercolonial road networks, supplementing water transportation, promoted travel and thereby the exchange of ideas. Improved transportation also made possible an improved postal system, and in 1710 Parliament passed an act to establish a "General Post Office for all Her Majesty's Dominions," replacing the functions and broadening the scope of the individual colonial post offices of the 17th century. This system in turn made possible the dissemination of printed materials. Beginning with John Campbell's Boston News Letter, which in 1704 launched colonial journalism, newspapers proliferated in the towns and cities of America.

The new intellectual preoccupation produced better educational opportunities, which reacted to deepen still more the intellectual interests. In many parts of New England, and to some extent in the middle Colonies also, an elementary education could be had at public expense. In the plantation colonies of the South, however, private tutors continued to furnish almost all early schooling. The colonies' two collegiate institutions of 1700, Harvard and William and Mary, had by 1775 increased to nine with the addition of Yale, Princeton, the University of Pennsylvania, Columbia, Brown, Rutgers, and Dartmouth. (See pp. 103–104, 175–176.)

Massachusetts Hall, built in 1718–20, is the oldest surviving building of Harvard University, the first institution for higher learning in the Colonies.

This distinguished architectural specimen, the Wren Building at Williamsburg, Va., was built between 1695 and 1702, after a design by Sir Christopher Wren. It was the original academic building of the College of William and Mary.

The cultural growth of the 18th century played its part in binding together the Colonies and instilling in the colonists a sense of common interest and purpose that, combined with strengthening economic and political bonds, had propelled the American Colonies to the brink of nationhood by 1775.

Architecture

Almost coincidental with the opening of the 18th century, Renaissance architecture finally reached the American Colonies. This "severely formal" adaptation of the classic Roman orders and design, born in Italy in the 15th century, first appeared in England around 1570 and reached its mature phase there 50 years later. The timelag of 130 years before it spread to the Colonies is a measure of the economic and social gap between the mother country and her offspring.

Colonial Renaissance architecture, influenced directly by that of the late Stuart period in England, became known as Georgian after the advent of the Hanoverian dynasty. Its general features included a balanced design; the use of classic orders to embellish doorways and entrance facades; predominantly brick construction, laid in Flemish bond (although the wood-building tradition was so strong in New England that many of the finer Georgian mansions there were clapboarded); low-pitched roofs, frequently hipped; sheathed and highly finished interiors; and such treatment of the entrance hall as to make it a room of major importance.   After midcentury the Late Georgian style evolved, with such features as the projecting central pavilion, giant pilasters at the corners, small entrance portico, larger windowpanes, roofs pitched progressively lower, balustraded roof decks, and dado interior decoration with wallpaper above paneling.

Although adapted from English antecedents, "Georgian architecture in America was singularly free from either the practice or the doctrine of exact imitation."   Professional and amateur American architects, and the humbler carpenter-builders who augmented the work of the few architects, all felt free to disregard their handbooks on occasion, "in accordance with necessity, invention, or taste." [4]   Many illustrations and descriptions of their work are found in part II of this book.

Only a score of professional and amateur American architects are known by name for their work during this period.   Among the professionals were James Porteus, of Philadelphia; John James of Boston; Peter Harrison, of Rhode Island; John Hawks, of North Carolina; Thomas McBean, of New York; William Buckland, of Virginia and

William Buckland designed the Hammond-Harwood house at Annapolis, Md., shortly before his death in 1774.

Maryland; and John Ariss, who appears to have confined himself entirely to Virginia. Notable in the category of architect-builders (where Buckland may also be placed), was James Wren, another Virginian practitioner. In recent years the name of Joseph Horatio Anderson has emerged as a designer with his own corps of craftsmen. He is believed to have been a Philadelphian, though his known work is located in Annapolis and vicinity. Among amateur architects the roster at Philadelphia is an imposing one: Drs. John Kearsley and William Shippen, Andrew Hamilton, Samuel Rhoads, Samuel Blodget, and Robert Smith. Noted amateur architects elsewhere were Richard Munday, of Newport, R.I.; Joseph Brown and Caleb Ormsbee, of Providence; Henry Caner, of New Haven, Conn.; Gov. Francis Bernard, of Massachusetts; Richard Taliaferro, of Williamsburg, Va.; and the painters, John Smibert and John Trumbull. To George Washington and Thomas Jefferson, architecture was an avocation and a gentlemanly pursuit. Both Mount Vernon and Monticello evolved under the watchful eyes of their masters, following a number of remodelings and continuing refinements.

In Charleston, S.C., the typical 18th-century dwelling was Georgian, but with a certain southern flavor. A disastrous fire in 1740 caused

Robert Brewton House, built about 1730 by Miles Brewton for his son. It is the earliest accurately dated example of the Charleston "single house."

the assembly to specify nonflammable future construction. Charleston became a city of brick houses, faced with tinted stucco and covered with red tile roofs, unlike any other colonial metropolis. Many were "double houses" of typical Georgian design; others were of that peculiarly Charleston type called the "single house," standing "with its shoulder to the street," only one room in width and having a long piazza on one side.

Not all 18th-century American architecture was Georgian, by any means. The cultural lag between England and the Colonies had its parallel within the Colonies. A progression from the seaboard to the frontier, or from top to bottom of the economic scale, would bring to view more humble dwellings—less durable, smaller, and of more antique design. Of these the best known was the log cabin, apparently introduced in New Sweden in the mid-17th century, but reaching its present familiar role of a frontier home a century later through its popularity among the Scotch-Irish frontiersmen.

Expansion and Conflict

The population growth and territorial expansion of the English colonies produced collisions. The French, the Spanish, and the Indians all contested English pretensions in the 18th century.

The French proved most formidable. Numerically inferior to the English and scattered in tiny islands throughout the wilderness, they nevertheless possessed important advantages. They had an authoritarian rather than a representative government. While the English depended mainly on poorly trained militia led by inexperienced officers, the French fielded disciplined regulars commanded by the best officers of France. While the colonial legislatures haggled and denied money and troops, the French could manipulate efficiently their money, men, and supplies. And whereas the Colonies treated individually with the Indians, and for the most part tactlessly, the French executed a uniform Indian policy with some skill.

The earliest clash of the 18th centry was Queen Anne's War, which broke out in 1702. In this New World counterpart of the War of the Spanish Succession, the French and Spanish joined in an 11-year struggle with the English. On the southern borders of the English Colonies, South Carolinians in 1702 destroyed the Spanish town of St. Augustine and in 1704 wrecked the Spanish mission system in western

Florida.   Two years later they repulsed a joint French-Spanish attack on Charleston.   On the northern borders, a series of barbarous French attacks on New England settlements, notably on Deerfield, Mass., in 1704 (see p. 178), led ultimately to a series of retaliatory expeditions against Port Royal, which was captured in 1710.   The war finally ended with the signing of the Treaty of Utrecht in 1713.

The older section of the Frary House, in the foreground, is the major surviving landmark of 17th-century Deerfield.

The Treaty of Utrecht was designed to insure peace through the maintenance of a balance of power, but it soon became evident that a piece of paper could not restrain the English colonists.   In 1716, Virginia's bold Lieutenant Governor, Alexander Spotswood, dramatized the possibilities of westward expansion by leading the "Knights of the Golden Horseshoe" across the Blue Ridge.   Ten years later, New Yorkers ignored French claims and planted Fort Oswego on the shores of Lake Ontario. (See pp. 212–213.) To the south, on lands claimed by Spain, James Oglethorpe founded a new English colony in 1733.

To Oglethorpe and his associates, Georgia was a humanitarian project designed to provide new lives for English debtors. To the English Government, it was a military outpost from which attacks could be

Rusted old artillery pieces and sturdy tabby walls of the King's Magazine are among the striking remains of Fort Frederica, Ga. The fort was established in 1736 by James Oglethorpe.

launched against Spanish Florida. To the Carolinians, even though they lost valuable western lands as a result, it was a welcome buffer against the Indian attacks from which they periodically suffered. Almost immediately, the Georgians and the Spanish Floridians began trying by force of arms to dislodge each other. Neither succeeded. In the last of a series of expeditions against St. Augustine, in 1739–40,

Georgians came within sight of their goal but failed to reach it. Span-iards fared no better. After an unsuccessful attempt to take the Geor-gia outpost of Fort Frederica in 1742 (see pp. 54–55), they gave up the effort to expel the intruders.

Relations with the French along the western and northern frontiers of the English Colonies, if less bloody, were equally explosive. France claimed everything west of the Appalachians by right of a tenuous oc-cupancy of the Mississippi Valley, a claim that England, because of the interests of her fur traders and land speculators, refused to acknowledge. England finally moved in 1754 to strengthen the Colonies for the ap-proaching conflict. Two imperial Indian agents were appointed to co-ordinate and improve Indian policy. (See sites associated with Sir William Johnson and John Stuart, pp. 128–130, 212, 213, 224.) An overall commander, Maj. Gen. Edward Braddock, took charge of the American military forces and, to counteract the advantage of the profes-sional French Army, British regulars began to arrive in America.

The French and Indian War broke out early in 1754 when the French seized and fortified the forks of the Ohio River. (See pp. 145–148.) Lt. Col. George Washington marched west with a force of Virginia militia to

The Forks of the Ohio, where the Allegheny and Monongahela Rivers meet, was a Gateway to the West held successively by France, Britain, and the United States. The sites of French Fort Duquesne and British Fort Pitt are preserved in Point State Park, at the apex of modern Pittsburgh's "Golden Triangle." Courtesy, Samuel A. Musgrave.

Fort Ticonderoga, on Lake Champlain, was the key post on the traditional path of invasion between Canada and the Hudson Valley, both in the French and Indian War and in the War for Independence.   Courtesy, Fort Ticonderoga Association.

contest the action but was besieged in Fort Necessity, southeast of the forks of the Ohio, and compelled to surrender.   (See pp. 65–66.)   The following summer, General Braddock's expedition against the French stronghold ended even more disastrously when the French and their Indian allies ambushed his command and all but annihilated it.

For 3 years the English tried in vain to drive back the French.   Then William Pitt rose to power in England in 1757.   He named young and vigorous men to commands in America, and the tide turned.   In rapid succession the French strongholds fell to the English armies: Louisbourg, Fort Duquesne, Fort Frontenac, Fort Niagara, Fort Ticonderoga, Crown Point, Quebec, and finally Montreal itself.   With the surrender of Montreal on September 8, 1760, the French gave up their claims to Canada and all its dependencies in North America.   The war flared again, briefly, in 1761 when Spain came to the aid of France.   The British, however, effortlessly seized Cuba and other Spanish possessions, and France and Spain had no choice but to sue for peace.

The Treaty of Paris, signed in 1763, ended the French and Indian War (in Europe, the Seven Years' War).   Besides losing Canada, France surrendered the eastern half of the Mississippi Valley to England.   For the return of Cuba, Spain had to relinquish Florida. To compensate her ally, France gave to Spain western Louisiana and the city of New Orleans. England thus emerged as the possessor of all North America east of the Mississippi River, and in the long run her mainland colonies profited very signally. No longer menaced by the French, they were free to expand westward in comparative security. They had gained from the war valuable military experience and a new sense of solidarity. Their ties with the mother country were weakened still further.

America Crosses the Mountains

The year 1763 found the western line of settlement stretching along the eastern base of the Appalachian barrier. Anglo-American frontiersmen had already penetrated the mountains beyond this line, exploring the interior rivers and trading for furs. This irregular penetration showed the way for the gathering flood of settlers who would soon pour through the mountains.

The fur interests vigorously opposed the overrunning of western preserves by settlers, who would inevitably drive away the Indian market. Balancing this influence, the land companies pressed to open new territories in the West. These and other interests were diligently at work while dogged pioneer farmers, who wanted only to find good land and build their homes, prepared to cross the mountains and claim the interior. The westward movement gathered momentum amid the clamor of land speculators and traders, presenting England with the bald fact that, no matter what the pressure groups wanted, or her own self-interest required, settlers were going to cross the mountains. The best that could be hoped for was the enactment of measures that would postpone western settlement until a policy could be formulated that would satisfy the vested interests and lessen the mounting threat of full-scale war with the Indians.[5]

The solution of the London policymakers was the Proclamation of 1763, which established the Appalachian highlands as the temporary boundary of settlement on the western border of the Atlantic colonies. At the same time, the proclamation established the Province of Quebec northwest of the Ohio River; East and West Florida; and the vast region north of the Floridas, west of the Appalachians, and south of the Ohio River as a reservation for the Indians, with land purchases from them forbidden. The Proclamation of 1763 and subsequent efforts in the same direction were, for the most part, hardly more than gestures.

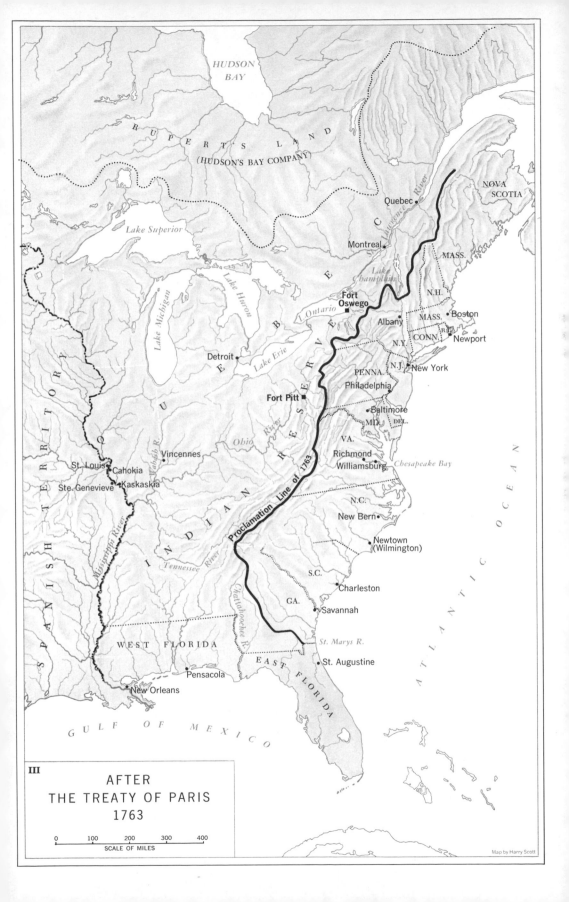

HUDSON
BAY

R U P E R T ' S   L A N D
(HUDSON'S BAY COMPANY)

Lake Superior

NOVA
SCOTIA

Quebec

Laurence River

Montreal

MASS.

Lake Champlain

C

N.H.

**Fort
Oswego**

Lake Michigan

Lake Huron

L. Ontario

Albany

MASS.   Boston

Detroit

Lake Erie

N.Y.   CONN.   R.I.
Newport

E

B

U

Q

N.J.   New York

PENNA.

Philadelphia

Fort Pitt

Wabash R.

Vincennes

Ohio River

Baltimore

MD.   DEL.

St. Louis   Cahokia

Ste. Genevieve   Kaskaskia

I N D I A N   R E S E R V E

VA.

Richmond
Williamsburg   *Chesapeake Bay*

Tennessee River

Proclamation Line of 1763

N.C.

New Bern

Newtown
(Wilmington)

S P A N I S H   T E R R I T O R Y

Mississippi River

S.C.

GA.

Charleston

Savannah

Chattahoochee R.

WEST   FLORIDA

St. Marys R.

EAST   FLORIDA

St. Augustine

Pensacola

New Orleans

A T L A N T I C   O C E A N

G U L F   O F   M E X I C O

III   AFTER
THE TREATY OF PARIS
1763

0   100   200   300   400
SCALE OF MILES

Map by Harry Scott

Events had passed beyond the control of the British authorities, who but dimly understood the forces at work in the Colonies.

Decrees from faraway London, intended to control the westward movement, could neither deal effectively with the surge of immigrants nor prevent conflict with the Indians. Indian fear and resentment expressed

The site of the "flourbag fort," Bushy Run Battlefield State Park. Courtesy, Pennsylvania Historical and Museum Commission, Harrisburg.

itself almost immediately in the bloody Pontiac uprising of 1763–64. For a time the frontier faced disaster, but the superior resources of the settlers ultimately prevailed, notably at the Battle of Bushy Run. (See pp. 140–141.)

The tide of pioneers flowed through the mountain passes. Trading posts sprang up on the Ohio below Fort Pitt, and the first settlement in the present State of Ohio was made at Schoenbrunn in 1772. (See p. 220.) In New York the thin line of settlement that pointed west along the Mohawk spread north up the Hudson Valley, and south toward the Delaware. German and Scotch-Irish immigrants filled the fertile valleys of western Pennsylvania, and rude cabins dotted western Maryland and northwestern Virginia.   Since the 1730's, indeed, settlers from Pennsylvania had streamed south and west to Springdale (see pp. 235–236) and other places in the Shenandoah Valley of Virginia.   This valley, in turn, offered a natural highway to the Carolina Piedmont, and from the farms

This marker stands at the traditional site of Fort Watauga, Tenn.

and settlements of the Piedmont and Southern Highlands colonists drifted into eastern Tennessee, along the Watauga River (see the Bean Cabin and Fort Watauga sites, pp. 228, 229), and through Cumberland Gap into Kentucky.

War with Indian and European rivals, treaties with these nations, land speculation, and the ceaseless coming and going of the hunters and fur traders—all these helped to plant the new frontier beyond the Appalachians. But the real strength of the westward advance lay in the sustained movement of thousands of settlers who left the safety of the Colonies on the Atlantic, or came directly from Europe, to wrest a new life from the wilderness across the mountains. In the 18th century the pattern of the frontier movement emerged. One day it would carry the Nation to the Pacific.

Mounting Political Tension

While wars with Indian and European enemies occupied the 18th-century English colonists, another conflict gained momentum, less spectacular but far more significant for the future. As the Colonies approached maturity, they increasingly resented efforts by the mother country in the direction of strict rule. The mother country responded to this resentment by trying to tighten the controls further. The result was growing friction that brought about an open rupture in 1775.

The friction expressed itself principally in a struggle between colonial Governors and colonial assemblies. Most of the Colonies had either a royal or a proprietary form of government. In the royal Colonies the Governors received their appointments from the Crown and answered directly to the Crown. In the proprietary Colonies they were appointed by and answered to the grantees or proprietors, who were usually favorites of the Crown. In both forms the Governors in theory ruled independently of the people and their elected representatives, the provincial assemblies. But in practice, the assemblies had a powerful weapon with which to contest the authority of the Governors—control of the purse. Because of the nearly constant need of the Governors for defense money, the legislative bodies were able to use their control of internal finances to assert progressively more authority.

By 1763 most of the colonial assemblies had, through this means, extended their powers to include freedom of debate, the right to judge the qualifications of their own members, regularly scheduled meetings, the right to fix their date of adjournment, and the exclusion of Crown-appointed officers from deliberations. Some had further gained the right to appoint provincial treasurers, customs and tax collectors, Indian commissioners, provincial military officers, and agents to represent them in London, as well as the right to authorize military expeditions and the construction of forts.

Reenactment of a meeting of the Virginia House of Burgesses, in their reconstructed hall, Capitol building, Williamsburg. At the far end of the room is the original Speaker's chair, used here in the 18th century. The Speaker occupied this chair and attempted to stop Patrick Henry during his famed "Caesar-Brutus" speech. Courtesy, Colonial Williamsburg.

Despite this legislative ascendancy, however, the fundamental question at issue remained unanswered, the relationship of the colonial constitutions to the imperial constitution. Colonial political thought, strongly influenced by John Locke, had evolved two ideas foreign to the British political system—a growing belief in written constitutions and a belief in direct representation on a territorial basis. Colonial legislators rejected the Crown's contention that the instructions issued to royal Governors automatically became part of the colonial constitutions. Denying the theory of "virtual representation" (that is, that all members of Parliament represented all British subjects, not merely the constituencies that elected them), the legislators maintained that none but themselves could properly legislate the internal affairs of the Colonies.

The home government struck back, on occasion. In 1749, for example, the Crown disallowed 10 laws passed by the Virginia House of Burgesses simply because they omitted the usual provision that the laws were not to take effect until approved by the Crown. Patrick Henry challenged the right of the Crown to disallow any Virginia law approved by the Governor, in 1763 in the famous "Parson's Cause," a years-long dispute over ecclesiastical salaries.   He argued that such action violated the British Constitution and the fundamental rights of British subjects.

The accent on self-government stimulated thinking on civil liberty and personal freedom.   The trial of John Peter Zenger in New York in 1735 was a notable expression of this trend.   Two important precedents were set by the Zenger case: first, that in a jury trial for libel the jury rather than the judge must decide on libelous matter; second, that a true statement cannot be libelous.   (See Federal Hall, p. 60.)

The widening gulf between England and her American Colonies inevitably influenced the complexion of political parties in the Colonies. There were not only well-defined "court" and "colony" parties, but also "gentlemen's" and "country" parties.   The conservative gentlemen's party, zealously guarding its power, stood for such things as a stabilized currency and political encouragement to land speculation.   The liberal country party, on the other hand, stood for unlimited paper money, free land, and adequate frontier defense.   This division, which identified conservatives with loyalists, had much to do with making the approaching break with England not only an imperial civil war but also a revolution.

Increasingly aware of problems with the mother country that were common to them all, many colonials also came to see that the whole range of issues could be handled best through concerted action by the Colonies.   Among them were relations with the Indians, control of the fur trade, and defense against foreign foes.   Seven Colonies went so far as to send representatives to Albany to devise a plan of union when war threatened in 1754.   Though rejected by the colonial assemblies, the Albany Congress was an important recognition of the need for solidarity and also a portent of things to come.

England adopted a series of measures in the decade following 1763 that dramatized the drift of colonial thinking away from the established concepts of imperial relationships and impelled the Colonies down the road to revolution.   After conclusion of the Treaty of Paris, the British Government found itself with the dual problems of recouping its strained finances and governing effectively its vastly expanded North American empire.   Since much of the cash outlay had been for colonial defense, imperial administrators considered it simple justice for the Colonies to make up a share of the deficit.   But the methods adopted to collect the money, coming at a time when the Colonies had achieved political and economic maturity and when their major foreign foe had been routed, had an effect completely unanticipated by the home government.

Parliament stirred up the Colonies between 1763 and 1765 by enacting one law after another that Americans regarded as oppressive.   Led

The home of John Dickinson, "Penman of the Revolution," was first built in 1740 by Dickinson's father.   Destroyed by fire in 1804, the house was rebuilt under Dickinson's supervision.

off by the Proclamation of 1763, which tried to halt the westward movement, the series reached its climax with the Stamp Act of 1765, which sought to tax every business transaction in the Colonies.   Patrick Henry rose to castigate Parliament, and his "Virginia Resolves," characterized by the Governor of Massachusetts as the "alarm Bell to the disaffected," echoed throughout the Colonies.   Nine Colonies sent representatives to New York in October 1765, where they placed themselves on record in opposition to the doctrine of "virtual representation."   The Stamp Act, a dead letter from the start, was repealed soon.

The furor had scarcely subsided, however, when it was revived by the Townshend Acts of 1767, aimed at tightening the system of collecting import duties in the Colonies.   Popular opposition broke out with renewed vigor, manifested boldly at Boston's Old South Meeting House (see pp. 105–107) and elsewhere.   British troops were sent to Boston, and the Massachusetts Assembly was dissolved for circulating a letter inviting the other Colonies to resist.   Virginia again led the opposition with

George Mason's "Virginia Resolves of 1769." John Dickinson, of Pennsylvania, the most outspoken critic of the Townshend Acts, circulated the widely read "Letters of a Pennsylvania Farmer," which argued that Parliament had no right to tax imperial commerce. Colonial merchants united to carry out nonimportation agreements, the most effective of all protest measures.

Although the Townshend duties were repealed in 1770, the fundamental issue remained. The breakdown of nonimportation that followed repeal brought 3 years of relative prosperity, but it marked the beginning of an even wider cleavage between "moderates" and "radicals." The first group was dismayed by the excesses of the other, while the latter was infuriated by the "desertion" of the merchants. Only the greatest necessity could drive them into alliance again. Parliament obliged by providing the necessity.

The Outbreak of War

The alliance of moderates and radicals formed again following passage of the Tea Act of 1773. This measure gave the East India Company a virtual monopoly of the colonial tea market. Even so, it probably would have aroused little antagonism had not the Company chosen as its agents the unpopular merchants who had earlier opposed the nonimportation agreements. At the "Boston Tea Party" on December 16, 1773, angry colonists retaliated by dumping shiploads of tea into Boston Harbor. Parliament's answer was to pass the "Intolerable" or "Coercive" Acts in April 1774. This body of legislation provided, among other things, for closing the port of Boston until the British East India Company was reimbursed for the tea destroyed. The other Colonies sprang to the aid of Massachusetts—with food and supplies for Boston, with heated words and fiery pamphlets, and with a call for a general meeting of representatives from all Colonies.

The meeting convened at Philadelphia on September 5, 1774. This First Continental Congress consisted of 55 delegates from 12 Colonies, Georgia alone being unrepresented. Before adjourning on October 26, the Congress adopted a Declaration of Rights and an intercolonial nonimportation agreement called "The Association," which also provided for the appointment of local committees to watch for acts of disloyalty to the colonial cause. A moderate plan of colonial union, offered by Joseph Galloway, of Pennsylvania, narrowly failed of adoption.

The actions of the First Continental Congress aroused much resentment in England, and the English people rallied to the support of Lord North's government. On March 20, 1775, Parliament passed the New England Restraining Act, which prohibited the New England Colonies from doing business outside the British Empire. The act was applied subsequently to all except four of the continental Colonies. By the end of 1774, however, the American situation seemed to be beyond restoration through either coercion or conciliation. Committees of Safety enforced effectively the provisions of The Association. Ten of the Colonies organized extralegal provincial congresses. Local groups began to accumulate stores of arms and ammunition. It was such arms and ammunition that finally, the following spring, converted the political struggle into a military struggle.

War began on April 19, 1775, when Gen. Thomas Gage's British regulars marched from Boston to seize American munitions reportedly stored at Concord. Alerted by swift-riding Paul Revere and others, the Massachusetts "Minutemen" turned out on Lexington Green (see pp. 91–92, 102–103, 104–105) to contest the advance. The professionals easily dispersed this "rabble" and continued to Concord. But they found, upon their return, that they had tipped the hornet's nest. (See pp. 55–57, 112–113.) When the weary British regulars stumbled into the

Here, on Lexington Green on the morning of April 19, 1775, were fired the first shots in the struggle for American independence. The boulder at the right marks the approximate location of one end of the line of Minute Men drawn up to face the approaching British. Courtesy, Boston National Historic Sites Commission.

The Bunker Hill Monument and surrounding 4-acre park denote the approximate center of the redoubt defended by American forces in the first full-scale action of the Revolutionary War, after the opening of hostilities at Lexington and Concord. Courtesy, Massachusetts Department of Commerce.

defenses of Boston at last, after a nightmarish retreat along miles of stone walls manned by the farmer militia, they were part of an army besieged.

The American position was strengthened early in May, when New England forces under Ethan Allen seized the British posts of Fort Ticonderoga and Crown Point, on Lake Champlain. (See pp. 127–128, 211–212.) Strategically important, the forts also supplied artillery and military material needed in the siege of Boston.

As more and more colonial troops arrived in the vicinity of Boston, the British garrison's position became steadily more precarious. In mid-June 1775, however, the Americans crowded the enemy too closely by entrenching Breed's Hill in Charlestown, overlooking Boston from the north. Disdainfully, Gen. Sir William Howe's British regulars attacked the American position frontally on June 17. Twice the British ranks were shattered by close-range fire. But, as American powder ran low, a third British attack carried the position at bayonet point, and the misnamed "Battle of Bunker Hill" was over. (See p. 93.)

George Washington arrived 2 weeks later to take command of the army around Boston. For the next 8 years he was to bear the hopes of America on his shoulders. From this army—for the most part raw

Independence Hall, Philadelphia.

militia, insufficiently supplied, indifferently officered, and enlisted for only short periods—he was to mold a fighting force that would win independence for the American Colonies.

A New Government

When the Second Continental Congress met in Philadelphia on May 10, 1775, war had begun. The delegates recognized this fact by formal declaration and went on to create a Continental Army, naming one of their own number as commander, George Washington. The Congress also issued a "Declaration of the Causes of Taking up Arms" on July 6, 1775, but moved for a final attempt at reconciliation in the "Olive Branch Petition." This document, asking the Crown to protect American rights from Parliamentary tyranny, was spurned by George III.

As 1775 passed, American sentiment gradually drifted away from

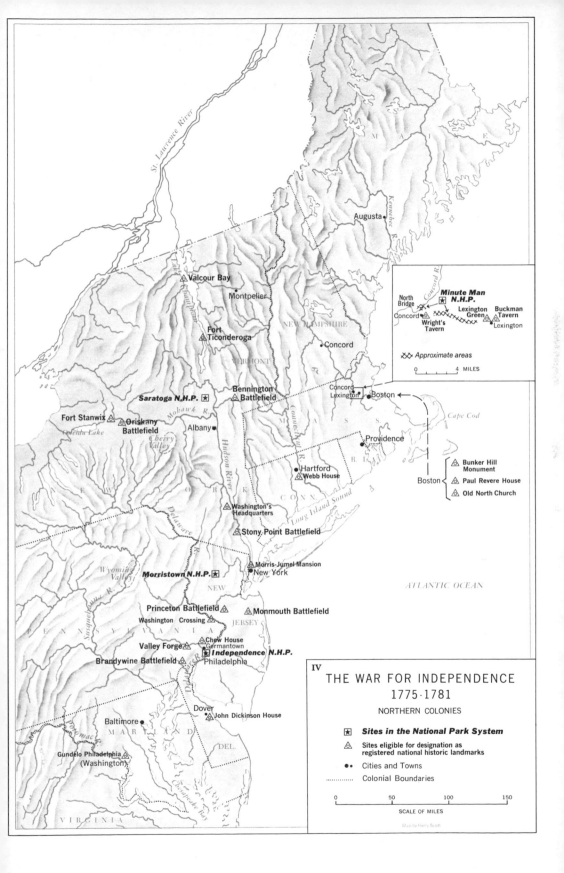

Augusta

Valcour Bay

Montpelier

Fort Ticonderoga

NEW HAMPSHIRE

VERMONT

Concord

Minute Man N.H.P.

North Bridge

Concord

Wright's Tavern

Lexington Green

Buckman Tavern

Lexington

⚔ Approximate areas

0   4 MILES

Saratoga N.H.P. ★

Bennington Battlefield

Concord
Lexington

Boston

Cape Cod

Fort Stanwix

Oriskany Battlefield

Cherry Valley

Albany

Providence

Bunker Hill Monument

Hartford
Webb House

Boston ⟨ Paul Revere House

Old North Church

CONN.

Long Island Sound

Washington's Headquarters

Stony Point Battlefield

ATLANTIC OCEAN

Morris-Jumel Mansion
New York

Wyoming Valley

Morristown N.H.P. ★

NEW

Princeton Battlefield
Washington Crossing

Monmouth Battlefield

JERSEY

PENNSYLVANIA

Chew House
Germantown

Valley Forge

★ Independence N.H.P.
Philadelphia

Brandywine Battlefield

Dover

John Dickinson House

Baltimore

MARYLAND

DEL.

Gundelo Philadelphia
(Washington)

VIRGINIA

IV
THE WAR FOR INDEPENDENCE
1775·1781
NORTHERN COLONIES

★   **Sites in the National Park System**

⚠   Sites eligible for designation as registered national historic landmarks

●•   Cities and Towns

··········   Colonial Boundaries

0   50   100   150

SCALE OF MILES

Map by Harry Scott

the original desire for a guarantee of rights within the British Empire. The King announced plans on October 26 to hire foreign mercenaries to subdue the colonists. In January 1776 Thomas Paine published "Common Sense," which sounded the call for a complete and final break with England. The tide soon ran strongly for independence, which was adopted on July 4, 1776.

With the Declaration of Independence, the Colonies faced the necessity of establishing a formal union to carry on the war. Although a committee to consider the problem was appointed in June 1776, Congress did not approve a draft of the Articles of Confederation and send it to the States for ratification until November 15, 1777. Most States acquiesced within a few months, but the required unanimous approval was lacking until March 1, 1781, when Maryland ratified.

With the beginning of the movement toward independence in late

A view of the room in Independence Hall where the Declaration of Independence was signed. The original silver inkstand used by the signers is visible on the table beneath the painting of George Washington.

1775, the Continental Congress appointed a secret committee to establish relations with foreign governments. Arthur Lee, Massachusetts colonial agent in London, was assigned to the task. He soon won the support of Caron de Beaumarchais, popular French playwright and secret agent of France.

Congress sent Silas Deane to France in 1776, and he helped obtain secret aid in the form of arms and supplies. During the summer of 1776 Deane was joined by Lee and Benjamin Franklin. The trio were charged with securing French recognition of the United States and, if possible, military assistance. Partly because of the diplomatic skill of Deane and his colleagues, and partly because of the course of military events in America in 1777, the diplomats attained both objectives in treaties signed on February 6, 1778. Efforts to win overt Spanish support failed, although Spain gave clandestine aid and entered the war against England as an ally of France in 1779.

Naval Operations

In addition to money and supplies, which more than once saved the American cause from disaster, the most conspicuous French contribution to American independence was at sea. Adm. Francois de Grasse, sealing off the mouth of Chesapeake Bay with his French Fleet in the fall of 1781, made possible the decisive American victory at Yorktown which marked the end of major operations. (See p. 73.)

Although the Continental Congress established an American Navy and a Marine Corps in the fall of 1775, the initiative at sea remained in the hands of the powerful British Navy until Yorktown. Most of the memorable exploits of the U.S. Navy took the form of small, individual engagements. Strangely enough, the most significant American naval "victory" of the war was fought on an inland lake by a force of soldiers under command of a brigadier general, and resulted in the loss of the American fleet (Valcour Bay, pp. 135–136).

Among the notable exploits on salt water were the spectacular raid on the Irish Channel coast of England by Capt. Lambert Wickes' three small ships in May 1777 and John Paul Jones' celebrated cruise around Great Britain in the late summer of 1779. The climax to Jones' exploit was the successful engagement of his flagship, the *Bonhomme Richard,* with the English *Serapis* on September 23, when he is reported to have said the immortal words, "I have not yet begun to fight."

This narrow bay between Valcour Island (in the distance) and the west shore of Lake Champlain was the scene of an 8-hour battle between Benedict Arnold's 15 hastily built vessels and a British fleet of 29 craft. Arnold lost his fleet, but won precious time for the American cause in the autumn of 1776. Courtesy, New York State Education Department.

Land Operations

The land war went well in the first year. George Washington built up his army in the Boston siege lines during the winter of 1775–76, and by spring had sealed off the British defenders so effectively that their position clearly became untenable. On March 17, 1776, General Howe's army sailed away to Nova Scotia, leaving Boston and 250 cannon in the hands of the Revolutionary Army.

Meanwhile, an ambitious campaign had been launched against Canada. Gen. Richard Montgomery was to advance up Lake Champlain toward Montreal while Gen. Benedict Arnold marched up the Kennebec River in Maine and down the Chaudiere to Quebec. It was a desperate gamble, but Canada was lightly garrisoned and the Americans hoped that France would come to their aid. Although Montgomery's army suffered from hunger, fatigue, and sickness, it moved swiftly and captured Montreal in mid-November 1775. Arnold also reached his objective. His decimated army arrived at Quebec after an epic march through the Maine wilderness, but was too weak to take the city alone. (See p. 200.) Montgomery joined Arnold, and the combined forces attacked Quebec on December 31, 1775. The assault failed after Montgomery was slain and Arnold badly wounded. The American Army held on until the following spring; in June 1776 Arnold's successor, Gen. John Sullivan, fell back to Lake Champlain.

The English had not been idle. Early in 1776 Gen. Sir Henry Clinton led an expedition down the Atlantic coast to cooperate with the strong Tory factions in the Southern States. The command got off to a late start and, by the time Clinton reached an appointed rendezvous, Tory forces in Virginia and North Carolina had been defeated and dispersed. He then decided to capture Charleston, S.C., for use as a base of operations. A 4-week siege, beginning on June 1, was beaten off by the determined resistance of Col. William Moultrie's small force on Sullivan's Island.

After the evacuation of Boston, British and American eyes turned to New York, strategically situated between New England and the Middle and Southern States. Washington moved his army to the vicinity of New York City in April and May 1776, posting part on Long Island and the rest on Manhattan Island. General Howe's British Army arrived in August and disembarked on Long Island. Attacking on August 27, the British outflanked Washington's forward line and drove the defenders back to fortifications on Brooklyn Heights. There Howe commenced siege operations. But Washington, appreciating his danger, skillfully evacuated Long Island on the foggy night of August 29–30.

Howe landed on Manhattan on September 15, forcing Washington to evacuate New York City. The Americans won a small but encouraging victory at Harlem Heights during the withdrawal. (See pp. 130–131.) Howe's command of the numerous waterways gave him an enormous advantage over Washington. In mid-October the British crossed to the mainland in Washington's left rear and forced him back to White Plains. After a sharp and skillfully fought action there on October 28, he withdrew again.

The American situation now deteriorated rapidly. Washington had left part of his force to hold Forts Washington and Lee, on opposite sides of the Hudson at the upper end of Manhattan Island, and now he left part to hold the highlands of the Hudson while he led the remainder across the river into New Jersey. Moving quickly to attack

Morris-Jumel Mansion. General Washington made his headquarters from mid-September to mid-October 1776 in this handsome home built by Roger Morris in 1765. Morris was a loyalist and had left the country at the outbreak of war. The house was later the property of Stephen Jumel. Courtesy, New York City Department of Parks.

the forts, Howe captured Fort Washington with its entire garrison on November 16, and 3 days later forced Gen. Nathanael Greene to evacuate Fort Lee. His army disintegrating, Washington began a rapid retreat across New Jersey. The British advance under Gen. Lord Charles Cornwallis followed closely. Washington's difficulties were compounded by the inexplicable refusal of Gen. Charles Lee, despite repeated orders, to join him with a major portion of the American Army. In early December, Washington crossed the Delaware River into Pennsylvania with the remnants of his army. Howe left garrisons at Princeton, Trenton, Bordentown, New Brunswick, and Perth Amboy, and withdrew the rest of his force to winter quarters at New York City. Another British detachment was sent to capture Newport, R.I., where it remained in garrison.

While Washington had been suffering these setbacks, affairs on Lake Champlain had taken a turn for the better. Gen. Horatio Gates, who was ordered on June 17 to take command of the American forces that had retreated from Canada, withdrew the force from Crown Point to Fort Ticonderoga. Learning that Gen. Sir Guy Carleton, British commander in Canada, was assembling a fleet for a drive up Lake Champlain, Gates ordered Arnold to build an American fleet. Arnold fell to work with furious energy, and his small "navy," manned by landsmen, fearlessly engaged Carleton's advance at Valcour Bay on October 11, 1776. In 2 days of fighting he lost most of the vessels, but the delay convinced Carleton that he could do nothing decisive before the onset of winter. (See pp. 135–136.) Early in November the British retired to the north end of Lake Champlain.

Meanwhile, Washington planned to inflict a stunning surprise on the British. He understood that, if he hoped to recruit his army for another year of service, he must win a victory. On Christmas night of 1776, he crossed the Delaware River and struck the Hessian outpost at Trenton, N.J. The surprised garrison quickly surrendered, and Washington recrossed the river with prisoners and materiel. (See pp. 121–123.)

Although the terms of enlistment of his army expired with the old year, Washington persuaded most of the men to serve for 6 weeks longer. He again entered New Jersey on the night of December 30–31, 1776, with them and reinforcements of militia. A British force under Lord Cornwallis confronted Washington, and the American position seemed hopeless. But by a swift march Washington eluded Cornwallis and

A Pennsylvania State Park preserves the site where Washington embarked his troops for the crossing of the Delaware on Christmas night, 1776. The brilliant raid on Trenton heartened the American cause at a critical period in the struggle for independence.

The Gilpin House, used by Lafayette as headquarters at the time of the Battle of Brandywine, has been restored and preserved in Brandywine Battlefield State Park, overlooking Chadd's Ford, Pa.

struck the British supply base at Princeton on January 3, 1777. (See pp. 119–121.) Driving the British out, he moved his army northeast to Morristown. The British evacuated New Jersey, and the front quieted down for several months.

With the opening of active operations in the spring of 1777, the War for Independence reached a crisis in the North. Strong British forces poised at opposite ends of the Hudson River-Lake Champlain line, and a coordinated advance by both almost inevitably would have produced a British victory of major proportions. Fortunately for the Americans, divided British command resulted in the defeat of one of the armies while the other stood idly by.

Faced with the double mission of guarding the capital at Philadelphia and preventing a move by Howe up the Hudson River, Washington spent most of the spring and summer of 1777 marching and counter-marching through New Jersey. In mid-August Howe decided on an offensive against the American Capital. He loaded his army on transports at New York and sailed south. After a long and circuitous voyage, he disembarked at the head of Chesapeake Bay. Washington moved his army to Brandywine Creek, southwest of Philadelphia, and there engaged the British advance on September 11. The Americans were outflanked and forced to withdraw (see pp. 139–140), and the British entered Philadelphia on September 26.

Washington launched an attack on the main British outpost at Germantown on October 4.   After a promising start, the American assault was blunted and the attackers driven from the field.   Howe was now

A view of part of the encampment area at Valley Forge State Park, used by the Continental Army in the winter and spring of 1777–78.

able to turn his attention to the American forts along the Delaware below Philadelphia, which were evacuated soon afterward.   Washington put his army in winter quarters at Valley Forge, 20 miles northwest of Philadelphia.

Meanwhile, expecting a simultaneous advance up the Hudson by Howe, Gen. John Burgoyne's British Army had started south from Canada in June 1777.   Another British force, under Gen. Barry St. Leger, was to advance eastward along the Mohawk Valley from Fort Oswego. St. Leger reached Fort Stanwix early in August, laid siege to the post, and shortly afterward ambushed a militia relief force at Oriskany. (See pp. 131–132.) Two weeks later, however, General Arnold arrived with another relief column and compelled St. Leger to lift the siege and retire.

Burgoyne reached Fort Ticonderoga on June 27 and speedily forced Gen. Arthur St. Clair's American garrison to evacuate.   Pursuing the retreating Americans southward, however, the British left the easier water route and began a difficult march overland.   Burgoyne's advance was opposed by a weak American force under Gen. Philip Schuyler, who hampered the British as best he could by felling trees and destroying bridges.   Weak as he was, Schuyler was farsighted enough to send Arnold with the relief expedition that saved Fort Stanwix from St. Leger.

The savage conduct of Burgoyne's Indian allies aroused the New York and New England militia, a circumstance that led to the first major defeat suffered by the invading force.   A Hessian foraging party, numbering about a tenth of Burgoyne's army, was nearly wiped out by militiamen from Bennington, Vt., on August 16, 1777.   (See pp. 124–125.)

Maj. Gen. John Stark, commander of a brigade of New Hampshire militia, was the victor at Bennington.   He had served in the French and Indian Wars and at the Battle of Bunker Hill, and participated in the defeat of Burgoyne at Saratoga.   U.S. Army photo.

By September, Burgoyne had learned that Howe was not coming to join him, but he decided nevertheless not to withdraw to Canada. He crossed the Hudson at Saratoga on September 13 and attacked the Americans, now under General Gates, 6 days later. Unable to break through, Burgoyne remained inactive for 3 weeks, having received word that reinforcements under Clinton were advancing north from New York City. Clinton successfully captured two forts below West Point, but failed to follow up his success. Burgoyne, his position growing daily more desperate, made another unsuccessful attack on October 7. Surrounded at Saratoga, he surrendered his army to Gates 10 days later. This victory at Saratoga, which encouraged the French alliance and boosted patriot hopes tremendously, is generally regarded as the turning point of the War for Independence. (See pp. 62–63, 211).

Washington's army suffered bitter hardships at Valley Forge during the winter of 1777–78. (See pp. 153–154.) The country was far from destitute, but the supply services were inefficiently managed. Short of food, clothing, and supplies of all kinds, officers and men lived the best they could in hope that spring would bring a lessening of their trials. Two events of 1778 augured well for the future. One was the French alliance. The other was a reorganization of the army command that brought the appointments of Nathanael Greene as quartermaster general, of Jeremiah Wadsworth as commissary general, and of a new arrival, "Baron" Frederick von Steuben, as drillmaster. During the last months of the winter encampment at Valley Forge, Steuben's tactical instruction and a vast improvement in supply transformed the Continental Army into a formidable fighting force.

France's entry into the war convinced the British Government that Philadelphia could not be held. On June 18, Clinton, who had replaced Howe in the British command, began an overland retreat to New York. Washington immediately pursued and, on June 27, 1778, caught the British at Monmouth Courthouse. A smashing Continental victory was prevented by the misconduct of General Lee, who was subsequently court-martialed and suspended from command. Nevertheless, the Americans held their position against heavy counterattacks, and after dark the British retreated. (See pp. 115–117.)

In furtherance of the alliance, a French fleet with 4,000 regular troops reached America on July 8. Washington planned a joint attack on New York City, but the French ships were unable to cross the sandbar blocking the entrance to New York harbor. The American commander then persuaded the French to support an attack on the British garrison at Newport, R.I.   An American Army under John Sullivan successfully landed on the island, but a gale scattered the French Fleet, which then sailed away and left Sullivan to extricate his men as best he could.   The American Army was saved, but the affair severely strained relations between the allies.

This fine old colonial mansion at Morristown, N.J., built just a few years earlier by Col. Jacob Ford, Jr., was Gen. George Washington's headquarters during the winter of 1779–80, while the Continental Army was encamped nearby in Jockey Hollow. Mrs. Washington, Alexander Hamilton, and other members of the staff resided here.

The war in the North settled into a stalemate after the abortive attack on Newport.   The British held New York City and Newport, while Washington's army held a semicircular line around those cities.   In the late spring of 1779, however, General Clinton sallied from the New York defenses to seize unfinished American works at Stony Point and Verplanck's Point, on opposite sides of the Hudson River below West Point. On the night of July 15, Gen. Anthony Wayne recaptured Stony Point in a daring attack at bayonet point.   The Americans were unable to hold the position, but after its abandonment it was not reoccupied in strength by the British.   (See pp. 133–135.)   Washington's command remained near Morristown, N.J., in the following winter.   (See pp. 58–59.)   One further serious threat to Washington's position came in September 1780 with Benedict Arnold's treasonable plan to surrender West Point to the British. The plot was discovered and Arnold was forced to flee for his life.

Failure of the British to win a decision in the North caused them to turn their attention to the South, which had enjoyed 2 years of comparative calm. In the fall of 1778 the situation changed. Savannah fell to a British Army under Gen. Archibald Campbell in December, and the British quickly overran the interior of Georgia, occupying Augusta the following month. The invaders abandoned Augusta in February 1779, however, after a body of South Carolina Tories en route to reinforce them was crushed by American militia at Kettle Creek.

General Benjamin Lincoln was assigned to command American forces in South Carolina, but despite his vigilance the British, now under Gen. George Prevost, temporarily besieged Charleston in May. In the autumn of 1779, the arrival of a French Fleet under Adm. Count D'Estaing gave the Americans a temporary superiority of numbers, and General Lincoln attempted to recapture Savannah. After a 4-week siege, the combined French-American army assaulted the city on October 9. The attack was repulsed with heavy losses, including the brilliant Polish cavalryman, Casimir Pulaski. D'Estaing sailed away to the West Indies, and the Americans once more were on the defensive.

General Clinton sailed from New York early in 1780 with an expedition to capture Charleston. The British Army, outnumbering Lincoln more than 2 to 1, began siege operations on March 29. The American commander unwisely allowed himself to be bottled up in the city and on May 12 surrendered his army. This disaster left only one other organized American force in South Carolina—a small band of militia under Col. Abraham Buford. It was surprised and wiped out by Lt. Col. Banastre Tarleton's British cavalry at Waxhaws on May 29. The British conquest of the South was nearly complete.

When Charleston fell, a small force of Delaware and Maryland Continentals under Baron Johann Kalb had reached Virginia en route to reinforce Lincoln. Kalb advanced into North Carolina, where on July 25 General Gates appeared to take command. Gates almost immediately marched for the British base at Camden, S.C. Lord Cornwallis, commanding in South Carolina after Clinton's return to New York, reinforced Camden and took personal charge. The two armies met a few miles north of the town on August 16. The American Army was quickly routed and driven from the State in disorder. (See pp. 160–161.) The collapse of organized American resistance brought a period of bitter

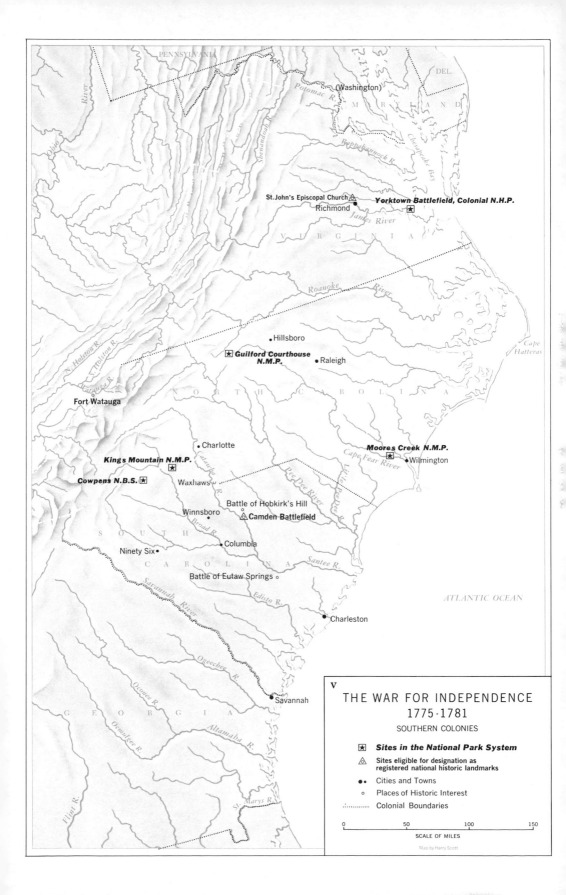

PENNSYLVANIA

DEL.

(Washington)

Potomac R.

M A R Y L A N D

Chesapeake Bay

Rappahannock R.

St. John's Episcopal Church △
Richmond ●

Yorktown Battlefield, Colonial N.H.P. ★

James River

V I R G I N I A

Roanoke River

Cape Hatteras

● Hillsboro

★ **Guilford Courthouse N.M.P.**

● Raleigh

N O R T H   C A R O L I N A

N. Holston R.   *Holston R.*   *Tolston R.*

Watauga R.

● Fort Watauga

● Charlotte

Kings Mountain N.M.P. ★

Cowpens N.B.S. ★

Catawba R.

Waxhaws ○

Pee Dee River

Moores Creek N.M.P. ★
● Wilmington

Cape Fear River

Little Pee Dee

Battle of Hobkirk's Hill ○

Winnsboro ●

△ **Camden Battlefield**

S O U T H

Broad R.

Ninety Six ●

● Columbia

C A R O L I N A

Santee R.

Battle of Eutaw Springs ○

Edisto R.

ATLANTIC OCEAN

Savannah River

● Charleston

Ogeechee R.

Oconee River

● Savannah

G E O R G I A

Ocmulgee R.

Altamaha R.

Flint R.

St. Marys R.

V

THE WAR FOR INDEPENDENCE
1775-1781
SOUTHERN COLONIES

★ *Sites in the National Park System*

△ Sites eligible for designation as registered national historic landmarks

●● Cities and Towns

○ Places of Historic Interest

⋯⋯ Colonial Boundaries

0	50	100	150

SCALE OF MILES

Map by Harry Scott

View from the eastern slope of the Kings Mountain ridge, looking north-eastward toward Henry's Knob, another ridge of the Kings Mountain chain.

civil war to South Carolina, with highly effective partisan warfare waged by Col. Francis Marion and Gens. Thomas Sumter and Andrew Pickens.

The defeat of Gates' army marked the nadir of American fortunes in the South. Within 2 months, however, the tide began to turn. In September Cornwallis invaded North Carolina, simultaneously sending Maj. Patrick Ferguson with his "American Volunteers" on a sweep through the back country of South Carolina. Ferguson's march aroused the Virginia and Carolina frontiersmen, who moved swiftly to surround and annihilate the Tories at Kings Mountain on October 7. (See pp. 71–72.) Cornwallis quickly withdrew from Charlotte, N.C., to Winnsboro, S.C.

Granite obelisk erected in 1909 by the U.S. Government at Kings Mountain to commemorate the battle.

General Greene relieved Gates in command of the American Army in the South early in December 1780. He divided his army, to retain the initiative, advancing with one part against the British right flank at Camden and sending Gen. Daniel Morgan toward the British left at Ninety Six. Cornwallis divided his own army three ways, sending Tarleton after Morgan and reinforcing Camden, while with his main

Maj. Gen. Nathanael Greene was in command of American forces at the Battle of Guilford Courthouse. This engraving was made from a painting by Charles Willson Peale.

body he marched northward to cut the American supply line. Tarleton pushed forward with customary dash and came upon Morgan's men at the Cowpens on January 17, 1781. Tarleton flung his men upon the American line, and Morgan, in a tactical masterpiece, wiped out the attackers. Tarleton escaped with a few men, but his major usefulness had ended. Morgan quickly rejoined Greene, and the American Army began retreating northward. (See pp. 70–71.)

Cornwallis was sternly determined that Greene should not escape. Stripping his army of everything not essential, he marched swiftly in pursuit. Greene stayed just ahead of him, meanwhile actively encouraging the guerrilla leaders to harass the British rear and disrupt the supply lines. The Americans barely won the race for Virginia, crossing the swollen Dan River a few hours ahead of their pursuers. Having failed to catch Greene, Cornwallis withdrew to Hillsboro and sought to rebuild his depleted army. Greene received reinforcements and advanced on the British. At Guilford Courthouse, on March 15, the armies collided. Although the British retained possession of the field, Cornwallis was so badly shattered that he moved his army to Wilmington, on the coast, where the British Navy could support and supply it. (See pp. 63–64.)

With Cornwallis out of the way, Greene returned to South Carolina. His ensuing operations were tactically unsuccessful. The Battle of Hobkirk's Hill on April 25 was an American defeat; the 4-week siege of Ninety Six ended in an American withdrawal when Lord Rawdon approached with British reinforcements; and the battle of Eutaw Springs on September 8, the last major engagement in South Carolina, ended indecisively. (See pp. 226, and 227–228.) Nevertheless, Greene's maneuvers resulted in strategic victory, clearing the British from the interior of South Carolina by the end of 1781. He was aided immensely in his campaign by the activities of the guerrilla leaders.

The War in the West

While British armies were attacking the Colonials from the seaward side, the long inland frontier from Maine to Georgia was exposed to assault by savage tribes. Most of the Indians sided with the English and, led by British officers, struck time and again at the frontier settlements. Happily for the Americans, the settlements stood firm. Otherwise, the coastal armies might have faced attack from two sides at once. On the southwestern frontier, the Indian threat was negated early. A series of joint campaigns by Georgia, Carolina, and Virginia militiamen in the summer and fall of 1776 reduced the Cherokees to virtual impotence, and a second drive 3 years later completed the job. In the north, the frontier was fairly quiet until 1778, when Tory-led Iroquois bands perpetrated fearful massacres in the Wyoming Valley of Pennsylvania and the Cherry Valley of New York. A punitive expedition under Gen. John Sullivan invaded the Iroquois country in the summer of 1779 to devastate the Indian villages. Another force under Col. Daniel Brodhead marched north from Fort Pitt about the same time to destroy crops and villages around the west end of Lake Erie.

In Kentucky, where settlement began simultaneously with the outbreak of war (see Fort Boonesborough and Fort Harrod, pp. 198–199), the situation was touch and go for 4 years. Boone's Wilderness Road became a tenuous supply line for the few Kentucky stations, which stood off numerous Indian assaults. The frontiersmen had learned well the lessons of Indian war, and knew that passive defense would never halt the raids on the settlements. But it remained for a young Virginian, George Rogers Clark, to prove to the embattled American Congress that offense was the best defense.

Clark's plans required more than his resources could provide, but Virginia, with an eye to cementing her western claims, agreed to subsidize his operations. In the summer of 1778 Clark swooped down on the old French Illinois base of Kaskaskia and a short time later induced the inhabitants of Vincennes, on the Wabash to the east, to switch their allegiance. The British at Detroit struck back and reoccupied Vincennes without a fight. Clark responded by taking the initiative. After a remarkable winter march across the flooded Illinois prairie, he captured Vincennes (Fort Sackville, see pp. 197–198) on February 24, 1779. Clark's daring subdued the Northwest for a time, but he lacked the men and supplies to seize Detroit, center of British power in the Northwest. Although the British were equally unable to win final victory in the Northwest, they were able to strike into Pennsylvania and Kentucky in hit-and-run raids in the closing years of the war. In the Battle of Blue Licks, on Kentucky's Licking River, August 18, 1782, an American frontier force was ambushed and suffered a disastrous defeat (see p. 198) that was only partially avenged by Clark's successful campaign into Ohio the following autumn. This punitive expedition was the last major action of the war in the West.[6]

Victory at Yorktown

In the autumn of 1780 the British commenced operations in Virginia. In October an army under Gen. Alexander Leslie landed at the mouth of the James River. Although called to South Carolina 2 months later, his force was soon replaced by a command under Benedict Arnold, now a general in the British Army. Washington, still in New Jersey, sent the Marquis de Lafayette with a small force to keep Arnold occupied. Although greatly outnumbered, the young Frenchman maneuvered skillfully to keep Arnold under surveillance without risking his own men. Then, late in April 1781, Lord Cornwallis marched into Virginia. After

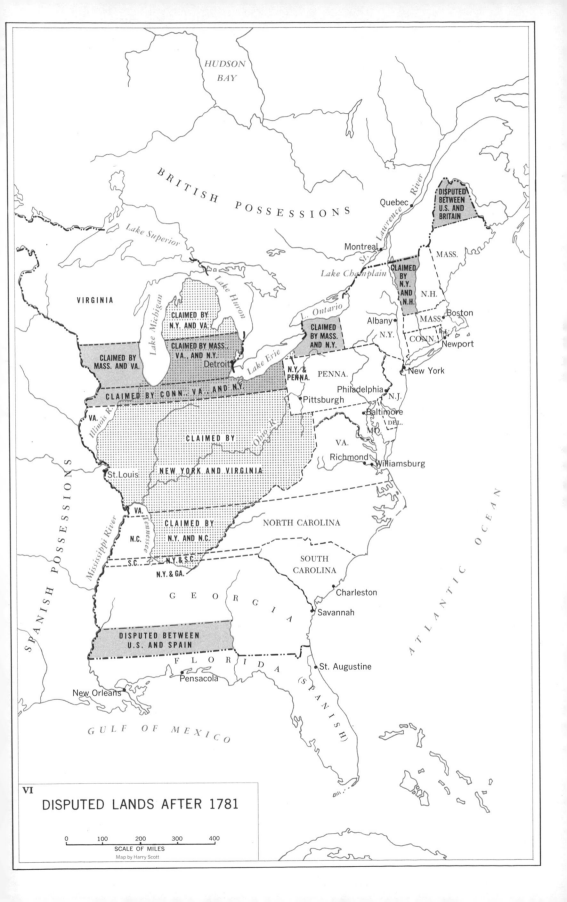

HUDSON
BAY

B R I T I S H   P O S S E S S I O N S

Lake Superior

Quebec

DISPUTED
BETWEEN
U.S. AND
BRITAIN

Montreal

St. Lawrence River

MASS.

Lake Champlain

CLAIMED
BY
N.Y. AND
N.H.

N.H.

VIRGINIA

Lake Michigan

Lake Huron

CLAIMED BY
N.Y. AND VA.

CLAIMED BY MASS.
VA., AND N.Y.

Detroit

Lake Erie

L. Ontario

CLAIMED
BY MASS.
AND N.Y.

Albany

Boston

N.Y.

MASS.

CONN.

Newport

CLAIMED BY
MASS. AND VA.

CLAIMED BY CONN., VA., AND N.Y.

N.Y. &
PENNA.

PENNA.

New York

VA.

Illinois R.

Ohio R.

Philadelphia

N.J.

Pittsburgh

Baltimore

DEL.

St. Louis

CLAIMED BY
NEW YORK AND VIRGINIA.

MD.

VA.

Richmond

Williamsburg

Mississippi River

VA.

CLAIMED BY
N.Y. AND N.C.

Tennessee

N.C.

NORTH CAROLINA

S.C.

N.Y. & S.C.

N.Y. & GA.

SOUTH
CAROLINA

S P A N I S H   P O S S E S S I O N S

G E O R G I A

Charleston

Savannah

A T L A N T I C   O C E A N

DISPUTED BETWEEN
U.S. AND SPAIN

F L O R I D A   (S P A N I S H)

St. Augustine

New Orleans

Pensacola

G U L F   O F   M E X I C O

VI

DISPUTED LANDS AFTER 1781

0   100   200   300   400
SCALE OF MILES
Map by Harry Scott

LOOK WELL UPON THIS SYMBOL · FROM LIKE HOMES CAME AMERICA'S GENIUS TO SHOW TO ALL THAT WHICH NURTURED LIBERTY

POST CARD

vainly pursuing Lafayette's small force for a month, he withdrew to the coast. Lafayette, his strength gradually increasing, followed closely. After a brisk encounter on July 6 at Green Spring, near Jamestown Island, Cornwallis crossed the James River and marched to Portsmouth. There he received orders to take up a position at Yorktown, on the Virginia Peninsula, which General Clinton thought would make a good naval station. The British reached Yorktown by water early in August, and Lafayette took station nearby.

Washington had been considering an assault upon Clinton's strongly positioned force in New York City. But word came in August that Admiral de Grasse's French Fleet would put into Chesapeake Bay in the fall, and Washington saw an opportunity to crush Cornwallis while the French warships protected him from the British Navy. Gen. Jean B. de Rochambeau, French commander at Newport, agreed to cooperate. A swift march took the combined French-American Army southward. Virginia militia flocked to the standard. By the end of September, Washington had concentrated almost 16,000 men around Yorktown, bottling up Cornwallis. Admiral de Grasse held off the British Fleet while Washington conducted siege operations. The genius of Washington's Yorktown campaign lay in his swift movement and concentration of forces. The siege was routine and had the result that was inevitable under the circumstances. On October 19, 1781, Cornwallis surrendered his entire army of 7,500 men. (See p. 73.)

The Peace of Paris, 1783

Although the main British Army under Clinton remained intact in the North, Yorktown proved the decisive event of the War for Independence. The British Cabinet fell, and the new Government sued for peace. Minor skirmishes plagued the South for another 2 years, but the outcome of the struggle had already been decided.

Negotiations between British and American peace commissioners, involving also French and Spanish diplomats, began in Paris in the spring of 1782. Although the United States and France had been allied in the war, the American negotiators saw that, in view of French and Spanish aspirations in North America, self-interest demanded that the United States conclude a separate peace with Britain. The Treaty of Paris, signed in September 1783, recognized American independence. The United States was to extend from the Atlantic to the Mississippi

Grand French Battery, part of the first Allied siege line, Yorktown Battlefield, Va.

and from Canada to the northern boundary of Florida, which England returned to Spain. The Mississippi was to be open to English and American vessels, but with Spain in control of its mouth a source of future trouble was left.

The Americans had won virtually all their demands. A new nation had been born.

PART II

National Survey

of Historic Sites

and Buildings

E NGLISH COLONIAL and Revolutionary War sites and buildings are abundant along the Atlantic coast, particularly in the New England and Middle Atlantic States. War and economic distress have taken a great toll in the South, and War for Independence sites were fewer there to begin with, but there are still many important locations. Selection was a major problem in almost all phases of the Survey's work. Even a rigid application of the criteria of exceptional value (see p. 254) barely reduced the field to manageable proportions. Approximately 650 places relating to the period 1700–1775 were noted and evaluated from written sources, for instance. Field historians then made formal visits to more than a hundred of these. The Advisory Board on National Parks, Historic Sites, Buildings, and Monuments has approved 38 sites and buildings and 5 historic districts in this period as meeting the criteria and therefore eligible for the Registry of National Historic Landmarks; and an additional 22 sites in the period of the War for Independence.

Many important sites have been "lost" in one way or another. The exact locations of some, such as Fort Moore, a South Carolina trading

post, are unknown in the light of present knowledge.   Others have lost
their integrity because of undesirable encroachments or the destruction
of original features.   Among these may be noted the Carlyle House, a
magnificent Georgian mansion built by one of the founders of Alexandria, Va., and the Lucas Plantation, where 16-year-old Eliza Lucas
demonstrated that indigo could become a major export crop in South
Carolina.   Most of the lost sites have been obliterated by the growth of
communities and industries since the colonial period.   For example, New
Post, Spotsylvania County, Va., headquarters of the General Post Office
for America for 23 years, has been destroyed by a sand-and-gravel operation; the Albany Congress site by the streets and buildings of downtown
Albany, N.Y.; the site of the Boston Tea Party by a commercial building; and battle areas of Long Island, Manhattan, Trenton, Germantown, and Savannah have been overwhelmed by urban expansion.

Most of the important 18th-century sites and buildings that survive
appear to be protected adequately against destruction. ⁄A number of
them are in State or municipal ownership while others—such as Boston's
Old South Meeting House and Virginia's Stratford Hall—are well maintained by private organizations.   Some notable restorations have been
accomplished within the past generation, of which the most famous is
Colonial Williamsburg.

The toll among less significant sites and buildings continues, however.
The boom period since World War II, with its accompanying accelera-
tion of industrial, housing, and highway development, has greatly increased the threat.   A particular threat, the full extent of which is not
yet known, is the interstate highway program.   The damage is being
offset and blocked to some extent by an increasing awareness of preservation needs by historical societies and the public at large.

Groups and individuals active in historic preservation are too numerous to mention individually.   They range from the National Trust for
Historic Preservation through such regional organizations as the Society
for the Preservation of New England Antiquities, State groups such as
the Association for the Preservation of Virginia Antiquities, to groups
such as the Historic Charleston Foundation, Inc., the Deerfield (Mass.)
Heritage Foundation, and the Elfreth's Alley Association of Philadelphia.
The work done by these groups, and many others like them, is invaluable
in the preservation of our historic heritage.

Six categories of historic sites are described and listed in the following
pages: First are units of the National Park System; second, National

Historic Sites in non-Federal ownership; third, sites eligible for the Registry of National Historic Landmarks; fourth, historic districts eligible for the Registry; fifth, sites of sufficient importance to merit attention but not considered nationally significant when measured by the criteria; and sixth, named but not described, sites of marginal importance which were examined by National Park Service field historians in the course of their studies and travels in preparing this work. The sites are listed, within these categories, alphabetically by States.

A. Sites in the National Park System

The principal aim of the National Survey of Historic Sites and Buildings is to identify nationally important historic sites that are not units of the National Park System, but no survey of historic sites would be complete without mention of historic areas in the Park System. The sites described below are those areas administered by the National Park Service that have primary or secondary associations with 18th-century English colonial development and the War for Independence. Park Service units are not included that are of a purely memorial character, such as Statue of Liberty National Monument, N.Y., and Thomas Jefferson Memorial and Washington Monument in the District of Columbia. Further information about each area described below may be obtained by writing directly to the superintendent.

1. Fort Frederica National Monument, Georgia

> *Location: St. Simons Island, 12 miles from Brunswick; address, Box 816, St. Simons Island, Ga. 31522.*

Fort Frederica was established in February 1736 by Gen. James Oglethorpe, colonizer of Georgia, to assert England's claim to the southern coastal area contested by France, Spain, and England. It consisted of a fortified town and a defensive bastion. Minor clashes with the Spaniards led Oglethorpe late in 1739 to attempt to seize the Spanish bastion of Castillo de San Marcos at St. Augustine, Fla. The attempt failed, and the Spanish retaliated by marching against Fort Frederica. Oglethorpe defeated them in July 1742 at the Battle of Bloody Marsh,

Excavation by archeologists has revealed much about the layout of the fortified town of Fort Frederica, and produced many objects used by the earliest settlers. The foundations of the Hawkins and Davison houses are shown here.

1½ miles from Fort Frederica. The Spaniards withdrew and never again tried to occupy Georgia. Deprived of its strategic location by the Treaty of Aix-la-Chapelle in 1748 and swept by fire in 1758, Fort Frederica was gradually abandoned.

Fort Frederica National Monument contains the sites of the town and the fort. Tabby ruins of some of the buildings are still standing, and the sites of others have been exposed by archeological excavations. A visitor center interprets the history of Fort Frederica.

2. Minute Man National Historical Park, Massachusetts

Location: Between Lexington and Concord; address Room 1400, Post Office and Courthouse Building, Boston, Mass. 02109.

At this writing, Minute Man National Historical Park has been authorized by Congress and its development is in the planning stage. In broad terms, its purpose is to acquire, restore, maintain, and interpret for public benefit retrievable portions of the historic setting intimately associated with events in the towns of Lexington, Lincoln, and Concord, Mass., that marked the outbreak of the American Revolution. The park will be made up of two units. The first, covering up to 600 acres of roadsides and rural landscape from circumferential highway Mass. 128 in Lexington to Meriam's Corner in Concord, will include more than 4 miles of the historic route over which the British marched in the early morning of April 19, 1775, and where, in their retreat from Concord later in the day, they were first exposed to attacks of minutemen and provincial militia that initiated the Revolution. Here, too, earlier in the morning, a British patrol captured Paul Revere and brought a sudden end to his famous ride.

The second unit of the projected park will consist of up to 150 acres on both banks of the Concord River at the historic North Bridge in Concord, where a detachment from the British expeditionary force, sent from Boston to seize military stores assembled by the patriots, was assaulted by a column of minutemen and militia who fired "the shot heard round the world." Features of major interest at the North Bridge include the Concord Monument, which was dedicated on July 4, 1837, on the site of the British position in the fight; the well-known Minute Man Statue by Daniel Chester French, occupying the American position on the opposite side of the stream and erected on the centennial in 1875; the "Grave of British Soldiers" killed or mortally wounded at the bridge, marked by a slate tablet with lines composed by the poet, James Russell Lowell; and a replica of "the rude bridge that arched the flood"—the most recent version of which was built in 1956. These features are part of a small public area developed and maintained by the town of Concord. It is intended not later than 1963 to complete negotiations with the town for a cooperative agreement to provide for the permanent management of the town-owned area at North Bridge as a part of the second unit of the park. By then, it is anticipated that important private holdings, including the muster field of the minutemen and militia on the west bank of the river, will have been acquired and will thus be ready for the inception of unified maintenance and interpretation with the town-owned area at the bridge.

Acquisitions of individual properties for the first unit of the park have already taken place and, before long, are expected to reach such proportions as to make feasible a program of development. A relatively unspoiled parcel of 8 acres, containing the site of the Josiah Nelson House and adjacent farm buildings, together with pastures and stone walls used as shelter by the minutemen, was acquired in 1959. In the west pasture behind a stone wall on this parcel is the Minute Man Boulder, from the cover of which William Thorning shot and killed two grenadiers retreating with the British main body on the nearby road.

Other historic properties acquired in the first unit of the park include parts of former farms, with farmhouses and other farm buildings, or the sites thereof, that were a part of the rural setting on April 19, 1775. In Lexington, possession has been taken of 17 acres of the Fiske Farm at Fiske Hill, including the cellar hole of the family home, which was looted by the fleeing enemy. The Muzzey House has been acquired also, the home of a father and son who were members of Captain Parker's company which at sunrise faced the British in the exchange of fire. In Lincoln, title has been obtained to the Brooks-Sturm House near a stream where, during the 18th century, the numerous Brooks family practiced their trade of tanners and curriers.

Based on further historical, architectural, and archeological study, a program of development will be initiated on properties acquired and consolidated in both units of the park. Exterior restoration will be performed on all remaining historic buildings, and inside restoration also, on structures to be treated as historic house museums. By far the largest task, however, will consist of obliterating later intrusions and reviving manmade features of the historic landscape of 1775.

3. Salem Maritime National Historic Site, Massachusetts

> *Location: Derby Street, Salem; address, Custom House, Derby Street, Salem, Mass. 01970.*

This National Historic Site preserves a group of structures surviving from the period of the town's maritime greatness. Salem and other New England shipping interests played a significant role in the colonial and early republican economy. Sailing vessels based on Salem plied the sealanes of the world, beginning early in the 17th century, building the commerce upon which Yankee prosperity came to rest. Salem and other New England ports engaged in the important "triangular trade" with Africa and the West Indies. During the Revolution, Salem provided a base for privateers that ravaged British shipping, and for nearly three-quarters of a century afterward, through the era of the great clipper ships, Salem continued to function as one of New

The Derby House, shown here, is the oldest surviving structure of the formerly important port of Salem. The house is a unit of Salem Maritime National Historic Site.

England's most important ports. The increasingly large sailing vessels of the mid-19th century, however, could not use the shallow, landlocked harbor, and the town gradually surrendered its prominence to other ports.

Derby Wharf, extending nearly 2,000 feet into Salem Harbor, was built in 1762 and restored in 1938. Opposite the wharf is the Custom House, built in 1819, where Nathaniel Hawthorne worked on "The Scarlet Letter." The Derby House (1761–62), home of a prominent shipping family of the 18th century, is the oldest surviving house in Salem. Other structures help to illustrate the significance of maritime activities to the development of early America.

4. Morristown National Historical Park, New Jersey

Location: Morristown, Morris County; address, Box 759, Morristown, N.J. 07960.

New York City was the principal British stronghold in the North, throughout the Revolutionary War. Only 30 miles distant but separated from the British lines on Manhattan and Staten Islands by a series of parallel ridges, the New Jersey village of Morristown took on important strategic values for Washington's army and was the scene of nearly continuous American military activity from 1776 to 1782. The American Army spent the winters of 1776–77 and 1779–80 encamped at Morristown. The Watchung Mountains, intervening between Morristown and New York, enabled Washington to keep watch on the British, to protect his own supply and communication lines, to guard the roads connecting New England and Pennsylvania, and to be ready to move swiftly on any point threatened by the enemy.

Morristown National Historical Park features the unspoiled natural setting on the edge of Morristown where the American Army passed the winter of 1779–80. The Ford Mansion, Washington's headquarters, and the Wick House, a farmhouse where Gen. Arthur St. Clair maintained his headquarters, have been restored and refurnished. Reconstructions include fortifications called "Fort Nonsense," nine log huts typifying the quarters of officers, and a representative camp hospital

This crude log structure, as reconstructed and pictured here, served the American patriot army as its hospital during the hard winter of 1779–80 at Morristown, N.J.

building. A large historical museum houses an extensive collection of artifacts illustrating the role of Morristown in the War for Independence, a library, and a unique collection of manuscripts.

5. Federal Hall National Memorial, New York

Location: Wall and Nassau Streets, New York City; address, Executive Director, Federal Hall Memorial Associates, Inc., New York, N.Y.

The old City Hall of New York was the scene of numerous significant events of the colonial and constitutional periods of American history. The imprisonment and trial of editor John Peter Zenger for publishing "seditious libels" took place here in 1734 and 1735. Zenger's acquittal marked a large advance toward winning freedom of speech and the press in America. Colonists expressed the first organized opposition to the Stamp Act when delegates from nine Colonies convened the Stamp Act Congress in City Hall in October 1765. The petition, declaration, and address that came from this meeting helped influence Parliament to

A print of City Hall, New York City, produced in 1790 by A. Doolittle of New Haven, Conn., and apparently intended to depict George Washington taking the oath of office as President, on the balcony. The seat of the Federal Government was removed to Philadelphia in 1790, however, and this building fell into ruin.

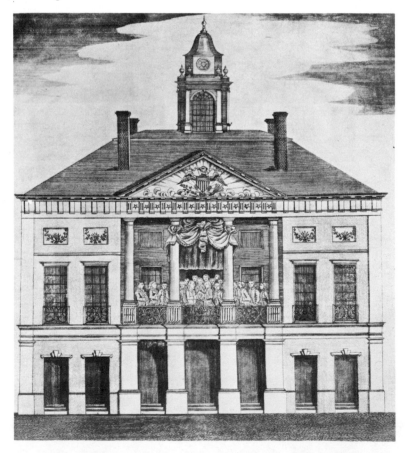

rescind the Stamp Act the next year.   After the Revolution, when New
York City served as the National Capital, the Continental Congress sat
in City Hall.   On its balcony Washington was inaugurated first Presi-

This outstanding example of Greek Revival architecture was built in 1842
on the site of City Hall, the first Capitol of the United States.   It served
first as the New York City Custom House, later as the United States Sub-
Treasury, and is now Federal Hall National Memorial.

dent of the United States, and within its walls were created the Departments of State, War, and the Treasury, as well as the Supreme Court.
Here, too, Congress adopted the Bill of Rights.

After the transfer of the Federal Government to Philadelphia in 1790,
City Hall fell into disrepair and was ultimately sold for salvage.   On its
site, however, Federal Hall was completed in 1842.   An outstanding
example of Greek Revival architecture, it served as the New York City
customhouse until 1862, then as a U.S. Subtreasury.   Designated a
National Historic Site in 1939 and a National Memorial in 1955, it now

exhibits documents and artifacts interpreting the role of City Hall in the colonial and early republican periods.

6. Saratoga National Historical Park, New York

Location: On Hudson River 28 miles north of Albany, between Stillwater and Schuylerville; address RFD 1, Box 113–C, Stillwater, N.Y. 12170.

Advancing down the Hudson River as part of a grand design for conquering the Northern States, the British Army of Gen. John Burgoyne clashed in September 1777 with the American Army of Gen. Horatio Gates.   The Battle of Saratoga and the resulting surrender of Burgoyne's army wrecked the British campaign.   Saratoga was the turning point of the war in the North.   Vastly more important, it was the turning point of the Revolution.   Not only did the colonists draw new hope at a critical moment when defeat would have been disastrous, but the victory also had a decisive influence on negotiations in Europe for an alliance with France.   Without French aid, the American cause would almost certainly have failed.

Saratoga National Historical Park preserves 1,429 acres of the rolling countryside along the Hudson where the two armies battled.   Paved roads give access to the sites of significant phases of the action, to the

A view looking northeastward over the Hudson River, from Stark's Knob at Schuylerville (Old Saratoga).   Gen. John Stark occupied these heights on October 12, thus closing the final gap in the American lines and trapping Burgoyne's army.

A view looking southeastward from the British River Redoubts at Saratoga. This shows the heart of the final British position, the Great Ravine in the foreground and the plains beyond.

opposing redoubts and fortifications, and to the headquarters of Burgoyne and Gates, all of which are identified and interpreted. A 25-acre detached section of the park at nearby Schuylerville includes the restored and refurnished Schuyler Mansion, summer residence of Gen. Philip Schuyler, who relinquished command of the American force to General Gates almost on the eve of the Battle of Saratoga.

The ceremony of surrender by the British took place at the Field of Grounded Arms, not part of the park, as Schuylerville. (See p. 211.)

7. Guilford Courthouse National Military Park, North Carolina

Location: 6 miles northwest of Greensboro on U.S. 220; address, Box 9145, Plaza Station, Greensboro, N.C. 27408.

Although it was a defeat for the Americans, the Battle of Guilford Courthouse, March 15, 1781, was a significant landmark on the road to victory at Yorktown. The determined assaults by Lord Cornwallis' army on the American lines at Guilford Courthouse finally led Gen. Nathanael Greene to abandon the field and concede victory to his opponent. But the assaults hurt Cornwallis so badly that he was forced to abandon the offensive and give up his plans for conquering the South. The British Army withdrew from North Carolina and ultimately established new

Monument at Guilford Courthouse National Military Park commemorating Pvt. Peter Francisco. Serving with William Washington's cavalry, Francisco, a huge man with an oversize sword, slew 11 enemy soldiers during the engagement.

positions at Yorktown, where Washington, with the aid of the French Fleet, compelled Cornwallis to surrender the following year.

Guilford Courthouse National Military Park contains 148 acres, including the most important parts of the battlefield and the site of the historic courthouse. Twenty-nine monuments and markers honor the participants and identify points of interest. A museum interprets the action and its significance.

8. Moores Creek National Military Park, North Carolina

Location: 25 miles northwest of Wilmington, Pender County, on N.C. 210; address, Currie, N.C. 28435.

The Battle of Moores Creek was the opening engagement of the Revolution in the South, and is often called the Lexington and Concord of the

The flooring of this bridge, reconstructed here, was removed by the Whigs (patriots) and the girders were greased in order to make the crossing of Moores Creek more difficult for the enemy loyalists. This view is eastward toward the patriot encampment.

South. Here on February 27, 1776, a force of 1,500 loyalist militia under Donald McDonald attacked a patriot force of about 1,000 men under Col. James Moore, entrenched on Moores Creek. The patriots turned back the loyalist assault and subsequently captured or dispersed the entire loyalist command. The action bolstered patriot morale and strengthened the movement for independence. The British, moreover, abandoned their plans for conquering the southern Colonies and did not resume major operations in the South until late in the war.

Moores Creek National Military Park contains 50 acres on which the engagement was fought. A self-guiding trail leads to remains of the patriot fortifications, cannon, field exhibits, monuments, and markers which unfold the story of the battle. A visitor center houses exhibits relating to the battle and its consequences.

9. Fort Necessity National Battlefield, Pennsylvania

Location: 11 miles east of Uniontown on U.S. 40; address, Star Route, Box 15, Farmington, Pa. 15437.

At Fort Necessity, which consists of a rude circular palisade and cabin in the Great Meadows of western Pennsylvania, George Washington rose to prominence in the conflict that opened the French and Indian War. Lieutenant Colonel Washington marched westward with an army of Virginians in April 1754 to contest French possession of the Forks of

A view of the Great Meadows and reconstructed Fort Necessity, from the southwest, the direction from which the French first approached the fort.

the Ohio, strategic site of modern Pittsburgh, where the French had built Fort Duquesne. He and his small advance guard skirmished at Great Meadows on May 24 with a French scouting party from Fort Duquesne, and drove it from the field. Washington next built Fort Necessity as a temporary defensive work. Reinforcements swelled his command to 293 officers and men, but the French attacked him on July 3 with a force more than twice this number and by nightfall had clearly won the battle. The Virginians surrendered and were permitted next day to withdraw with the honors of war. They returned to Virginia.

Visitors now see at Fort Necessity a stockade, storehouse, and entrenchments, faithfully reconstructed in 1954 on the exact site of the original structures. Most of Great Meadows is included in the surrounding Federal area. In the vicinity are the site of the skirmish between Washington and the French scouting party and the grave of Gen. Edward Braddock, killed in a famous battle with the French and Indians in 1755.

10. Hopewell Village National Historic Site, Pennsylvania

Location: Berks County, 5 miles south of Birdsboro; address, R.D. No. 1, Elverson, Pa. 19520.

Hopewell Village was founded in 1770 by ironmaster Mark Bird and is typical of the ironmaking villages that dotted the Colonies during the

The ironmaster's house, Hopewell Village National Historic Site, Pa.

18th century. The vicinity afforded an abundance of iron ore, hardwood for charcoal, and labor. The undertaking prospered, and Hopewell became the thriving center of a larger community. The ironmakers supplied Washington's army with cannon and shot during the Revolution, and Bird himself served in the field as a colonel of militia. The village and its industry continued to expand after the war and, passing through a succession of owners, turned out iron products until new industrial techniques after the Civil War made it obsolete.

Although the buildings deteriorated thereafter, they remained basically sound. In 1935 the Federal Government acquired the site, now 848 acres, and since 1950 has been carrying out a program of restoring the historic structures to their 19th-century appearance. Today the restored

Abandoned employees' houses, Hopewell Village National Historic Site, Pa.

ironmaster's house, charcoal house, furnace, blacksmith shop, office-store, and barn of Hopewell Village provide an outstanding illustration of an early American industrial community.

11. Independence National Historical Park, Pennsylvania

Location: Philadelphia, between Second and Sixth, Chestnut and Walnut Streets, plus detached areas; address, 420 Chestnut Street, Philadelphia, Pa. 19106.

Independence Hall is the heart of Independence National Historical Park. It was originally the statehouse for the Colony of Pennsylvania, built beginning in 1732. The Liberty Bell, displayed here, was ordered from England in 1751, and its famous "Proclaim Liberty" inscription was intended as a 50th anniversary memorial to William Penn's Charter of Privileges of 1701. The Second Continental Congress met in Independence Hall in May 1775 and took the crucial steps which converted a protest movement into a resistance and independence movement. Fighting had already broken out in Massachusetts when this Congress met, and they chose George Washington to be General and Commander in Chief of the Continental Army, in June 1775. He delivered his acceptance in Independence Hall. Next year, on July 4, 1776, the Dec-

Archeological excavations in Independence Square. The foundation walls shown here belonged to buildings designed by Robert Mills, early 1800's.

laration of Independence was adopted by Congress meeting here. It was written largely by Thomas Jefferson and stands as perhaps the finest statement of democratic rights and principles ever written, and the basis of the free government of the United States throughout its history.

During the War for Independence and the ensuing period under the Articles of Confederation, Congress met in various towns and cities, but Philadelphia remained the chief city of the United States. Thus, beginning on May 25, 1787, the Federal Constitutional Convention met here under Washington, as President of the Convention. Benjamin Franklin, Alexander Hamilton, James Madison, and other eminent leaders made up the Convention, which labored for 4 months and produced the Constitution which, with amendments, continues today as the supreme law of the land. The meetings were held in strictest secrecy and the results submitted to every State for ratification. Americans will never fail to honor the wisdom and courage exhibited by the writers of the Constitution. The City of Philadelphia purchased Independence Hall from the Commonwealth of Pennsylvania in 1818—a financial and spiritual investment unequaled in the history of American cities—and thus took the first step to preserve it and surrounding structures for posterity. Great progress has been made recently by the Commonwealth in converting the three blocks directly north of Independence Hall into a mall, to enhance the setting of the park.

Independence National Historical Park includes a number of other historic structures in addition to Independence Hall. Those in the Independence Hall group are owned by the City of Philadelphia and administered by the National Park Service; some others are owned and occupied by certain associations. Carpenters' Hall is among the most important of the latter. It was built in 1770 as a guildhall for the Carpenters' Company of Philadelphia, and was the scene of action for the First Continental Congress in 1774. This building is open to the public under a cooperative agreement between the Carpenters' Company and the U.S. Department of the Interior, and is located on Chestnut Street between Fourth and Orianna Streets.

The structures most closely associated with Independence Hall are on Independence Square. The former County Court Building is on the west, the Old City Hall on the east, with the American Philosophical Society Building (Philosophical Hall) next to it. All but Old City Hall were completed before 1790, when Philadelphia became the Federal Capital. During this period the Court House became known as Congress

Hall because Congress sat there and, similarly, City Hall in 1791 became the Supreme Court Building. Philosophical Hall is not open to the public. It is still the headquarters of the American Philosophical Society, founded in 1743 by Benjamin Franklin, the oldest society of its kind in the United States. Its library is in Library Hall, on Fifth Street, a reconstruction of the original home of the Library Company of Philadelphia, which was built in 1789–90.

Other features of, or associated with, Independence National Historical Park include: The First Bank of the United States, erected in 1795–97; The Second Bank of the United States, 1819–24; New Hall, 1791; Philadelphia Exchange, 1832–34; Bishop White House, 1786–87; Dilworth-Todd-Moylan House, 1775; Franklin Court, site of Benjamin Franklin's home from 1763 to 1790; Christ Church, 1727–54; St. Joseph's Church, 1838, but in earlier structures from 1733; St. Mary's Church, established in 1763; Deshler-Morris House, 5442 Germantown Avenue, erected 1772–73; St. George's Church, 1769; and Mikveh Israel Cemetery, 1738.

12. Cowpens National Battlefield Site, South Carolina

Location: 11 miles northwest of Gaffney and 2 miles southeast of Chesnee at intersection of S.C. 11 and 110; address, Box 31, Kings Mountain, N.C. 28086.

The American victory at Kings Mountain in October 1780 (see below) was the first setback to Lord Cornwallis' strategy for conquering the South. Falling back to Winnsboro, he learned that part of Gen. Na-

The United States monument, at the right, honors the patriot soldiers who fell at the Battle of Cowpens.

thanael Greene's army had been sent to the northwestern part of the State under Gen. Daniel Morgan. Cornwallis dispatched his cavalry leader, Lt. Col. Banastre Tarleton, with more than 1,000 men, to dispose of Morgan's 970. At Cowpens on January 17, 1781, the two forces joined battle, and in little more than an hour the British were driven from the field. Barely a fifth of Tarleton's command escaped, while Morgan lost only 12 killed and 60 wounded. Along with the results of Kings Mountain and Guilford Courthouse, Cowpens renewed American hope and ultimately led Cornwallis to abandon his attempted conquest of the Carolinas.

A commemorative monument stands in the angle of the highway intersection near the rear of the American lines. The fighting took place for a distance of about 600 yards southeast along present S.C. 11. The National Park Service administers 1¼ acres on which the monument stands, but no attendant is on duty, the superintendent of Kings Mountain National Military Park exercising general supervision.

13. Kings Mountain National Military Park, South Carolina

> *Location: 4 miles south of U.S. 216, on S.C. 216, between Charlotte, N.C., and Spartanburg, S.C.; address Box 31, Kings Mountain, N.C. 28086.*

Lord Cornwallis' triumphant northward thrust through Georgia and the Carolinas in 1778–80 left the scattered settlers of the Appalachian foothills comparatively undisturbed. Preoccupied with pushing the frontier across the mountains and defending themselves against Indians, they took little interest in the war to the east. Cornwallis, however, detached Maj. Patrick Ferguson to operate in the Carolina Piedmont. Aroused by this threat, frontiersmen from both sides of the mountains rallied to meet the invader. On October 7, 1780, a force of about 900, under Cols. Isaac Shelby, John Sevier, Joseph McDowell, and William Campbell, surrounded Ferguson's 1,100 posted on Kings Mountain. In a 1-hour battle the frontier marksmen stormed up the slope and overwhelmed the British. Ferguson was slain and his entire command killed, wounded, or captured, with a loss to the Americans of 28 killed and 62 wounded. Kings Mountain compelled Cornwallis to withdraw from North Carolina and go on the defensive. Subsequent reverses caused him to abandon the southern campaign altogether.

Aerial view of George Washington Birthplace National Monument, from northeast. Popes Creek in foreground. U.S. Department of Defense photo.

The Kings Mountain ridge on which the battle occurred rises from the center of the 4,012-acre Kings Mountain National Military Park. A self-guiding trail leads from the visitor center and museum to the scenes of action on the mountain, marked by four large commemorative monuments.

14. George Washington Birthplace National Monument, Virginia

Location: Potomac River 38 miles east of Fredericksburg; address, Washington's Birthplace, Va. 22575.

George Washington was born at his father's tidewater plantation on February 22, 1732 (February 11 by the old-style calendar). Here he spent the first 3 years of his life before moving to the plantation farther up the Potomac that became Mount Vernon. The earlier plantation passed to his half brother, Augustine Washington, Jr., and the home burned to the ground during the Revolutionary War.

Part of the birthplace site became a Federal area in 1882, and the Wakefield National Memorial Association later helped to acquire additional land. This organization also conducted extensive research to determine the original appearance of the plantation, but failed. A memorial mansion was therefore built. Patterned on tradition and surviving structures of the period, it is intended to represent the typical 18th-century Virginia plantation house such as Washington was probably born in. A mile northwest of the memorial mansion is the family burial ground containing the graves of many of Washington's forebears.

15. Yorktown Battlefield, Colonial National Historical Park, Virginia

Location: 13 miles east of Williamsburg on U.S. 17; address, P.O. Box 210, Yorktown, Va. 23490.

In the spring of 1781 Lord Cornwallis transferred the scene of his operations from the Carolinas to Virginia, and in July, receiving orders to move his army to New York, he established a base at Yorktown preparatory to embarkation. The Americans and their French allies moved swiftly to trap Cornwallis in Yorktown. The French Fleet under Admiral de Grasse blockaded Chesapeake Bay and cut off the British from all aid by sea. Washington and Rochambeau dropped down from the North and laid siege to Yorktown. With superiority of numbers— 15,700 to 7,500—Washington quickly rendered the British position untenable. On October 17, after 2 weeks of siege operations, Cornwallis asked for terms. On the 19th the British Army marched out of its fortifications and surrendered. Although a treaty of peace was not signed until 2 years later, Yorktown was the decisive military event of the Revolution and virtually ended the fighting.

Yorktown Battlefield lies in and around the colonial town of Yorktown. The park contains the restored fortifications and gun emplacements of the opposing armies. A self-guiding tour road with interpretive markers and field exhibits leads to the principal historic features. One mile from Yorktown is the restored Moore House, where the articles of capitulation for Cornwallis' army were drafted. Several historic buildings within the town itself have also been restored. A visitor center provides information and orientation service and houses museum exhibits relating to the events that ended the Revolution. Yorktown Battlefield is linked with Jamestown Island, scene of the first permanent English colony in America, by the Colonial Parkway, and all three units are administered as Colonial National Historical Park. Together with nearby Williamsburg, the park offers a unique panorama of America's colonial and Revolutionary history.

B. National Historic Sites in Non-Federal Ownership

Scattered throughout the United States are a number of National Historic Sites in non-Federal ownership. These are not units of the National Park System but, as authorized by the Historic Sites Act of 1935, are administered under the provisions of cooperative agreements to which the Secretary of the Interior is a party. In order to retain the designation of National Historic Site, the other parties to the agreement must maintain the property in a manner consistent with good preservation practices, and for this purpose they may receive technical assistance from the National Park Service. The Federal Government also normally provides a bronze plaque for mounting at the site. All sites so designated have been approved by the Advisory Board as meeting the criteria of exceptional historical value.

1. Dorchester Heights National Historic Site, Massachusetts

Location: Thomas Park, South Boston.

The seizure and fortification of Dorchester Heights in March 1776 was the first real stroke of military success enjoyed by the Continental Army in the War for Independence. Not only were the British forced to evacuate Boston by Gen. George Washington's unexpected move, but this success served also to inspire hope and confidence in the leadership and capabilities of the Continental Army.

This masterful operation was launched from Dorchester and Roxbury, and was very carefully planned, utilizing about 2,400 troops and militia with a continual procession of carts and wagons, screened partially by bales of hay, carrying long bundles of birch saplings (intended for facines for building up breastworks on exposed ledges and on frozen ground) and other materials. The labor began on the night of March 4, under a bright moon. It proceeded so rapidly that by daylight the forts on the two highest hilltops of what is properly Dorchester Heights were well enough advanced to offer some defense against assault. When Gen. William Howe looked on the redoubts from his bedchamber that morning, he is said to have remarked, "The rebels have done more in one night than my whole army would have done in a month."

Colonel Henry Knox had brought overland from Fort Ticonderoga 70 artillery pieces which, promptly placed on Dorchester Heights, rendered the city untenable by the British and threatened also the vessels in the harbor. Howe determined to attack immediately, and the Americans waited resolutely "in a position twice as strong as Bunker Hill, with a force more than twice as large, and under the immediate eye of the General-in-Chief." They were snug in their works, with rows of stone- and sand-filled barrels ready to roll down upon any attacking force. The intended attack never came. The British artillerists found that they could not elevate their guns sufficiently to reach the American parapets, and a boisterous storm prevented the movement of troops needed for a planned night attack. Washington worked all the while to perfect the fortifications, and soon made them, as far as Howe's army was concerned, impregnable. The British evacuated on March 17—an army of 11,000 men, with 1,100 loyalist refugees, in their transports.

Every side of the heights is now built up, but the white marble monument at the summit looks sufficiently high even today to reveal a position that was naturally strategic and, with fortifications, very formidable. The monument is 115 feet high, consisting of a tower and steeple reminiscent of a New England meeting house of 200 years ago. It was dedicated on March 17, 1902, the 126th anniversary of the British evacuation of Boston.

Under the terms of a cooperative agreement signed by the Secretary of the Interior and the Mayor of Boston on March 17, 1951, Dorchester Heights was designated a National Historic Site. The monument and Thomas Park, named for Gen. John Thomas who commanded the troops on Dorchester Heights, are under the jurisdiction of the Department of Parks, City of Boston.

2. St. Paul's Church National Historic Site, New York

Location: South Columbus Avenue (old Boston Post Road) between South Third and Fulton Avenues, Eastchester, Mount Vernon.

St. Paul's Church was founded in 1665, not long after the founding of the village in 1642 by freedom-loving refugees from Puritan Massachusetts under Anne Hutchinson. Her consistent stand during her life, and her death in 1643 at the hands of Indians, created something of a reaction in the Colonies in favor of religious freedom and tolerance. Later the "Great Election of 1733" here led to the famous trial of John Peter Zenger, his vindication, and a reaction in favor of freedom of the press. Connected in these and other ways with the history of civil liberties in the United States, the present effort toward the protection and preservation of St. Paul's Church is being spearheaded by the Society of the National Shrine of the Bill of Rights. The objectives of the society are to assist in the upkeep of the church, to restore the village green in front to its colonial appearance, to help maintain the planned Zenger Memorial Museum Building, and to carry on educational activities.

The present structure of stone and brick was started in the 1760's and evidently not completed until after the War for Independence. It is of simple Georgian colonial style and replaced an earlier wooden structure, said to have been destroyed for firewood when the newer church was used as a hospital and barracks by Hessian troops. In its tower hangs Freedom Bell, 1,800-pound twin of the more famous Liberty Bell at Independence Hall, Philadelphia. Freedom Bell was cast in 1752 by the same foundry that manufactured the Liberty Bell, and it was preserved during the Revolutionary War by being buried secretly, along with other precious objects belonging to the church. The entire area along the Boston Post Road was ravaged severely by armed men of both sides during the war. About a hundred Hessians were buried in a mass grave, now marked, in the cemetery. Other identifiable graves in the cemetery date from as early as about 1700.

St. Paul's Church was restored faithfully to its 1787 appearance in 1942 as the result of work of a committee of eminent citizens headed by Mrs. Sara Delano Roosevelt. It was designated a National Historic Site in 1943. It has been faced by serious problems of maintenance because of the industrial nature of its modern environment and its lack of religious function since the former congregation has joined the recent trend in the evacuation of cities to the suburbs.

3. Gloria Dei Church National Historic Site, Pennsylvania

Location: Delaware Avenue near Christian Street, South Philadelphia.

Gloria Dei, or "Old Swedes'," Church is the oldest church building in Philadelphia, having held services first in the year 1700. The structure is of red brick in Flemish bond, with glazed headers. Its Swedish origins are revealed in the steep gable roof, square belfry, and small spire. There were Swedish settlers on the ground long before William Penn came to establish the city of Philadelphia, and Gloria Dei Church is perhaps the best evidence of the fact.

Gloria Dei, or "Old Swedes'," Church, in Philadelphia, stands today as a reminder that the first European inhabitants of this region were Swedes.

689–192 O–64—8

The first Swedish settlers came to the banks of the Delaware River in the 1630's, and one of the villages that developed was called Wicaco, a place now known as South Philadelphia.   A mission of the state church of Sweden was begun about 1646 which developed into Gloria Dei Church, using first a small square log blockhouse originally provided for defense against Indians.   The present structure was dedicated in 1700 and was the greatest public building in Philadelphia.   The bricks were manufactured close at hand and the interior furnished in part with articles brought from Sweden, including a cherubim or decorative carving brought from Sweden in 1643, still to be seen hanging below the organ loft, and a baptismal font from Gothenburg dating to the same year.   The church treasures include silver altar appointments, among them the Vanderspiegel tankard of 1773, executed by the Philadelphia silversmith, Young; a Breeches Bible presented to the church by William Penn, published in London in 1599; and a cherished reproduction of the Gustav Vasa Bible of 1541.   These and other relics and documents add up to a museum-archival collection of considerable value.

Betsy Ross was among the notable persons connected with Gloria Dei Church—she married her second husband here in 1777.   Resting in the churchyard are the last remains of Gustavus Hesselius, first American portrait painter; Alexander Wilson, father of American ornithology; Capt. John Douglas, General Washington's aide-de-camp; and Margaret Boone, sister of Daniel.   Gloria Dei separated from the mother church of Sweden in 1789, and was admitted in 1845 into the Convention of the Protestant Episcopal Church of the Diocese of Pennsylvania.

The church is the center of an active parish, filling the current religious needs of hundreds of communicants of the area and carrying on an extensive social service program on the waterfront, as well as giving inspiration to history-minded visitors.   Well preserved and useful, it has been likened to a jewel in its drab environs.   It was declared a National Historic Site in 1942.

4. Touro Synagogue National Historic Site, Rhode Island

Location: 85 Touro Street, Newport.

Touro Synagogue symbolizes the spirit of religious freedom that arose during the colonial period and found its way into the principles upon which the political system of the new Nation was founded. The Code of Laws for Rhode Island in 1647 proclaimed religious freedom, and a Jewish sect that had been persecuted in Europe sought haven in this new colony founded by Roger Williams, himself a victim of religious persecution in Massachusetts. For nearly a century the Newport Jews

Strikingly different from other colonial houses of worship in its appearance, Touro Synagogue, in Newport, R.I., represents an element of the colonial population whose important contributions are sometimes overlooked.

prospered and made important contributions to Newport life before they were able to build a synagogue. In 1759, however, ground was broken, and the edifice that was dedicated 4 years later was a distinguished addition to Newport architecture as well as the highest achievement of Architect Peter Harrison. The Revolution sapped the vitality of Newport, and its Jewish community revived only partially after the war. By the end of the 18th century the doors of the synagogue had closed, but the building was preserved and maintained by descendants of the Reverend Isaac Touro, spiritual leader of the Newport Jews when it was opened, until services resumed in 1883. It still serves the purpose for which it was built.

An expert modification of Georgian architecture to accommodate the Sephardic Jewish ritual, Touro Synagogue exhibits a plain brick exterior and an ornate interior. Inside, 12 Ionic columns support a gallery, above which rise 12 Corinthian columns supporting a domed ceiling. Five massive brass candelabra hang from the ceiling. The Holy Ark at the east end contains sacred, hand-lettered Scrolls of the Law mounted on wooden rollers. In the center of the room is the Bimah, an elevated platform where the cantor intones the liturgy and reads the Torah. The profusion of holy objects gives to the synagogue a profoundly religious atmosphere.

Designated a National Historic Site in 1946, Touro Synagogue is administered under the terms of a cooperative agreement between the Secretary of the Interior, the Shearith Israel trustees of New York City, and the Congregation Jeshuat Israel of Newport. The Society of Friends of Touro Synagogue National Historic Shrine, Inc., aids in preservation and restoration work.

C. Sites Eligible for the Registry of National Historic Landmarks

This group of historic sites has been judged to meet the criteria of "exceptional value" (see p. 254) and therefore to possess importance to the Nation for commemorating and illustrating the history of 18th-century English colonial development in North America and the separation of these Colonies from England. The Secretary of the Interior has declared them eligible for inclusion on the Registry of National Historic Landmarks. Some are already designated Registered National Historic Landmarks; the others may receive the designation upon application of the owners. The whole list is subject to reappraisal each 5 years for possible additions and deletions.

1. Webb House, Connecticut

Location. 211 Main Street, Wethersfield.

Ownership and Administration. The Connecticut Society of the Colonial Dames of America (Headquarters of the Society).

Significance. In the spring of 1781, when the weight of active campaigning had shifted to Virginia and the Carolinas, Washington's army lay inactive in and around West Point. It was obvious that a combined offensive must be undertaken by the allies if the American cause were not to languish. War weariness had settled on the land, and much of the Continental Army was scattered along the frontier and in the South. The Webb House, in Wethersfield, Conn., was destined to be the scene of a conference that started the Americans and their French allies on the road to victory.

Washington learned in the middle of May that Count de Rochambeau, the French commander in America, desired a meeting to discuss the plan of campaign. Washington immediately accepted this opportunity to

At the Webb House in Wethersfield, Conn., in May 1781, Generals Washington and Rochambeau planned American-French operations against the British in the closing campaigns of the War for Independence.

break the stalemate. The old Connecticut town of Wethersfield, lying about halfway between Washington's Hudson River headquarters at New Windsor and Rochambeau's headquarters at Newport, was selected as the place of meeting. On May 19 Washington arrived at Wethersfield and, in his own words, "lodged * * * at the house of Joseph Webb, Esq." On May 21 Washington rode to Hartford to meet Rochambeau, and the party returned to Wethersfield. The next day the French general confirmed that a French Fleet was en route to the West Indies and would be off the American coast by midsummer.

Here at last lay an opportunity for concerted action. Rochambeau, however, gave Admiral de Grasse, the French naval commander, the option of joining the allied forces against the British in New York or in Virginia.

As a result of the conference Rochambeau brought his forces, numbering nearly 5,000 men, to join Washington in New York. Part of the original plan of attack by the allies was aimed at the British forts on Manhattan Island, but after thorough reconnaissance of the British fortified lines the effort was wisely abandoned, and Washington turned his attention to the developing situation in the south. On August 14 Rochambeau heard from Admiral De Grasse that the fleet, with a strong land force aboard, would sail from the West Indies for Chesapeake Bay, where it would be available only until October. Washington acted quickly to take advantage of this substantial reinforcement. He notified De Grasse that the Franco-American Army would march south to cooperate with the fleet in cornering Cornwallis in Virginia. If the trap failed, an attack on Charleston could be undertaken. This decision bore fruit in the entrapment and surrender of Cornwallis at Yorktown.

Although it is too much to say that the conference in the Webb House laid the specific plans for the victorious Yorktown campaign, it nevertheless marked the implementation of the Franco-American alliance in terms of actual field operations. The American and French Armies were united in time for them to move south and operate in conjunction with the French Fleet from the West Indies.

Present Appearance. The Webb House was built in 1752 by Joseph Webb, who occupied it for 9 years before his death. With its well-proportioned exterior design and steep gambrel roof, the two-story house has considerable architectural interest. The south parlor, traditionally identified as the conference room, has been repaneled, and the house is excellently furnished, mostly by gifts from members of the Society of Colonial Dames. Several items of furniture, silver, and china belonged to the Webb family. The setting, suggestive of the 18th century, is enhanced by the broad, tree-lined street that passes in front, and by a number of old homes adjacent to it.

2. John Dickinson House, Delaware

Location. 5 miles southeast of Dover, .3 mile east of U.S. 113 on Kitts Hummock Road, Kent County.

Ownership and Administration. State of Delaware, administered by Delaware State Museum, Dover.

Significance. John Dickinson is known as the "Penman of the Revolution." A writer has said, "In the literature of that struggle, his position is as preeminent as Washington in war, Franklin in diplomacy, and Morris in finance." [8] Thomas Jefferson commented that "his name will be consecrated in history as one of the great worthies of the Revolution." [9] The restored John Dickinson House near Dover is the surviving structure most intimately associated with him.

It was built in 1740 by his father, and young Dickinson lived there until he was 18 in 1750, when he left for Philadelphia to study law. Dickinson lived in the house at various times after 1750, although his role in public life kept him most of the time in Philadelphia, Wilmington, and elsewhere.

Dickinson's career is briefly summarized: He read law with John Moland in Philadelphia, studied at London's Middle Temple, and in 1757 began the practice of law in Philadelphia. He was a prolific writer of political pamphlets, then the chief medium of argument and exposition, and he served in the colonial assemblies in both Delaware and Pennsylvania. His convictions were generally conservative and he disliked violence, but as a member of the Stamp Act Congress in 1765 he helped draft the Declaration of Rights and the Petition to the King adopted by that body.

In 1768 he published "Letters of a Farmer in Pennsylvania to the Inhabitants of the British Colonies," his most famous pamphlet. As leader of the conservative faction which opposed both British colonial policy and the radicals' drive for independence, and because he was fearful of a war in which Americans would have neither allies nor a central government, Dickinson refused to sign the Declaration of Independence. Nevertheless, he headed the committee which made the first draft of the Articles of Confederation, in July 1776, and he was one of the few Members of Congress who entered upon active duty with the Army during the war.

After the conflict ended Dickinson continued to be active in the public affairs of both Delaware and Pennsylvania until his death in 1808. He headed the Delaware delegation to the Annapolis Convention in 1786 and was elected chairman of the convention. In this capacity he presented the report recommending the Constitutional Convention to be held in Philadelphia in 1787, where he was a leader in fighting for the rights of small States and in urging prompt ratification of the Constitution. Delaware was the first State to ratify.

Present Appearance. The Dickinson mansion near Dover, its Flemish-bond front facing south, is one of the most interesting architectural examples of the plantation house of the region. Cultivated fields, all around it, produce a scene similar to that of the plantation period.

The original dwelling was a two-story brick structure, with hip roof. A fire gutted it in 1804, leaving little but the four walls, after which it was restored under Dickinson's close supervision. A gable roof was added and a small brick kitchen wing built at the west end. The interior of the rebuilt house was substantial but plain in keeping with its intended use from this time as a tenant house.

The National Society of Colonial Dames of America presented $25,000 to the State of Delaware in 1952 to preserve the Dickinson House, when it was threatened with destruction. The State matched this donation with a similar amount, the house and surrounding tract were acquired, the necessary research accomplished, and it was restored to its appearance as Dickinson last knew it, by means of State funds and private gifts. The reconstruction was based on Dickinson's correspondence and written instructions during the period 1804–6. Materials of the original structure were reused when found in good condition. A furnishing committee provided the interior with items typical of the region, some of which once belonged to the Dickinson family. A garden adjacent to the house has been developed with the aid of garden clubs and by private donations. The house was formally opened to the public on May 2, 1956.[10]

3. The Gundelo *Philadelphia*, Washington, D.C.

Location. Smithsonian Institution, Washington, D.C.

Ownership and Administration. Smithsonian Institution, U.S. Government.

Significance. The U.S. Gundelo *Philadelphia* is the only surviving gunboat built and manned by American forces during the Revolutionary War. Moreover, the vessel is one of the 15 small craft with which Benedict Arnold fought 29 British vessels in the battle off Valcour Island, Lake Champlain, on October 11, 1776. The year of grace won by the building of Arnold's "fleet" and the battle off Valcour Island paved the way for the decisive American victory at Saratoga in the autumn of the following year.

Little more than a rowboat compared with modern vessels, the *Philadelphia* was one of the hastily built fleet constructed in the early summer of 1776 at present Whitehall, N.Y. In late September 1776, the fleet took station in a small bay west of Valcour Island, about 7 miles south of what is now Plattsburgh, N.Y. The sound between the island and the mainland was about three-quarters of a mile wide, divided by a high bluff projecting from the west side of the island. Arnold's fleet formed a line south of the bluff and in this position on October 11 fought the heavier British Fleet to a standstill. The American force was badly damaged in the action, and only with considerable luck did Arnold elude the enemy and escape southward during the night. The *Royal Savage,* the former American flagship, was lost, and the *Philadelphia* was sunk on October 11, and only four of Arnold's vessels managed to escape the British pursuit during the next 2 days.

Arnold's action on Lake Champlain wrecked the plans of Gen. Sir Guy Carleton, British commander in Canada, to push down the Hudson and unite with Sir William Howe, a move that would have split the northern Colonies. Carleton moved on to Crown Point after the battle off Valcour Island, but the time lost in building his fleet to oppose Arnold, together with the hard fight with the Americans, led him to reconsider his plans. Deciding that it was now too late in the season to prosecute the invasion to a successful conclusion, Carleton withdrew to Canada.

In 1934 the wreck of the *Royal Savage* was recovered and the pieces saved. In the following year the *Philadelphia,* remarkably well preserved by the cold water, was identified and salvaged from the sandy lake bottom near the midchannel of Valcour Bay. After her guns were lifted, a 12-pounder and two 9-pounders, the hull was raised 57 feet to the surface and towed to the beach. In addition to her guns, hundreds of other relics were found on the vessel—shot, cooking utensils, tools, buttons, buckles, and human bones. The vessel was exhibited at various places on Lake Champlain and the Hudson River and finally, in 1960, was placed at the Smithsonian Institution.

Present Appearance. The *Philadelphia's* hull is 54 feet in length, 15 feet in beam, and approximately 5 feet deep. Construction was almost entirely of oak. The mast, nearly 36 feet high, was found intact except for the top section, and the oaken hull timbers were still in place. Three shotholes were visible in the hull, and in one of them a cannonball remained lodged. Considering the punishment it took in battle and its long years under water, the *Philadelphia* is exceptionally well-preserved.[11]

The Lady Pepperrell House, Kittery Point, Maine, was built in 1760 by the widow of Sir William Pepperrell, successful merchant and commander of the victorious expedition against Louisburg.

4. Lady Pepperrell House, Maine

Location.   Maine 103, Kittery Point, York County; near Portsmouth, N.H.

Ownership and Administration.   Society for the Preservation of New England Antiquities, 141 Cambridge Street, Boston 14, Mass.

Significance.   The home built at Kittery Point by the widow of Sir William Pepperrell is a notable example of northern colonial architecture in the closing years of British rule.   Its owner, Mary Pepperrell, was the daughter of Grove Hirst, wealthy Boston merchant, and a granddaughter of Judge Samuel Sewall, of the Massachusetts Bay Colony. Her husband commanded American land forces at the siege and capture of Louisburg, off Nova Scotia, in 1745.   For his services in this major victory over the forces of New France, Pepperrell was commissioned a colonel with authority to raise and command a regiment of regulars in the British line, and was given the title of baronet—the first native-born American to receive this honor.   By successful business ventures, he amassed a fortune estimated at a quarter of a million pounds and was known as one of the wealthiest men in the Colonies.   Sir William died in 1759, and about 1760 his widow built the great Georgian house in which she lived for 30 years and which today bears her name.

Present Appearance.   The house is a two-story frame structure with hip roof and two pairs of end chimneys, its whole appearance being one of simplicity.   Walls are clapboard, and the plain facade is distinguished only by the projecting pavilion of smooth white boards that give a masonry effect.   Ionic pilasters, two stories high, frame the door.   The window trips, caps, and sills project well forward of the wall line, to provide space for inside shutters.   The piazzas at either end are later additions.

The spacious center hall provides access to handsomely furnished rooms featuring great fireplaces and fine woodwork.   On the first floor are the living room to the left of the hall, and the drawing room to the right. Behind the living room is the dining room, from which a kitchen ell extends.   A large chamber is situated in the rear of the drawing room. On the second floor are five chambers, the smallest of which is located over the kitchen.

The furnishings point up the dignity of the interior design and construction.   Chippendale, Hepplewhite, Sheraton, and Duncan Phyfe furniture, with fine glass, china, mirrors, and paintings, do much to preserve the stately atmosphere that surrounded Lady Mary Pepperrell, who weathered the storms of revolution and, to the day of her death, demanded the deference due her title.[12]

5. Hammond-Harwood House, Maryland

Location.   Maryland Avenue at King George Street, Annapolis.

Ownership and Administration.   Hammond-Harwood House Association, Inc., Annapolis.

Significance.   Annapolis is a city containing many distinguished 18th-century houses, of which three, the Brice, the Chase-Lloyd, and the Hammond-Harwood, are the most notable.   Although all three are of first rank architecturally, the last appears to be the most significant in terms of English colonial associations.   Not only is it a superior example of the Georgian dwelling but, of the three, each attributed to William Buckland, the Hammond-Harwood House appears also to have the soundest claim to this distinction.   One authority has said of Buckland's design, "Here at last, it seems, he merits the appellation of 'architect' rather than 'decorator'." [13]   The writer notes further that the house marks the period of Buckland's architectural maturity, achieved in the years just preceding his untimely death at the age of 40. As an example of period architecture and a reflection of the genius of William Buckland, the Hammond-Harwood House is an outstanding survivor of the flowering of American architecture at the end of the colonial period.

Present Appearance. Probably completed in 1774, the year of Buckland's death, the Hammond-Harwood House is a symmetrical building typical of Georgian houses in the area. Its five-bay center section, constructed of salmon-colored brick laid up in Flemish bond, is flanked by two-story wings with polygonal bays. One wing served the house's builder, Matthias Hammond, as a law office, and the other housed kitchen and service rooms. Hammond is worthy of notice in his own right, for he was one of Maryland's distinguished leaders on the eve of the Revolution.

The low-pitched hip roof and center pavilion are typical of the late Georgian period. The arched fanlight doorway features tall Ionic columns and rich moldings. A wealth of carved woodwork gives ornamentation to the first-floor dining room and the second-floor ballroom. Decorations and furnishings, including many pieces that were in the house originally, adhere faithfully to the period. A number of portraits by Charles Willson Peale adorn the interior.[14]

6. Whitehall, Maryland

Location. Outskirts of Annapolis, off St. Margaret's Road, Anne Arundel County.

Ownership and Administration. Private.

Significance. Superlatives become Whitehall, not alone for its distinction of being the first colonial dwelling with temple-type portico, and as an exemplar of 18th-century "country life" in America, but also as the embodiment of a great many composite factors that contribute luster to a building and a site. Built by Maryland's bachelor Governor, Horatio Sharpe, at the close of the French and Indian War as a retreat and entertainment pavilion, it was shortly afterward enlarged. It served as his residence from the time of his enforced retirement in 1769 until his return to England in 1773. Whitehall was designed and built under Sharpe's direct supervision, along with the surrounding landscape development of gardens, parks, and entrance court in the shape of a semioctagon. The latter feature, capable of being fortified, undoubtedly

Whitehall, on the outskirts of Annapolis, was started by Maryland's Governor Horatio Sharpe at the close of the French and Indian War. Enlarged a short time later, it was Sharpe's residence from 1769 until 1773 when he returned to England.

reflected his military interests and concern for defense. As commander of colonial forces for the protection of Virginia and adjoining Colonies until superseded by Maj. Gen. Edward Braddock, Sharpe had firsthand experience with Indian warfare and depredations on the frontier. He was a capable civil and military administrator, and his Whitehall plantation recalls other roles as well: those of gentleman-farmer, fancier of fine horses, hospitable host, and friend of George Mason and George Washington.

Whitehall was an outstanding achievement in colonial design and elaboration of detail. All the more remarkable is the available documentation concerning the architect and a few of the craftsmen associated with its construction. This mansion is a key to the career of Joseph Horatio Anderson. Anderson's plans, now in the possession of the owner, were characterized by Fiske Kimball as the "most professional" to come from the hands of an 18th-century American designer—Jefferson's early drawings for Monticello excepted. A notable sketch in the same group, dealing with design and placement of carved ornaments in the great hall, is attributed to William Buckland. Buckland is credited with supplying the delicate Corinthian caps, the rich entablature, and the refined woodwork of the interior. John Rawlins, newly settled in Annapolis from London, executed the elaborate plaster cornices, enriched with color and gilt.

Present Appearance. Whitehall is a five-part brick house of Palladian character and unusual length, about 200 feet. The central block is one room deep, placed above a basement that is exposed on the north facade only. The great portico to the south opens into a salon, or great hall, that extends through two floors. Arcaded hyphens connect with end wings covered by pyramidal roofs, projecting northward to give the effect of two-story units. Extant plans and specifications reveal that the building was designed as a seven-part composition with a half-underground kitchen extension containing a well, and at the other end a unique water-closet development just off the bedroom wing. Archeological studies indicate that the kitchen addition was built as planned, although the other development was apparently never carried out. An unusual cistern, however, fed by rainwater from the roofs, was incorporated into the foundation of the original unit and extended under the portico and across the entire central block, apparently in anticipation of some such development. Archeological research has established another remarkable detail in the carved, sanded, and painted presentment of the great seal of Maryland placed in the pediment on the riverfront. Archeological activity likewise has uncovered the ruins of the Whitehall brick kiln at the river landing.

The exterior appearance of the mansion was restored in 1957, based upon painstaking studies. The original acreage is nearly intact.[15]

7. Buckman Tavern, Massachusetts

Location. Hancock Street, opposite east side of Lexington Green, Lexington.

Ownership and Administration. Town of Lexington, administered by Lexington Historical Society.

Significance. Buckman Tavern is an integral and important part of the historical setting of the first conflict of the War for American Independence, and it appears in the background of nearly every illustration depicting the brief fight between the British light infantry and the minutemen. One of Lexington's better hostelries, it was built about 1690 by Benjamin Muzzey, who in 1693 received a license to maintain a public house. In 1775 it was owned and operated by John Buckman, a member of the Lexington Minuteman Company, and was a favorite gathering place for the citizen-soldiers on days when they trained on the Lexington Green. Captain Parker's minutemen assembled at the tavern during the night and early morning as Major Pitcairn's British regulars

Buckman Tavern, facing Lexington Green, looks here almost exactly as it did on the morning of April 19, 1775, when it was the mustering place for Lexington's company of minutemen.

approached from Boston, and the building still exhibits scars left by British musket balls fired at Parker's men drawn up on the Green. Buckman Tavern housed the first village store in Lexington, and later, in 1812, the first town post office.

Present Appearance. Some structural changes were made in Buckman Tavern between 1690 and 1775, but it appears today virtually the same as at the time of the battle on Lexington Green. A two-story white clapboard building, the tavern retains its 18th-century taproom with large fireplace and central chimney. Acquired by the town of Lexington in 1913, it constituted a significant extension of the triangle formed by the Battle Green. The Lexington Historical Society, already the owner of the Hancock-Clarke House and the Munroe Tavern, made a generous contribution toward the purchase and, under a 99-year lease, assumed the task of furnishing the building and showing it to the public. Buckman Tavern is now maintained by the Lexington Historical Society as a historic house museum. It also serves as headquarters for the Lexington Minute Men, Inc., an organization that perpetuates the traditions of Captain Parker's company.[16]

8. Bunker Hill Monument, Massachusetts

Location. Breed's Hill, Charlestown.

Ownership and Administration. Commonwealth of Massachusetts, Metropolitan District Commission, 20 Somerset Street, Boston.

Significance. The Battle of Bunker Hill was actually fought on nearby Breed's Hill, June 17, 1775. It was the first full-scale action between American militia and British regulars following the running fight at Lexington and Concord, 2 months earlier. The raw American Army was driven from its position after repulsing two assaults, although the costly British victory did not alter the situation for the besieged redcoats. The battle convinced the British command that defeating the rebellious colonists would not be an easy task, however, and in later years the American defeat was translated into virtual victory by the folklore that sprang from the fight. Actually, the struggle for Breed's Hill had a harmful effect in creating the myth that raw militia, suffused with patriotism, could always take the measure of professional troops. Indecisive as it was, the battle has remained in the American tradition as one of the key episodes of the Revolution.

Present Appearance. The present monument marks the approximate center of the American redoubt on Breed's Hill and is surrounded by a 4-acre park in a residential section of Charlestown. The monument itself possesses considerable interest as an example of early historical monumentation. The Bunker Hill Monument Association was organized in 1823, a year after 3 acres of the battlefield had been purchased to keep it open. In 1825 an additional 15 acres was purchased. When the association ran short of funds, however, most of this land was sold in 1834 and the proceeds applied to completing the 220-foot obelisk. The cornerstone of the monument was laid in 1825, the 50th anniversary of the battle, although construction was not completed until 1842. A statute of Col. William Prescott, commander of the American troops on Breed's Hill, stands at the base of the monument. A small museum is open to visitors. The monument is much in need of rehabilitation and development, particularly in regard to its interpretation of the battle story.[17]

9. Christ Church (in Cambridge), Massachusetts

Location. Garden Street, opposite George Washington Memorial Gateway, Cambridge.

Ownership and Administration. Christ Church, Cambridge.

Significance. This warm and dignified Episcopal church is a memorable evocation of 18th-century America in the last years of British rule and the period of the War for Independence. Christ Church was built between 1759 and 1761 on a design by the great Peter Harrison, then approaching the peak of his genius. It was the religious center for Cambridge aristocrats until the outbreak of the Revolution. Cambridge Common, in front of the church, served as a mustering ground for American troops. Most of the loyalist Anglican congregation had departed before the British evacuated Boston in March 1776, and the church was used as a barracks by the Americans. In December 1775 Martha Washington, who had come to join her husband, requested that the church be readied for religious services. On New Year's Eve, and infrequently afterward, services were held during Washington's stay in Cambridge. After Burgoyne's surrender at Saratoga in October 1777, his captive army was held for a time in Cambridge. A funeral

Christ Church faces the Common in Cambridge, Mass., and is the only structure in the immediate area which survives from colonial times. It was designed and built by Peter Harrison in 1759–61.

was held in Christ Church for a young British officer who was killed in this period. After the service a mob attacked and heavily damaged the church. Not until 1790 were services resumed in the building.

Present Appearance. Christ Church today is the only surviving landmark of colonial Cambridge Common. The exterior of the church is dominated by a simple, squat, wooden tower, topped by a commonplace cruciform belfry with some lunette windows on the front and sides. The church has no interior galleries and the sidewalls of rusticated planking are low. A row of seven arched windows of plain glass, topped by a Roman Doric cornice, relieves the plainness of each side. The simple exterior is in sharp contrast to the interior. Six Ionic columns along each side support the ceiling over the aisles. The recessed ceiling over the nave curves up to a flat panel, from which are suspended fine crystal chandeliers given in memory of Jessie B. Sayre, a daughter of Woodrow Wilson. The windows have heavy two-piece slatted shutters on the inside. When folded back, they partly cover the pilasters between the windows. The interior originally was 45 by 60 feet, but in 1857 the nave was lengthened by the addition of two bays.

The finest original surviving feature is the organ loft, although tradition has it that the original lead organ pipes were melted into bullets during the Revolution. The pew of George and Martha Washington is marked by a bronze plaque. Several bullet holes, one of which is marked by a plaque, are said to date from the period of the American military encampment. Modern restoration has been very conscientious, and later interior features are in keeping with the period of the church's original construction.[18]

10. Faneuil Hall, Massachusetts

Location. Dock Square, Boston.

Ownership and Administration. City of Boston, Real Property Department, City Hall Annex, Boston.

Significance. Often called "the Cradle of Liberty," Faneuil Hall was a focal point in the organization of colonial resentment and protest against acts of the British Parliament in the years immediately prior to the Revolution. Here James Otis, Samuel Adams, and other leaders of opposition to the Crown built colonial dissent into powerful sentiment for American self-government. Faneuil Hall heard the voices of the most notable leaders in the fight for the abolition of slavery in the 19th

century, and it remains today a significant symbol of the struggle for
American freedom.

In 1740 a market house was offered to Boston by Peter Faneuil,
"the topmost merchant in all the town." The question of fixed market-
places had long been debated, the countrymen favoring competition-
free, door-to-door peddling, and the city dwellers favoring a convenient
central market. Faneuil's offer was accepted by a narrow margin, and
on September 10, 1742, the building was completed. Perhaps to allay
opposition to the market, Faneuil arranged for a long room above the
marketplace to serve for town meetings and municipal purposes. The
building was designed by John Smibert, a noted painter turned amateur
architect for the project. Originally two stories high, 40 by 100 feet,
the structure was Georgian in style, with open arcades to the public
market on the ground floor. The large center cupola on the roof was
topped by a famous weather vane, a huge grasshopper with green glass
eyes and long antennae, turned out by Deacon Shem Drowne in May
1742. The hall was destroyed by fire on January 13, 1761, and only
its brick walls were left standing. It was rebuilt and opened again in
1763, becoming for several years thereafter the scene of many of the
public meetings that foreshadowed the Revolution. By 1768 the size
of the protesting crowds often made adjournments to the Old South
Meeting House necessary.

Faneuil Hall's great role in the Revolutionary movement had not
ended, however, for in a town meeting there on November 2, 1772,
Samuel Adams succeeded in creating the extralegal Committee of
Correspondence, the first of the bodies that produced the union of
the American Colonies. During the siege of Boston, the hall was used
as a playhouse for amateur theatricals offered by British officers and
Tory ladies in the town.

Present Appearance. As Boston grew in the years following the
Revolution, an enlargement of the hall and market became necessary.
This was accomplished during 1805–6 in accordance with plans drawn
by Boston's Charles Bulfinch. The building was tripled in size by
increasing its original three bays to seven and adding a third story.
The second-floor hall was thus expanded in area and in height, permitting the construction of galleries resting on Doric columns. Bulfinch
moved the large cupola with the grasshopper weather vane to the east
end, creating a more imposing effect. The attic of the enlarged building
became the armory of the Ancient and Honorable Artillery Company.

The exterior of the original building had an applied order of brick pilasters in the Doric style, capped by a heavy entablature of stone at the eaves. Bulfinch retained the entablature and from it ran an order of Ionic brick pilasters up the new and higher third story. A series of barrel-shaped dormers was placed on the new roof, lighting the attic. The arched open arcades that had provided access to the market area on the first floor were filled in with windows corresponding to the arched windows of the second floor. Faneuil Hall ceased to be the scene of town meetings after Boston obtained a city charter in 1822, but remained a popular meeting place and forum during the 19th century. From 1827 until 1858 there was no market activity in the hall, the space being given over to eight stores occupied by vendors of drygoods and hardware. After 1858, when the market was restored, the space was appropriated by butchers, as it is today.

The great hall on the second floor displays a collection of paintings, many of the portraits being copies of originals that once hung there but that are now protected in the Boston Museum of Fine Arts. The attic is still the armory of the Ancient and Honorable Artillery Company and contains a collection of military and other objects dating from the colonial period and afterward.

In 1898–99 the city of Boston reconstructed the hall, substituting iron, steel, and stone for wood, as far as practicable. In general, the Bulfinch plans were followed. Despite these efforts, the building is now considered substandard from the standpoint of safety.[19]

11. Isaac Royall House, Massachusetts

Location. 15 George Street, Medford.

Ownership and Administration. Royall House Association, 15 George Street, Medford.

Significance. "Few houses in Colonial history possess the interest of this one and the Royall House stands unique and distinctive among the many colonial houses of the period."[20] This evaluation of nearly half a century ago is clear evidence of the high place long accorded to this outstanding house of the 18th century. Actually, the building had its origins in the middle of the 17th century. About 1637 Gov. John Winthrop had built a house on the site, which gave way about 1692 to a more imposing brick house 2½ stories high and one room in depth. This was purchased in 1732 by Isaac Royall, a wealthy merchant of

The Isaac Royall House, Medford, Mass., is named for the wealthy merchant of Antigua who acquired the property in 1732. The house was extensively remodeled by Royall and later greatly enlarged by his son.

Antigua, and extensively remodeled in the period 1733–37. Royall's son came into its possession in 1739, and greatly enlarged it between 1747 and 1750. The younger Royall, a loyalist, fled the country at the outbreak of the Revolution and his estate was confiscated. The house served thereafter at various times as headquarters for American officers, among them Gen. John Stark. Generals Washington, Lee, and Sullivan were frequent visitors. The house was later returned to the Royall heirs, and they in turn sold it to a syndicate.

Present Appearance. The Royall House reflects the wealth and position of its owners; it also exhibits the alterations and additions made by each. Isaac Royall added a full third story to the original house and encased the east facade in clapboard, ornamenting the exterior with profuse architectural details in wood. He was also responsible for the outstanding feature of the exterior—continuous strips of spandrel panels uniting all the tall windows on the three stories of the east facade and emphasizing the vertical lines of the structure. Outbuildings were erected at the same time, including brick slave quarters—the only such known to survive in Massachusetts today. Between 1747 and 1750 Royall's son made other changes. He more than doubled the depth, extended the end walls correspondingly, and constructed great twin chimneys at each end of the house, connected by parapets. Other features added by the younger Royall were the rusticated wood siding on the new west facade and great Doric pilasters inserted at the corners. The interior was redone in Georgian detail possibly unsurpassed by any surviving house of the period.

Rented by the Daughters of the American Revolution in 1896, and acquired by the present owners 12 years later, the Royall House has received expert treatment in recent years in the restoration of interior colors, furnishings, and wallpapers. Among the historic objects displayed is one of the teaboxes dumped into Boston Harbor on the night of December 16, 1773. The frontage provided by a small city park between the eastern edge of the lot and Main Street enhances the setting, which is otherwise isolated by the residential growth of Greater Boston.[21]

12. Jeremiah Lee Mansion, Massachusetts

Location. Washington Street opposite Mason Street, Marblehead.

Ownership and Administration. Marblehead Historical Society, Marblehead.

Significance. This mansion, one of the best surviving examples of colonial architecture, demonstrates the wealth and position of the New England merchant princes whose ships plied the oceans in the 18th century. Col. Jeremiah Lee came to America in the early part of the 18th century. By 1760 he had become one of Marblehead's most prominent citizens and his home, built in 1768, was the center of the town's

The Jeremiah Lee Mansion, Marblehead, Mass., was the home of an 18th-century "merchant prince."

social life.   Originally a loyalist, Lee took up the colonial cause early and, although he died shortly after the outbreak of the Revolution, he played a leading part in preparing Massachusetts for the war.   After Lee's death his widow continued to live in the mansion, which remained a center of Marblehead social life.   Among its distinguished visitors were the Marquis de Lafayette, George Washington, James Monroe, and Andrew Jackson.   The house later passed into other hands and, for a century after 1804, was used as a bank.   The Marblehead Historical Society acquired the property in 1909.

Present Appearance.   Lee's three-story house was built of pine timbers and brick, over which were placed rusticated clapboards which, with the sand mixed into the final coat of limestone-gray paint, gave an appearance of masonry to the exterior.   The line of the facade is somewhat plain, broken only by a simple portico of two fluted Ionic columns. Surmounting the hip roof are two massive chimneys and a cupola from which Lee could watch for incoming ships flying his private flag.   The 16 rooms contain a wealth of intricate wood carving.   Much of the original wallpaper remains, and careful restoration has preserved to a remarkable extent the features of construction and decoration that characterized the house when it was home to a wealthy merchant and civic leader of 18th-century New England.   The mansion's historical collection includes original letters, diaries, account books, and genealogical records of old Marblehead.[22]

13. King's Chapel, Massachusetts

Location.   School and Tremont Streets, Boston.

Ownership and Administration.   King's Chapel Society, Boston.

Significance.   King's Chapel is an outstanding specimen of the work of Peter Harrison of Newport.   It was the first important building in British America to be built of cut stone, providing the first recorded use of Quincy granite in its construction, 1749–54.   Harrison took his design details for the most part from the *Book of Architecture* by James Gibbs, English master of the mid-Georgian style.   The interior has been called by one authority "without question the finest of Georgian church architecture in the Colonies." [23]   The architect intended that a tower with a lofty spire should surpass those on London churches of the period, but it was never built.

The massive stone walls of King's Chapel form a rectangle about 65 by 100 feet. The chapel was built around an earlier wooden structure that was the first Anglican church permanently established in New England. When the stone church was completed in 1754, the earlier

King's Chapel in Boston, built in 1749–54, is a superb example of the work of Peter Harrison.

wooden building was taken apart and its pieces removed through the arched windows of the new church.

Harrison's plan for King's Chapel included a front porch with stone Ionic columns, 25 feet high, to be crowned by an elaborate balustrade. These details were not added until 1785–87 and were done in wood rather than stone. The most striking feature of the interior is the series of Corinthian columns projecting in pairs to divide the elaborately paneled gallery fronts.

After the evacuation of Boston by the British in 1776, King's Chapel was finally separated from the Church of England and for a time was called simply the "Stone Chapel." The society that owns it now is an independent one, but it is regarded as the first church in the United States avowedly of the Unitarian fellowship.

Present Appearance. King's Chapel has undergone little modification or alteration. The stone floor was laid over the original wooden one in the present century, and a sprinkler system has been installed in the attic and basement. An iron catwalk provides access to the copper roof at the eaves to facilitate removal of ice, which was formerly a serious winter hazard on the School Street side of the building. The ice problem has now been overcome by the use of steam conductors at the edge of the roof. The interior contains a number of relics dating from the chapel's affiliation with the Anglican Church. These include the communion table and the chancel tablets given to the original church in 1696 by King William and Queen Mary. The raised pulpit also came from the earlier building, where it had been placed in 1718. The interior painting reflects a period later than that of its original construction. The building is well preserved and in good condition.[24]

14. Lexington Green, Massachusetts

Location. Massachusetts Avenue and Hancock Street, Lexington.

Ownership and Administration. Town of Lexington.

Significance. On Lexington Green on the morning of April 19, 1775, occurred the short but momentous skirmish between the minutemen and the British expeditionary force from Boston that initiated the struggle for American independence. Maj. John Pitcairn, commanding the British, saw the minutemen confronting his column at Lexington Green and formed his troops in line of battle. Realizing the hopelessness of the situation, Capt. John Parker, commanding the Americans, ordered his men to file away, but before they could do so a British volley and a charge with the bayonet killed 8 of the Americans and wounded 10 more. These were the first American fatalities in a war that would drag on for 8 years.

Present appearance. Lexington Green and nearby Buckman Tavern have been preserved as historic sites since the Revolution, and by State legislation enacted in 1956 they now comprise one of three protected historic districts in Lexington. On the east side of the common, facing the road by which the British approached, Henry H. Kitson's famous statue of a minuteman stands on a pile of rocks over a stone fountain. The historic Revolutionary Monument, erected in 1799 to commemorate the eight minutemen killed here, occupies the southwest corner of the green, and behind it is a tomb to which the remains of the dead were moved from the old burying ground in 1835. Two inscribed

boulders have also been placed on the green.   One identifies the site
of the old belfry, which was separate from the meetinghouse.   The
other, near the northwest corner, marks one flank of Captain Parker's
line.   It bears, in addition to designs of musket and powder horn,
Parker's immortal words: "Stand your ground.   Don't fire unless fired
upon.   But if they mean to have a war, let it begin here."   Lexington
Green and its monumentation recall vividly the opening military event
of the American Revolution.[25]

15. Massachusetts Hall, Massachusetts

Location.   Harvard University Campus, Cambridge.
Ownership and Administration.   Harvard University.
Significance.   Erected between 1718 and 1720, Massachusetts Hall
is the oldest surviving building of the first colonial institution for higher
learning.   As such, it possesses great significance not only in the history
of American education but also in the story of the developing English
Colonies of the 18th century.

Harvard College was founded in 1636, although it did not receive
its name and begin its active existence until 2 years later.   Even though
the founding and early years of the college belong to the 17th century,
Masachusetts Hall, built in the early years of the 18th century, illustrates
notably the striving for intellectual development and the first groping
toward education liberalism in the century that saw the Colonies become the United States of America.   Although a leading function of
Harvard was to supply clergymen for the Colonies, its graduates in fact
entered all walks of colonial life.   The liberal arts course was patterned
on that of Oxford and Cambridge, both of which recognized degrees
from Harvard.   The college was the site of the first laboratory for
experimental physics prior to the Revolution, and it developed a strong
curriculum in mathematics and physical sciences.   Most of the students
in the 18th century came from New England, but the college rolls reveal
also a scattering of young men from more southerly mainland Colonies,
Bermuda, and the West Indies.

Massachusetts Hall was designed by Harvard Presidents John Leverett
and his successor Benjamin Wadsworth.   It was originally a dormitory
containing 32 chambers and 64 small private studies for the 64 students
it was designed to house.   During the siege of Boston, 640 American
soldiers took quarters in the hall.   Much of the interior woodwork and

hardware, including brass doorknobs, disappeared at this time.

Present Appearance. The building has three full stories with a fourth under the broad gambrel roof. "The walls are plainly treated," Hugh Morrison has commented, "marked only by brick belt courses between stories; the brick masonry is laid in English bond below the water table and in Flemish bond above, except at the ends where there is a mixture of English and common bonds. The simple mass and heavy woodwork of the windows give a very satisfactory effect of solidity, and it is this effect—an early Georgian simplicity and weight—which has been sought in the recent buildings of Harvard." [26]

16. Old North Church (Christ Church in Boston), Massachusetts

Location. 193 Salem Street, Boston.

Ownership and Administration. Corporation of Christ Church in the City of Boston.

Significance. Old North Church was built in 1723 by William Price, a book and print seller of Boston, from designs based on Christopher Wren's great London churches. Historically and architecturally, it is one of the Nation's most cherished landmarks. The signal lanterns hung in the church belfry—"One, if by land, and two, if by sea," as Longfellow put it—were not intended for Paul Revere, who had arranged for the signal. Nevertheless, despite the almost legendary quality of the story today, the lanterns did hang in the belfry on the night of April 18 to alert patriots on the opposite side of the Charles River that British troops were moving out of Boston by water. In addition to its role as a signal station on the eve of the Revolution, Old North possesses further distinction as Boston's oldest surviving church. With the adjacent equestrian statue of Paul Revere, it is a memorable evocation of the night when the call to arms went out and the War for Independence began.

Present Appearance. Old North Church was built of brick walls laid in English bond 51 feet wide and 70 feet long, with two tiers of arched windows. A projecting square brick tower nearly 100 feet high was added to the original structure in 1724–37 and topped by a wooden steeple 191 feet high in 1740. This first steeple was blown down in 1804 and replaced several years later by a similar one possibly designed by Charles Bulfinch. The second tower was toppled by a hurricane on August 31, 1954, and has since been replaced.

The interior is particularly valuable as an early example of the then-new "church" plan of a two-storied structure, with longitudinal aisles separating the groups of box pews, in contrast to the 17th-century "meetinghouse" plan that had a raised pulpit on one long side of the building with galleries at the other three sides. The origin of the new plan in Wren designs is shown also by the use to support the galleries of superimposed pillars, the lower square and the upper fluted.

The interior was restored carefully and thoroughly in 1912–14, when a number of 19th-century alterations were eliminated. A stone tablet placed on the tower in 1878 identifies it as the place where the signal lanterns burned on the night of April 18, 1775. The church is well maintained, although its crowded surroundings detract from the setting and constitute a fire hazard to the building. More than 200,000 people visit the landmark annually.[27]

17. Old South Meeting House, Massachusetts

Location. Milk and Washington Streets, Boston.

Ownership and Administration. Old South Association, Boston.

Significance. Old South Meeting House—the "Sanctuary of Freedom"—belongs to two distinct triumvirates of historic buildings in Boston. The first group is made up of outstanding religious edifices from the colonial period, and includes Christ Church and King's Chapel. The second group is made up of structures that gained a lasting place in the American heritage as scenes of public assembly and deliberation in the stirring period of the Revolutionary movement. In the latter group Old South, because of its large seating capacity, shared distinction with the Second Boston Town House and Faneuil Hall. In many instances the last two could not accommodate certain mass gatherings that were the prelude to the final break with England. The mass protest meetings that gave Old South lasting fame took place during the tumultuous interval between the passage of the Townshend Acts in 1767 and the outbreak of war in 1775.

The first in the series of significant assemblies in Old South was held on June 14 and 15, 1768, when public feeling ran high immediately after the liberty riots and the ill-advised attempt by a captain of the British Navy to impress Yankee sailors in Boston Harbor. In this instance, the Colonials were somewhat mollified by the intercession of the Governor and the assurance that the Navy would be more cautious in seeking men for service. Not quite 2 years later the Boston Massacre (March 5, 1770) brought an inflamed throng of citizens to the Old South Meeting House. A committee headed by Samuel Adams, fresh from a conference with British officials concerning the removal of the redcoats from Boston, reported to the people on the afternoon after the "massacre" in King Street. Master James Lovell of Boston Latin School delivered the first anniversary oration commemorating the Boston Massacre in Old South.

The most significant of the gatherings were the antitea meetings which led to the Boston Tea Party on the night of December 16, 1773. The 1775 anniversary observance of the Boston Massacre was the last and most eventful such assemblage in Old South. Dr. Joseph Warren is supposed to have entered through the window behind the pulpit to avoid the British officers who had crowded the aisles and seated themselves on the pulpit steps, presumably hoping to break up the meeting.

During the siege of Boston, the Old South congregation dispersed, many of the members seeking refuge outside town. The church parsonage nearby was torn down by British troops and its material used as firewood. Old South's brick construction probably saved it from a similar fate, although most of its interior furnishings were used for fuel and the building turned into a riding school for British cavalry. This unhappy period ended with the evacuation of the British Army in March 1776. The congregation slowly reassembled and, in 1783, restored the interior much as it had been half a century earlier.

Old South, a large structure for its day, was built in 1729–30 for Third Church, the third body of Congregationalists to be organized in Boston. This group had gathered in 1669 to protest the narrower views of the congregation of North Church. In 1717 a new body of Congregationalists had taken the name "New South Church." To keep its identity clear, Third Church was called "Old South," the name it bears today. The new meetinghouse of brick, replacing an earlier wooden church, was designed by Robert Twelves and laid up in Flemish bond by Joshua Blanchard, a master mason who was later to win even higher recognition as the builder of the Thomas Hancock House on Beacon Hill and the original Faneuil Hall. The exterior of the new meetinghouse showed a marked reflection of the new Georgian style. It had two tiers of arched windows and a projecting tower in front, with a spire rising from an octagonal base. The interior plan is typical of a 17th-century New England meetinghouse, consisting of a side entrance with a central aisle leading across the auditorium to a high pulpit at the middle of the opposite long side. Galleries extended around the other three sides, with a second gallery added over the first at the east end.

When the interior of the meetinghouse was restored after the Revolution, the original design was generally followed, although subsequent repairs and improvements reflected the styles and taste of the early Republic. A number of changes occurred during the 19th century until, in the great fire of 1872, a considerable area around the meetinghouse was burned, with some damage to the building itself. Because of the removal of many of its members to the developing Back Bay area, the congregation decided in 1874 to move to a new building at the corner of Boyleston and Dartmouth Streets. Having no further use for the old house, the congregation decided to tear down the building and sell the valuable land on which it stood. When demolition started, however, public sentiment was aroused to save the structure. The outcome was the purchase of the meetinghouse for $400,000 by a committee of citizens. In the next few years the growth of the Old South preservation fund assured the success of this early undertaking in the cause of historical preservation.

After necessary repairs had been made, Old South became a historical museum. Of particular note was its role as headquarters for the Old South work in history and the program of publication of the extensive series of Old South leaflets covering a broad range of American history.

Present Appearance. Old South Meeting House has been maintained in a satisfactory state of repair and some efforts at restoration have been undertaken with the limited financial resources of the Old South Association. Box pews, for instance, have been installed again on the floor of the auditorium.[28]

18. Paul Revere House, Massachusetts

Location. 19 North Square, Boston.

Ownership and Administration. Paul Revere Memorial Association, 19 North Square, Boston.

Significance. Although it has been restored extensively, the Paul Revere House retains its original framework and, in addition to its significance as the home of a leading Revolutionary patriot, is important as downtown Boston's only surviving 17th-century dwelling. It was

The Paul Revere House, built soon after the Boston fire of 1676, was the patriot's home from before the Revolution until 1800. Restoration of the house reflects its 17th-century origin. Courtesy, Boston National Historic Sites Commission.

occupied by Paul Revere for about 5 years before the outbreak of the Revolution and was his home until 1800. The original portion of the house was built, probably by John Jeffs, soon after the Boston fire of 1676, on the site of the Increase Mather Parsonage. Architectural investigation indicates that the house was originally of the simple and characteristic 17th-century hall or one-room plan with an end chimney, of 2½ stories, but when Revere moved into it almost a century later it had probably been enlarged to three full stories. In the 19th century, after Revere's death, the dwelling degenerated into a tenement and store and was considerably altered. In 1908 it was studied and restored by Architect Joseph Everett Chandler, who worked to preserve it as an example of a 17th-century urban house. This architectural significance, in addition to intimate association with the patriot and craftsman, Paul Revere, make the house a treasured landmark in downtown Boston.

Present Appearance. The Paul Revere House consists of the main portion, fronting on North Square, and an early kitchen ell at the rear. It was through the back door in the kitchen ell that Revere probably passed for his famous ride on the night of April 18, 1775. North Square was full of British soldiers, and the front door would not have been safe. The main house has a deeply recessed fireplace in the hall and a small porch and winding stair in front of the chimney. The ceiling of the large room or hall is spanned by two summer beams. The main house has the characteristic 17th-century overhang, and the pendants, windows, front door, and roof have been restored in the 17th-century fashion, but the second-floor chamber is plastered, paneled, and painted as it might have been when occupied by the Reveres. The house is well maintained and is open to the public.[29]

19. Second Boston Town House (Old State House), Massachusetts

Location. Washington and State Streets, Boston.

Ownership and Administration. City of Boston; custody vested in the Bostonian Society.

Significance. In the troubled years prior to the Declaration of Independence in 1776, the Second Boston Town House was the scene of proceedings of greater moment than those at any other building in the Thirteen Colonies. In February 1761 James Otis struck sparks here that helped to ignite the Revolutionary movement with his impassioned argument against the legality of writs of assistance. Of this occasion John Adams wrote: "Then and there the child Independence was born." The building figured prominently in the Stamp Act riots and in the affray later called the Boston Massacre, March 5, 1770.

It was erected in 1712–13 to replace an earlier structure of wood completed in 1658 and destroyed in the great fire of October 2–3, 1711. The Second Town House, like its predecessor, served a variety of purposes for the Province, for Suffolk County, and for the town of Boston. The second building was itself destroyed by fire on December 9, 1747, and was rebuilt the following year, utilizing the walls that had survived the fire.

Almost from the day of its completion, the Second Town House was the center of political activity and controversy in the Province of Massachusetts Bay. Representatives of the Crown came into conflict here with the deputies of the people in the house of representatives, whose membership was popularly chosen in the town meeting. In the Second Town House Gov. William Shirley worked out his plan for the expedition to capture the French fortress of Louisburg on Cape

Breton Island, one of the most notable military operations of the colonial period. Upon the return of the expedition in July 1745, its commanders were honored by a ceremony at the Second Town House. In 1766 the house of representatives voted to install a gallery for the accommodation of visitors, a noteworthy step forward in the democratic procedure of legislative assemblies opening their doors to the public. As the people of Boston grew increasingly restless, British General Gage was sworn into office as military governor in the council chamber of the town house. On June 7, 1774, Gage moved the final session of the general court to Salem, and the town house ceased to be the seat of popular representation until legislators of the new State government returned in November 1776. The town house then became the state house.

With the completion of Charles Bulfinch's new statehouse, the members of the legislature on January 11, 1798, marched in a body from the old structure to the new. In 1803 the Commonwealth of Massachusetts sold its interest in the building to the town of Boston, and the counties of Suffolk and Norfolk followed suit. For more than a quarter of a century the building housed private offices and served as a Masonic meeting hall. In 1830 Boston appropriated space in the building for a city hall. While rehabilitating the building for this purpose the architects introduced new details and made alterations. The changes made at this time and perpetuated in work done later, when the building was rescued from oblivion and rededicated in 1882, largely obliterated the features that had given it identity with the period of the stormy movement toward revolution.

Present Appearance. Ill-conceived attempts at restoration have marred seriously the interior of the Second Town House. The present plan of the all-important second floor has a circular foyer in the center, opening onto four small rooms and into corridors that lead to the representatives' hall at one end of the building and the council chamber at the other. Architects and historians have shown that in the building's most important period, 1766 to 1776, the representatives' chamber was in the center of the second floor. The restoration of the second floor would be very desirable, as well as that of the ground floor and basement, which contain a subway entrance and exit. The building is occupied by the Bostonian Society and is open to the public under the auspices of this group.[30]

20. Shirley-Eustis House, Massachusetts

Location. 31–37 Shirley Street, Roxbury.

Ownership and Administration. Shirley-Eustis House Association, % Director, Society for the Preservation of New England Antiquities, 141 Cambridge Street, Boston.

Significance. This house was built for William Shirley, eminent colonial figure of the generation preceding the Revolution. Shirley was the Royal Governor of Massachusetts Bay, 1741 to 1756, and his imposing home, built about 1747, became a colonial showplace. Governor Shirley personally organized the expedition that captured the French fortress of Louisburg in 1745. After the death of British General Braddock in 1755, he was named commander of British forces in North America. In 1761 he was appointed Governor of the Bahamas. He returned to his country seat at Roxbury in 1769 and died there on March 24, 1771.

The proposed restoration of the Shirley-Eustis House, Roxbury, as pictured in this drawing, would give this distinguished dwelling the setting merited by its historic and architectural significance. Courtesy, Boston National Historic Sites Commission.

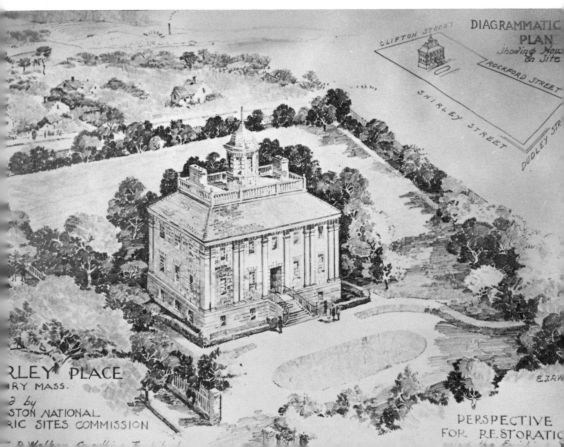

The house, often called Shirley Place, was confiscated during the Revolution and used by the patriots as a barracks and hospital during the siege of Boston. Thereafter the property passed through several hands until it was purchased in 1819 by Dr. William Eustis. He had been a surgeon in the Revolutionary War and was twice elected Governor of Massachusetts. He made a number of alterations in the building, adding a broad staircase in the salon.

Present Appearance. Manifestly Georgian in design, the Shirley-Eustis House is a 3½-story structure framed in solid oak, with hipped roof and a cupola. The facades are adorned by giant pilasters, the first in New England except for the Hutchinson House in Boston. A large salon, two stories high, divides the house and was used for State banquets and receptions. The high stone basement contained kitchens and offices. The house was sold in 1867 and moved 30 feet in order to lay out Shirley Street. Before rescue by the Shirley-Eustis House Association in 1911, it had been cut up into tenements and its original rural setting wholly destroyed by streets and unsightly buildings crowding upon it. In recent years the house has been kept in a state of temporary repair pending definite plans for restoration. The interior is not furnished, and the entire building is in urgent need of repairs. Although the Shirley-Eustis House Association has been unable to do more than provide the most necessary preservation, it has made the house available for architectural investigation. Much has been learned about the changes in the structure from the period of Governor Shirley to that of Governor Eustis, and most of the changes after 1867 have been removed. The house is protected by a resident caretaker who occupies quarters in the basement story.[31]

21. Wright's Tavern, Massachusetts

Location. Center of Concord on Lexington Road.

Ownership and Administration. Society of the First Parish, Concord.

Significance. Wright's Tavern stood in the center of Concord. With the public meetinghouse on one side and the militia training ground on the other, it was a favorite resort of Concord's leading citizens for both business and pleasure, and thus played an important role in the transaction of the town's civil and military business. Built in 1747 by Ephraim Jones, who operated it until 1751, the tavern was managed during the portentous days of April 1775 by Amos Wright, whose name it has borne ever since. On April 19, when the courthouse bell announced the ap-

Wright's Tavern, built in 1747 at Concord, played a colorful role in events leading up to the War for Independence, and in the fighting which marked the war's first day.

proach of Major Pitcairn's British troops, the Concord minutemen assembled at Wright's Tavern. Later, after Pitcairn's arrival in the public square, the British officers took refreshments in the tavern. As the scene of these events, the tavern has important associations with the opening military episode of the Revolution.

It also has associations with the Provincial Congress of Massachusetts Bay which met next door, in the First Parish Church, in October 1774. This congress, with John Hancock as president and Benjamin Lincoln as secretary, consisted of 300 delegates from Massachusetts towns who passed measures ending taxpayments to the Crown and organizing a militia force to defy the King by arms if necessary. Wright's Tavern was used as a meeting place for committees of the Congress during the 5-day session, and also provided refreshments for the delegates.

Present Appearance. With red clapboards and monitor or double-hipped roof, low-studded Wright's Tavern is still in good condition. Until recently it functioned in its original role as a public house. Since the Revolution, however, it has seen many uses and was finally saved from a doubtful future by the efforts of the Society of the First Parish and the generosity of two of Concord's public-spirited citizens.[32]

The Macpheadris-Warner House, Portsmouth, N.H., is one of New England's finest urban brick dwellings of the early 18th century.

22. Macpheadris-Warner House, New Hampshire

Location.   Corner of Chapel and Daniels Streets, Portsmouth.

Ownership and Administration.   The Warner House Association, Portsmouth.

Significance.   This house was built about 1716 by Archibald Macpheadris, a wealthy merchant of Portsmouth, and is typical of the superior early Georgian homes of New England.   It is commonly known in Portsmouth as the Warner House, after Jonathan Warner, who married Captain Macpheadris' daughter.   Warner, a figure of note in his own right, played an important role in town and provincial affairs.   The house descended to Warner's niece, Mrs. Nathaniel Sherburne, and remained in her family until 1931, when it was purchased by the Warner House Association.   The mansion is probably the oldest brick dwelling in Portsmouth and architecturally is one of New England's most significant urban brick dwellings surviving from the early 18th century.

Present Appearance.   The Macpheadris-Warner House has been spared major changes and retains a profusion of original construction details.   It is three stories high, with brick walls 18 inches thick.   The brickwork is exposed except on the south end wall, which is clapboarded.

The plain exterior is enhanced by a 12-panel door. Beneath the present roof, topped by balustrades and an octagonal cupola, have been discovered two parallel gabled roofs that originally covered the house. The deep cleft between these parallel roofs was later covered by a low-pitched roof to make the present gambrel treatment. The interior arrangement is on the center-hall plan. On the ground floor the kitchen and dining room are on one side of the hall and the parlor and a small chamber on the other. A small scullery extends from the rear of the kitchen. Among the unusual features of the interior are a unique set of frescoes on the walls of the staircase and a very early marbleized wood panel, which was a guide for the restoration of the other panels in the dining room. Among the furnishings is a series of five portraits of members of the Warner family painted by Blackburn in 1761. Many of the furnishings are on loan from a number of outstanding collections, including the Metropolitan Museum of Art in New York. The house is now well maintained by the association and is open to the public during the summer.[33]

23. Monmouth Battlefield, New Jersey

Location. N.J. 522 northwest of Freehold, Monmouth County.

Ownership and Administration. Privately owned farmland, public roads, and abandoned line of Pennsylvania Railroad.

Significance. The Battle of Monmouth, June 28, 1778, marked the debut of the American Army after the hard winter's training at Valley Forge. Although Washington failed in his design to thwart the British movement across New Jersey, this last major battle in the North demonstrated to both sides that the Prussian drillmaster, "Baron" Frederick von Steuben, had succeeded in molding an American Army that was able to meet the British on even terms.

On June 18, 1778, British Gen. Sir Henry Clinton abandoned Philadelphia and headed toward the Jersey coast, where he planned to embark his 10,000 men and return to New York by water. Washington, his army now numbering about 14,000 men, pursued. Against the advice of most of his lieutenants, he determined to attack Clinton and his vulnerable wagon train. The American striking force, commanded by Gen. Charles Lee, was poorly managed and after a feeble blow at the enemy near Monmouth Courthouse fell back on the main army led by Washington. Enraged, Washington peremptorily relieved the erratic Lee and took over the conduct of the battle in the face of a strong

British counterattack. The fighting raged throughout the day with sun and 100° temperature taking almost as heavy a toll as gunfire. Neither side would yield. The fighting raged back and forth in the fields and swamps between Old Tennent Church and the little settlement around Monmouth Courthouse. The engagement stands as the

A survivor from pre-Revolutionary times, the Old Tennent Church is a reference point for tracing the actions of the Battle of Monmouth, fought on the slope southeast of the church on June 28, 1778.

longest sustained action of the Revolutionary War. Clinton pulled away and made his escape during the night, his precious wagon train intact. Washington failed to prevent Clinton's escape, but he had demonstrated his own superb qualities of leadership and the new prowess of the army created in the misery of Valley Forge.

Present Appearance. The present town of Freehold, which in 1778 consisted of a courthouse and a few scattered dwellings, is a modern commercial city. The area northeast of Freehold, where General Lee's initial attack was made, has been largely built up and the character of the wartime scene lost, although the preliminary movements of the two armies can still be followed on the ground. In contrast is the remarkably open and unspoiled condition of the major scene of battle northwest of town. The battle area, about 1½ by 3 miles in extent, has undergone superficial change, but despite widening of fields and draining of swamps the terrain has retained its historical character to an unusual degree. One of the traditions that arose from the battle of Monmouth is the story of Molly Pitcher, who carried water to her husband and other artillerymen during the sweltering day of battle. Two places on the battlefield are marked as sites of the Molly Pitcher Spring. Of much greater significance as a historical landmark and survivor of the battle is the fine Old Tennent Church, dating from 1751. The battlefield slopes away southeast to the town of Freehold, from the high ground on which the church stands. The building serves as a handsomely preserved point of reference for tracing the combat action. The wartime road from nearby Englishtown to Monmouth Courthouse, employed by the Americans in their approach on Monmouth, passes near the church. Six farms are included in the battle area, and several houses of the Revolutionary period still stand on the field, including the Craig House, now much in need of restoration.

Although never accorded formal preservation, Monmouth Battlefield is one of the best preserved of the Revolutionary War battlefields. It has survived by accident, not design; however, at this writing the State of New Jersey is planning a State Park for the area.[34]

24. Nassau Hall, New Jersey

Location. Princeton University, Princeton.

Ownership and Administration. Princeton University.

Significance. Nassau Hall was the first important college building in the Middle Atlantic Colonies and the first permanent building at Princeton University, which was founded in 1746 as the College of New Jersey. Although established by Presbyterian churchmen, the college was not intended for the education of clergymen only. The founders emphasized that the principle of religious freedom would be observed carefully. In 1752 the college was formally located at Princeton, and

2 years later ground was broken for Nassau Hall, named to honor the memory of King William III of the House of Nassau. Seventy undergraduates moved into Nassau Hall in the autumn of 1756, and for almost half a century thereafter it was the only college building, containing dormitory, dining room, chapel, and classrooms.

Nassau Hall provided sleeping and dining accommodations as well as chapel and classrooms for the entire student body of the College of New Jersey (now Princeton University), from 1756 for almost half a century. Courtesy, Princeton University.

Nassau Hall served on occasion during the Revolution as a barracks and hospital for both British and American troops. It was the scene of the last stand of the British in the Battle of Princeton. From June to November 1783, the Continental Congress convened in Nassau Hall, receiving there the news of the signing of the treaty that ended the Revolution. Here also the first diplomatic representative accredited to the new Nation was received, the Minister of the Netherlands. The hall has been visited by scores of distinguished public figures in the course of its long history, including Washington, Jefferson, Madison, Lafayette, the Adamses, and virtually every other President of the United States.

As an outstanding example of the growth of educational facilities in the Colonies, and as the principal edifice of an institution that has played a major role in the cultural growth of the Nation, Nassau Hall is a notable historical resource.

Present Appearance. The building was designed by Robert Smith and Dr. William Shippen, of the Carpenters Company of Philadelphia. A central pavilion, topped by a pediment, breaks the 170-foot facade, and three doors lead to corridors separating the various classrooms and offices. Brownstone dug from a nearby quarry makes up the walls, which are unadorned except for the quoined and corniced entrances and the keyed flat arch lintels of the windows on the first two stories. A cupola and many chimneys crown the low-pitched hipped roof. The simple, solid lines appear to have influenced the design of later college buildings elsewhere, including Hollis Hall at Harvard (1762–63), University Hall at Brown (1770–71), and Dartmouth Hall at Dartmouth (1784–91).

Nassau Hall was damaged during the Battle of Princeton and virtually destroyed by fires in 1802 and 1855. The fire of March 6, 1802, left only the walls standing. The architect for the reconstruction was Benjamin H. Latrobe. On March 10, 1855, Nassau Hall was destroyed again by a fire that left only the walls standing. The building was reconstructed and reopened on August 7, 1856, reflecting architectural changes more drastic than those of 1802. Architect John Notman's rebuilding employed a pseudo-Renaissance design of massive character.

Memorial Hall, in the center of the building, was installed after World War I to honor Princetonians killed in all wars. It was altered after WorldWar II. The bronze tigers flanking the main entrance of Nassau Hall were executed by A. Phemister Proctor and were presented in 1911 by the class of 1879, a member of which was Woodrow Wilson. Nassau Hall is now used solely for administrative offices.[35]

25. Princeton Battlefield, New Jersey

Location. N.J. 583, south edge of Princeton, Mercer County.

Ownership and Administration. Department of Conservation and Economic Development, Forests and Parks Section, State of New Jersey.

Significance. Washington's victory at Princeton on January 3, 1777, like that at Trenton a week earlier, heightened the morale of the American Army as well as that of the citizens, and strengthened the reputation and authority of Washington himself. The twin victories of Trenton and Princeton came at a time when the spirits of the American people had reached a dangerously low ebb, when another defeat might have been fatal to the cause of independence. The situation brightened with these successes at the year's end, and from every corner militiamen flocked to the colors. A new Continental Army emerged.

Following his defeat of the Hessians at Trenton on December 26, 1776, Washington returned to the Pennsylvania side of the Delaware River. Safely across, he determined to hit the enemy again and returned to New Jersey on the night of December 30–31. Lord Charles Cornwallis, British commander in New Jersey, took a position confronting Washington, who stood with his back to the Delaware. Confident that the rebels could not escape, Cornwallis decided to wait until morning to strike the Americans. In a daring maneuver, Washington slipped away in the night, got in the rear of the British forces, and early on January 3 struck two British regiments just leaving Princeton to join Cornwallis. In the sharp fight that followed, several American assaults were thrown back in confusion. For a time the Army appeared on the verge of defeat, but Washington rallied his forces and finally drove the enemy from the field. One detachment of the enemy sought refuge in Princeton's Nassau Hall, where it was easily captured. The 15-minute fight at Princeton cost the Americans 40 killed and wounded, including Gen. Hugh Mercer, who died of wounds shortly after the battle.

Present Appearance. The scene of heaviest fighting in the battle is preserved in a 40-acre State park on the southern outskirts of Princeton. A handsome oak tree marks the spot that tradition identifies as the place where General Mercer received his death wound. The Clarke House at the edge of the battlefield was the scene of Mercer's death. A memorial arch on the west edge of the field marks the site where unknown American dead were buried in unmarked graves. The battlefield tract is surrounded by urban housing but, because of the small-scale nature of the action, the 40 acres of the field now preserved is sufficient to protect the scene. The park is undeveloped and there is as yet no attempt to interpret on the field the action that occurred there. Of the sites of the two crucial battles of Trenton and Princeton, only Princeton remains. The scene of the fighting at Trenton has been obliterated by the growth

The "Mercer Oak" marks the traditional site where Gen. Hugh Mercer was mortally wounded in the Battle of Princeton, January 3, 1777. Courtesy, New Jersey Department of Conservation and Economic Development.

of the city, although an extensively restored and altered barracks building dating from 1759 still stands.[36]

26. Washington Crossing, New Jersey and Pennsylvania

Location. N.J. 546 on Delaware River south of Titusville, Mercer County, N.J.; Pa. 32 and 532, on Delaware River at community of Washington Crossing, Bucks County, Pa.

Ownership and Administration. State of New Jersey, Department of Conservation and Economic Development, Forests and Parks Section; Commonwealth of Pennsylvania, Department of Forests and Waters, Washington Crossing State Park Commission.

Significance. Washington's crossing of the Delaware River on Christmas night 1776, for the brilliant raid on Trenton, was a crucial episode in the struggle for independence. Despite an almost legendary character in the American tradition, the crossing was in fact a realistic and carefully planned stroke designed to rescue a waning cause. Washington carried the war to the enemy by his daring act, and gave the new Nation and his often-defeated army a taste of victory at the war's lowest ebb.

The close of 1776 found the cause of independence staggering under a succession of defeats. The Continental Congress had made provision for a long-term military force in October, but at the end of the year this establishment was on paper, not in the field where it was desperately needed. In his camp on the Pennsylvania side of the Delaware, Washington realized that he must strike a blow at the enemy before his army melted away, and he determined to hit the Hessian garrison at Trenton. The American main force was ferried across the Delaware on the night of December 25 by Col. John Glover's hardy Marblehead fishermen, and in the bleak early morning hours assembled on the New Jersey shore for the march on Trenton, about 10 miles downstream. The surprise was complete, and within an hour and a half after the action opened the Hessians surrendered. Their loss was about 1,000 men captured, wounded, and killed, at a cost to the Americans of fewer than 10 casualties. Learning that the other column of his command had failed to cross the Delaware to join him, Washington returned to the Pennsylvania side of the river. A few days later he crossed again to New Jersey and defeated another enemy force at the battle of Princeton. A critical turning point was successfully passed, and valuable time won for the creation of the new military establishment. The epic crossing of the Delaware was a key to final victory.

Present Appearance. On the Pennsylvania side of the Delaware, a well-maintained State park of 478 acres preserves the site of the embarkation of Washington's main force. On the riverbank is the old Ferry Inn, the present structure containing an ell which was part of the original ferryhouse of the Revolutionary period. Emanuel Leutze's famous painting, "Washington Crossing the Delaware," is displayed in the auditorium of the handsome park memorial building. Whatever the artistic merits and historical accuracy of the picture, it constitutes an inspiring interpretation of the event in spirit if not in factual detail. The Washington Crossing Monument, erected in 1916, overlooks the embarkation site. The Thompson-Neely House, headquarters of American officers in 1776, is at Bowman's Hill, a detached section of the park 4 miles north of the crossing site. The older section of the house was built in 1702, and the building is furnished and open to the public. An old mill nearby, still standing, ground grain for the American Army.

The McKonkey Ferryhouse overlooks the New Jersey bank of the Delaware River, where Washington's troops landed on Christmas night, 1776, for the surprise attack on Trenton. The general warmed himself here, according to tradition, before moving on to rout the Hessians.

Beneath the memorial flagstaff are the graves of unknown American soldiers who died during the encampment of 1776. The Bowman's Hill section of the park also contains a State wildflower preserve and a memorial observation tower.

On the New Jersey side of the river is a 372-acre State park preserving the scene of the landing above Trenton. A short distance from the riverbank is the McKonkey Ferryhouse, now a museum. An interesting park feature is the preserved trace of the old road used by the American Army in its march from the riverbank. Trees planted on either side of the "Continental Lane" preserve this historic roadway.

The parks on either side of the Delaware, connected by an automobile bridge, constitute an outstanding preservation of a key site in the winning of American independence.[37]

Here at Bennington Battlefield, N.Y., American militia defeated a detachment of Burgoyne's invading army on August 16, 1777. This was a major setback to the English general's drive down the Hudson, foreshadowing the decisive American victory at Saratoga a few weeks later. Courtesy, New York State Education Department.

27. Bennington Battlefield, New York

Location. N.Y. 67, near Walloomsac, Rensselaer County.

Ownership and Administration. State of New York, administered by New York State Education Department, Albany.

Significance. The American militia's victory at the Battle of Bennington, August 16, 1777, was a significant contribution to the defeat of Burgoyne's British Army at Saratoga, 2 months later. The Battle of Bennington cost Burgoyne about 10 percent of his entire strength and denied the army supplies sorely needed for the planned offensive down the Hudson River. The British defeat greatly discouraged their uneasy Indian allies and encouraged militia enlistment in the American Army.

General John Burgoyne, camped near Fort Edward, N.Y., desperately needed supplies and horses for his descent upon Albany. Consequently, a force of some 800 men, mostly German mercenaries, was ordered to seize supplies stored at Bennington, Vt. Apprised of the enemy raid, Gen. John Stark aroused the countryside and on August 16 the farmers swarmed out to deal the Germans a crushing blow before they could cross the New York line into Vermont. Enemy reinforcements threatened to undo Stark's work, but timely help from Seth Warner and his Green Mountain Rangers threw back the relief column. The day's end found the foraging expedition virtually annihilated and Burgoyne's army in a more dangerous position than before. The shortage of supplies and loss of troops was to have a telling effect in the campaign around Saratoga, now about to open.

Present Appearance. The 208-acre Bennington Battlefield State Park includes the scene of heaviest fighting on the high ground overlooking the little village of Walloomsac and affords a wide view of the battle terrain. A bronze relief map indicates the various units and their battle positions, while other monuments commemorate the service of the Vermont and Massachusetts volunteers and their leader, General Stark.[38]

28. Fort Stanwix, New York

Location. Downtown Rome; site bounded approximately by Dominick, Spring, Liberty, and North James Streets.

Ownership and Administration. Owners of commercial and public buildings, and private dwellings.

Significance. The stand by an American garrison at Fort Stanwix during August 1777 was chiefly responsible for the repulse of the western wing of the British invasion of the northern Colonies from Canada, and checked the possibility of a loyalist uprising in the Mohawk Valley. The retreat to Canada of the western column after its failure to take Fort Stanwix was a blow to the British strategy of concentration at Albany, contributing thereby to the defeat of Burgoyne at Saratoga a few months later. In addition to its role in the War for Independence, Fort Stanwix was the scene of the treaty of that name, signed on November 5, 1768. By the Treaty of Fort Stanwix the Iroquois ceded a vast territory south and east of the Ohio River, as far west as the mouth of the Tennessee. The treaty thus cleared the way for a new and significant surge of westward settlement.

689–192 O–64—11

Fort Stanwix was situated at the Oneida Carrying Place, a key spot on the route between the Great Lakes and the Mohawk River, and was built originally during the French and Indian War but played no significant part in this conflict. It was reestablished in June 1776 (sometimes called Fort Schuyler by the patriots) and garrisoned with perhaps as many as 800 men in time to block British invasion objectives in the Mohawk Valley in the summer of 1777. Gen. John Burgoyne advanced south from Canada along the Champlain route at this time, expecting to meet the main British Army under General Howe which he believed would move up to the Hudson. Col. Barry St. Leger with more than 1,000 regulars, Tories, and Indians was to move down the Mohawk Valley to Albany and join the larger British forces there after rallying Tories and Indians on his route.

St. Leger invested Fort Stanwix on August 3 but was rebuffed when he demanded its surrender. The action was limited to sniping until August 6 when the bloody battle was fought at Oriskany, some 6 miles to the east (see pp. 131–132), between St. Leger and an American militia force under Gen. Nicholas Herkimer. The patriots were badly mauled and did not succeed in raising the siege of Stanwix, but during the action a detachment from the fort raided the British position, destroying provisions and camp equipment. This encouraged the besieged, who held firm while St. Leger began formal siege operations. He had advanced his works to within 150 yards of the fort when word came of the approach of an American relief force under Gen. Benedict Arnold. Having lost the confidence and support of his Indian "allies," St. Leger was obliged to abandon the siege near the end of August, retiring in considerable disorder to Canada. Fort Stanwix still stood and the American Army on the Hudson could give its full attention to Burgoyne, who surrendered at Saratoga on October 17, 1777.

Present Appearance. The site of Fort Stanwix occupies approximately a city block in the heart of Rome, and no physical evidence of the post is visible. The site is built over with roads, houses, and commercial developments. The remains of the fort were cleared away prior to the middle of the 19th century. Near the end of that century, after some controversy about the location, an effort was made to mark the outline at several points. Barring archeological investigation, it is difficult to say how successfully this was done. Authenticating the precise location of the fort through archeology appears somewhat impractical in view of the extensive development on the site.[39]

29. Fort Ticonderoga, New York

Location. N.Y. 8 and 9N, Ticonderoga, Essex County.

Ownership and Administration. Fort Ticonderoga Association, Ticonderoga.

Significance. Strategically located at the junction of Lake Champlain and Lake George, Fort Ticonderoga was the key to both Canada and the Hudson Valley in the 18th century. It saw more of the English-French struggle for North America than any other post, and its story is one of the most dramatic and colorful in American military annals.

The first military post on the site was Fort Vaudreuil, later Fort Carillon, built by the French in 1755–57. On July 8, 1758, an army of 15,000 British regular and colonial troops attacked the fort and was repulsed with heavy loss by the French under Montcalm. On July 27, 1759, however, Gen. Jeffrey Amherst captured the fort and renamed it Ticonderoga. This loss by the French, coupled with British pressure elsewhere on the frontier between New France and the American Colonies, was a severe blow to French plans. The capture of Ticonderoga gave the British undisputed possession of the strategically important Hudson River Valley. The French blew up part of the fort before they withdrew, and Amherst had repairs made in accordance with the original design. In the years between the defeat of France in North America and the outbreak of the Revolution, a small garrison manned the work. On May 10, 1775, Ethan Allen with 83 "Green Mountain Boys" surprised and defeated the few British defenders, and the post became a base for the projected advance on Canada. The following winter Col. Henry Knox hauled the fort's cannon overland to serve in the siege of Boston. Ticonderoga changed hands again when it fell to Burgoyne's British Army in the summer of 1777, but upon Burgoyne's defeat at Saratoga it again passed into American possession. Although reoccupied from time to time by scouting parties and raiding detachments, the post was never again garrisoned by a military force.

In 1816 William F. Pell, a merchant of New York, leased the grounds and 4 years later bought them. In 1908 the late Stephen Pell began restoration. By the following year the west barracks had been opened to the public, and the work has gone forward since that time. At this writing only the east barracks have not been rebuilt. The task of reconstruction was a major undertaking. Over the years the stones had been carted away by settlers for use as building materials. The upper part of the walls and most of the stone barracks disappeared, and the earth behind the walls washed over the remnants of the original walls. These remains were uncovered in the restoration that began in 1908. The present work was erected on the original foundations and utilized parts of walls that had survived.

Present Appearance. The fort is four-sided with bastions extending from its four corners. Outlooks or demilunes on the north and west, and an outer wall on the south, cover the approaches. Facing the central parade ground are the reconstructed west and south barracks, the ruins of the still-to-be-restored east barracks, and the long rampart joining the northwest and northeast bastions. The west barracks houses the administrative office, a library, and, in the basement, the armory, featuring the most important part of the Fort Ticonderoga gun collection. In the south barracks are displayed many artifacts excavated in the course of the restoration; furnished quarters of the officer of the day; exhibits of furniture, household goods, and other items used by early settlers in the region; Indian relics; and a model of the fort as it existed in 1758. Below the walls are the remains of a French village that probably served the fort. Research on the village is underway.[40]

30. Johnson Hall, New York

Location. Hall Street, one-quarter mile north of intersection with N.Y. 29, Johnstown, Fulton County.

Ownership and Administration. Department of Education, State of New York, Albany.

Significance. Johnson Hall was the home for the last 11 years of his life of Sir William Johnson, Superintendent of Indian Affairs for the Northern Colonies and the foremost frontier leader of pre-Revolutionary New York. Johnson's powerful influence on the Iroquois was of decisive importance in defeating the French in North America and in advancing the English colonial frontier. He played a major role in opening the Mohawk Valley to white settlement and proved an able military leader in the closing years of the war that ended in the fall of New France. At the close of the conflict Johnson made a notable contribution to the transition from French to English rule. (See pp. 212, 213.)

Johnson Hall was built in 1763 and became the center of British authority on the New York frontier. It was one of the most elaborate estates in the northern Colonies. Here most of the important Indian treaties of the latter colonial period were negotiated, and here Johnson entertained important officials from the Colonies and from abroad. In 1774, during a conference with the Iroquois, Johnson died at his home.

Johnson Hall was the home for the last 11 years of his life of Sir William Johnson, foremost frontier leader of pre-Revolutionary New York. The stone blockhouse at left, a rare example of its type, is one of two which originally flanked the house.

His enlightened handling of Indian affairs, his wide range of intellectual interests, and his generally successful efforts in furthering peaceful white settlement of the region north of the Ohio River attest to Johnson's remarkable talents and energy. His role as an outstanding personage in America's colonial history is fittingly commemorated by the imposing dwelling where he spent the last years of his life.

Present Appearance. Johnson Hall has undergone extensive repair and is in excellent condition. It is a rectangular frame building in Georgian style, with two stories, basement, and attic. The white rusticated siding and the ornamented cornices under eaves and over windows give the house a dignified appearance in keeping with its owner's character and position. The interior, arranged with two rooms on either side of the wide, central hallway, upstairs and down, has been restored faithfully with furnishings that include a room of pieces belonging to the Johnson family.   An inventory of the furnishings taken 3 weeks after Sir William's death made possible a highly authentic interior restoration.   The stone blockhouse adjacent to Johnson Hall on the west is an original structure, one of two that guarded the home; it is the only survivor in New York of this type of structure.   Dioramas and other exhibits interpreting the life of the Johnsons are housed in the basement of the home, and a scale model of the original estate is displayed in the blockhouse.[41]

31. Morris-Jumel Mansion, New York

Location.   160th Street and Edgecombe Avenue, Washington Heights, New York City.

Ownership and Administration.   City of New York, operated by Washington Headquarters Association, Daughters of the American Revolution, under direction of New York City Department of Parks.

Significance.   In addition to its distinction as the only important pre-Revolutionary house still standing in Manhattan, the Morris-Jumel Mansion is the major surviving landmark of the Battle of Harlem Heights.   Although it was a small-scale affair, the important effects of the battle were immediately evident, including the restoration of the offensive spirit of the American Army following a succession of defeats and retreats.

The Morris house served as the headquarters of Washington from September 14 to October 18, 1776.   Following their victory of Long Island, the British occupied New York City easily on September 15, routing a portion of the American Army at Kip's Bay the same day. The Americans retreated to fortified lines on the heights north of present 125th Street.   In this vicinity the Battle of Harlem Heights was fought on September 16.   Here, for the first time in the campaign, the patriots succeeded in forcing the British to give ground.   Hoping to lure the enemy into ambush, Washington feinted an attack in front and sent a flanking party to catch the advancing enemy in a crossfire.   The British withdrew, re-formed their battleline, resumed firing, and retreated again. As the fight went on, both commanders threw in more troops, and at about 2 o'clock in the afternoon the British withdrew again, this time to within a short distance of their massed reserve.   Washington had no desire to bring on a general engagement and called off the advance, a difficult feat because of his army's reluctance to give up the unusual opportunity of actually chasing the enemy. Lord Howe, surprised by the determined stand of the Americans, spent the next 4 weeks in fortifying his lines, leaving Washington to the comforts of his headquarters in the Morris Mansion. After Washington left the house it was occupied for the remainder of the war by General Clinton and other British officers.

The Morris-Jumel Mansion was built by Lt. Col. Roger Morris in 1765. Morris had come to America in 1746 and during the Braddock expedition in 1755 became a friend of Washington. A loyalist, Morris fled the country at the outbreak of the Revolution, and at the end of the war his house and land were confiscated and sold. In 1810 the house became the property of Stephen Jumel, and was restored in Federal period style. After passing through a succession of owners the house was saved from demolition in 1903 when the City of New York purchased it for $235,000, and by special legislation gave its care to the Washington Headquarters Association of the Daughters of the American Revolution. This group restored the house and again in 1945 renovated and refurnished it. At the same time, the grounds were landscaped.

Present Appearance. The white-painted house is mid-Georgian in design, built of brick encased in wood. The giant entrance portico has four columns two stories high, with a pediment at the top. The flattened top of the hip roof is surmounted by a balustrade. The spacious rooms are handsomely furnished in the styles of the late 18th and early 19th centuries, in consideration of the two distinguished families that lived there at different periods. The earlier period is carried out on the lower floor, while the American Federal and French Empire of the 19th century is used upstairs, where furniture belonging to the Jumels is displayed. The third-floor rooms, probably utilized formerly as guest chambers, house a collection of early American household utensils. The kitchen and servant quarters are in the basement. Of particular interest is a suite of three small rooms on the second floor, which served as Washington's quarters during his stay on Harlem Heights. The house is open to the public daily except Monday throughout the year.[42]

32. Oriskany Battlefield, New York

Location. 5 miles east of Rome on N.Y. 69.

Ownership and Administration. Education Department, State of New York.

Significance. The battle of Oriskany on August 6, 1777, was the key to the success of the garrison at Fort Stanwix in holding out against the siege by Barry St. Leger (described on pp. 125–126), which thwarted the British invasion plan in the Mohawk Valley. General Burgoyne was thus deprived of reinforcements which might have prevented the necessity of his surrender at Saratoga later in the year.

General Nicholas Herkimer was ambushed at Oriskany when he led a contingent of 800 Tryon County militiamen toward Fort Stanwix in an attempt to relieve the garrison. The patriot troops were green, and Herkimer was mortally wounded in the first fire, but they succeeded in holding the field. The British force was composed of both loyalists and Indians, and after a bloody struggle at close quarters the latter abandoned the field to return to the lines around Fort Stanwix, whose garrison had in the meantime come out to raid the British camps.

Herkimer and his soldiers retreated, and he died 10 days later. The Battle of Oriskany and the siege of Fort Stanwix not only discouraged the British and their Indian "allies" but also demonstrated the courage and determination of the militiamen, standing in defense of their homes.

Present Appearance. Gently rolling hills dropping away to the valley lands on the north preserve the scene of Herkimer's hard-fought battle, and a tall monument commemorates the action. Included in the site is the ravine between two low hills where the Indians and loyalists sprang their ambush. The heavy forest that covered the battlefield in 1777 has disappeared, but the area has otherwise retained its natural features with a minimum of modern encroachments. Restoration of the field appears practicable. Oriskany State Park, containing the battlefield, is well maintained and offers picnic facilities.[43]

33. St. Paul's Chapel, New York

Location. Broadway between Fulton and Vesey Streets, New York City.

Ownership and Administration. Corporation of Trinity Church, 74 Trinity Place, New York City.

Significance. An outstanding example of Georgian architecture, St. Paul's Chapel stands serenely among the skyscrapers of modern New York, the city's sole surviving church of the colonial era. St. Paul's was erected in 1764–66 to serve as the chapel of First Trinity Church, which was destroyed in the great fire of 1776 a few days after the British occupation of the city. New York's royal Governor had a pew in St. Paul's, as did, during the Revolution, Lord Howe, Maj. John Andre, and other officers of the British army of occupation.   After Washington's first inauguration, April 30, 1789, the Congress accompanied the new President to St. Paul's for a special service.   A painting of the arms of the United States now hangs above Washington's pew.

Present Appearance.   St. Paul's was designed by Thomas McBean, who took his inspiration from London's St. Martin's-in-the-Fields.   The body of the church, built of native stone, is distinguished by two tiers of arched windows.   The Ionic-columned portico and spire were added in 1794–96, when the chancel was extended.   The 220-foot spire was the work of Architect James C. Lawrence.   The spacious interior is a center-barrel vault supported by slender columns, and has a gallery and gallery vaults on each side.   The nave has been described as second only to that in King's Chapel, Boston, in architectural interest.   In 1950, at a cost of $200,000, St. Paul's was restored to its colonial appearance.   The wooden spire was reinforced with steel and the interior of the church was painted in white, gold, and blue.   Fourteen Waterford glass chandeliers hang from the vaulted ceiling.[44]

34. Stony Point Battlefield, New York

Location.   U.S. 9W and 202, north of community of Stony Point, Rockland County.

Ownership and Administration.   State of New York, administered by Palisades Interstate Park Commission, Bear Mountain.

Significance.   The small-scale battle at Stony Point, July 16, 1779, was the last military action of importance in the northern theater of war. It was important as a morale builder for the patriots and as a demonstration of the developing skill of the American Army, and it had other significant consequences.   A recent study has noted that "the assault paralyzed Clinton [the British commander].   When his reinforcements failed to show up, he dared not, after his loss of men in Connecticut and at the [Stony] Point, make an offensive move." [45]   By the action at Stony Point, Washington tightened his grip on the Hudson and especially on West Point, "the key to the Continent."

The Battle of Stony Point came after the long period of stalemate in the North that followed the Battle of Monmouth in June 1778.   At the beginning of June 1779, the British took without opposition the unfinished American fort at Stony Point, a few miles below West Point.   Verplanck's Point, on the east side of the river opposite Stony Point, was captured at the same time. Stony Point is a steep promontory jutting half a mile into the Hudson River and rising 150 feet above the water, which all but surrounds it. A marsh, under water at high tide, protected the inland side of the post. Having secured this strong position, Clinton pushed the fortifications to completion and manned them with a garrison of about 600 men. Washington was greatly concerned over the loss of the two strongpoints on either side of the river and after a thorough reconnaissance ordered Gen. "Mad Anthony" Wayne to regain Stony Point. He moved in after dark on July 15, and at about midnight his elite corps

"Mad" Anthony Wayne's Continentals stormed and captured this Hudson River promontory, Stony Point, on July 16, 1779. Washington's grip on the Hudson at West Point was thus assured.

launched its assault with muskets unloaded and with orders to use the bayonet. Within 20 minutes the fort had been secured and its surprised garrison made prisoners. The American loss was 15 killed and 80 wounded. Washington concluded that the post could not be held by his troops and ordered the fortifications dismantled and abandoned. The

British reoccupied Stony Point but Clinton, alarmed by his losses, had lost heart for further offensive action. Washington had retained his grip on the Hudson River line and won time in which to fortify West Point more strongly than ever.

Present Appearance. Stony Point Battlefield is preserved in a 45-acre State reservation. There are extensive earthwork remains, and historical markers trace the course of the American assault up the steep slopes into the fort. A small museum administered by the American Scenic and Historic Preservation Society contains relics of the battle and tells the story of the action. The point is heavily wooded, but foot trails give access to the important points of interest. A spectacular view of the Hudson River Valley may be had from the summit of the point.[46]

35. Valcour Bay, New York

Location. 7 miles south of Plattsburgh, between Valcour Island and west shore of Lake Champlain, Clinton County.

Ownership and Administration. State of New York.

Significance. Benedict Arnold's daring fleet action off Valcour Island on October 11, 1776, had a far-reaching effect on the outcome of the War of Independence. Although the American force was defeated, its very presence on the lake and its stubborn fight proved to be a strategic victory by delaying the British invasion of the northern Colonies in 1776. By the time the lake had been cleared of American vessels the British commander concluded that the season was too far advanced to carry out his projected movement toward Albany. The invasion did not resume until the following year, by which time the Americans were better able to meet and repulse it. This they did at Saratoga, the turning point of the Revolution. Alfred T. Mahan, the naval historian, wrote: "That the Americans were strong enough to impose the capitulation of Saratoga was due to the invaluable year of delay secured to them in 1776 by their little navy on Lake Champlain, created by the indomitable energy, and handled with the indomitable courage of the traitor, Benedict Arnold." [47]

Not until early fall of 1776, was Gen. Sir Guy Carleton, British commander in Canada, ready to cooperate with Howe in New York by moving down Lake Champlain and the Hudson River on Albany. By early October, Carleton's fleet was built and ready for action—29 vessels, mostly gunboats carrying a single gun, against the American fleet of 16 vessels—3 taken from the enemy and others hurriedly built on the lake.

Between Valcour Island and the west shore of Lake Champlain is a sound about three-quarters of a mile wide. Midway on the island a high bluff juts into the sound, dividing it into a north and a south bay. On the day of battle, October 11, 1776, Arnold's fleet—15 vessels were present—lay anchored in line across the bay south of the bluff, concealed from the enemy fleet approaching from the north. Carleton's vessels sailed down the eastern side of Valcour Island and were south of it before the crewmen caught sight of Arnold's fleet. Carleton had to attack against the wind, a decided disadvantage in the age of sail. Closing to short range, the opposing battlelines hammered each other from about 11 a.m. until dusk. One of the two American ships lost that day was the Gundelo *Philadelphia,* which sank about an hour after the battle. This vessel, recovered from the lake bottom in 1935, is described on pp. 85–86.

The end of the day found Arnold's surviving vessels heavily damaged and low on ammunition. Further fighting was out of the question. The British line still lay between Valcour and escape to the south, but in darkness and a providential fog the survivors of the fight slipped past the left flank of the enemy line. In the next 2 days, Carleton's pursuing vessels knocked out ship after ship, and Arnold burned some to keep them from enemy hands. Arnold and other survivors of the action eluded capture, but when the final score was counted it was discovered that of the ships engaged at Valcour only 4 had reached safety. The American Fleet on Lake Champlain was destroyed, but its work had been done. The invasion from Canada had been halted for 1 crucial year.

Present Appearance. Valcour Island is about 2 miles long from north to south and approximately 1¼ miles wide. It is rocky, high, and wooded, and, as seen from the west shore of Lake Champlain, it probably looks much as it did when it sheltered Arnold's makeshift fleet. The sound or bay between the island and the west shore of the lake is three-quarters of a mile wide. Although the shore of Lake Champlain has been built up to some extent, and Valcour Island is the property of several private owners, the island and, more importantly, the bay where the fighting took place have suffered little loss of integrity as landmarks of the War for Independence. No effort has been made to preserve or interpret the scene of the battle, and the only marking is a small monument on the mainland about 5 miles south of Plattsburgh, in view of the island. This was erected in 1928 by the State Education Department and the Saranac Chapter, Daughters of the American Revolution.[48]

The Hasbrouck House, Newburgh, N.Y., was Washington's headquarters from April 1782 to mid-August 1783, pending the conclusion of peace with Great Britain.

36. Washington's Headquarters (Hasbrouck House), New York

Location. Liberty and Washington Streets, Newburgh, Orange County.

Ownership and Administration. Education Department, State of New York.

Significance. None of Washington's military headquarters during the War for Independence is of greater historical significance than the Hasbrouck House at Newburgh. Arriving at Newburgh on April 1, 1782, the Commander in Chief remained at the Hasbrouck House, save for occasional brief absences, until August 19, 1783. This was a longer period than Washington spent at any other headquarters. More importantly, Washington drafted three memorable documents at his Newburgh headquarters. In these he reaffirmed the fundamental principle of subordination of the Military Establishment to civilian control and helped lay the foundation for the Nation's orderly transition from war to peace. The first document was Washington's vehement rejection of the suggestion that the new Nation become a monarchy, with Washington at its head. The second was his address in the "Temple" at the nearby New Windsor army encampment (see p. 215) on March 15, 1783. Here he effectively quelled an incipient movement provoked by the so-called Newburgh Addresses, looking toward the coercion of Congress by the Army to secure settlement of officers' claims against the Government prior to demobilization. Washington's third notable act at Newburgh was drafting an oft-quoted circular letter to the Governors of the States, in which he outlined his views on the future development of the Nation. These views were elaborated around four cardinal points: "An indissoluble Union of the States under one Federal Head," "A sacred regard to public justice," "The adoption of a proper peace establishment," and a "pacific and friendly disposition among the peoples of the United States which will induce them to forget their local prejudices and policies, to make mutual concessions which are requisite to the general prosperity, and in some instances, to sacrifice their individual advantages to the interest of the community."

In addition to these statements at Newburgh, an act of some interest was the establishment of the military award, the "Order of the Purple Heart," proposed by Washington and noted in the General Orders of the Day, August 7, 1782. Aside from its intimate association with Washington, the Hasbrouck House has the distinction of being the first historic house preserved by a State. The State obtained the property in 1850, and the building was dedicated on July 4 of that year.

Present Appearance. The widow of Joseph Hasbrouck bought the property overlooking the Hudson River on which the headquarters building now stands, in 1749, and next year her son, Jonathan, erected the northeast portion of the building. The southeast section was added sometime before 1770, and in that year an addition extending the length of the west wall of both earlier sections was constructed. An initialed date-stone confirms the date of this last addition. The walls of all three sections are of fieldstone. The house includes a large seven-doored chamber used as a dining room and living room, two bedrooms, parlor and kitchen on the ground floor, another bedroom on the second floor, and a spacious attic where can be seen the maze of hand-hewn timbers that support the roof. The large chamber on the first floor served Washington as a reception and living room. Period furnishings give the house great charm. The building is the original, except the kitchen and dining room floors. Adjacent to the headquarters building is a museum offering exhibits of local historical interest as well as material relating to General and Mrs. Washington and the role of the Newburgh headquarters in the Revolution. Maintenance of both the house and museum is excellent.[49]

37. Brandywine Battlefield, Pennsylvania

Location. U.S. 1, near Chadd's Ford, Delaware County.

Ownership and Administration. Commonwealth of Pennsylvania, administered by Brandywine Battlefield Park Commission.

Significance. The Battle of Brandywine on September 11, 1777, was the only major clash of the two main armies during the campaign that ended in the British capture of Philadelphia. Although the battle was an American defeat, Washington extricated his force in good order and the Continentals demonstrated their ability to withstand the determined attack of British regulars.

In the spring and early summer of 1777, Washington and Sir William Howe engaged in fruitless maneuvers in New Jersey. At the end of June, Howe moved to New York and on July 23 set sail from Sandy Hook with more than 15,000 men, bound for the American Capital, Philadelphia. The British Fleet sailed up Chesapeake Bay while Washington moved to the south to meet Howe's advance. The American Army, numbering about 11,000 men, took up a defensive position east of Brandywine Creek, its center on high ground overlooking Chadd's Ford. In this position it blocked the main road to Philadelphia, 30 miles distant. On September 11 the two armies renewed the contest they had waged from Boston to the banks of the Brandywine.

Washington deployed his army in three wings, one under his own eye at Chadd's Ford, another under Gen. John Sullivan guarding the right flank upstream, and a small detachment covering a crossing on the left, 2 miles below Chadd's Ford. Instead of delivering the expected frontal attack, Howe made a wide flanking movement to take Sullivan in the rear. Washington mistakenly believed that a diversionary attack in his front was the main British thrust. Only at the last minute, when Sullivan was under heavy attack, did Washington conclude that the major effort was against the right wing. Gen. Nathanael Greene with two brigades was ordered to support the collapsing right flank. Washington and his staff galloped toward the sound of heavy firing. Greene's stout action saved the Army from entrapment, but by his move to the right Washington's defenses at Chadd's Ford were weakened and he was forced to retreat. Although confused and scattered, most of the Army got away and returned to Chester. Helping to restore order was the young Marquis de Lafayette, active despite a bullet wound in his leg.

A few days later, still between Howe and Philadelphia, Washington attempted to strike a blow at the British but was thwarted by bad weather. After further skirmishing, marked by the disastrous defeat of "Mad Anthony" Wayne's American rearguard at Paoli, Howe occupied Philadelphia on September 26. Brandywine gave no new luster to Washington's generalship, but the Army's quick recovery was a tribute to both the quality of its ragged troops and its determined leadership.

Present Appearance. Brandywine Battlefield Park includes approximately 50 acres of rolling ground overlooking Chadd's Ford and the main battle areas to the north and west. Situated within the park are the restored quarters of Lafayette and the reconstructed headquarters of Washington. Part of Lafayette's headquarters dates from the late 17th century, and the restoration today exhibits three periods of construction: the original frame structure, a mid-18th-century stone addition on the west, and the north wing, added in 1782. The treatment of Washington's and Lafayette's headquarters was carried out by C. Edwin Brumbaugh, an authority on the early houses of southeastern Pennsylvania. The park contains well maintained picnic areas and excellent roads.[50]

38. Bushy Run Battlefield, Pennsylvania

Location. North of Jeanette, near Harrison City on Pa. 993, Westmoreland County.

Ownership and Administration. Department of Forests and Waters, Commonwealth of Pennsylvania, Harrisburg.

Significance. The Battle of Bushy Run was a major English victory in the most serious Indian threat against the 18th-century colonial frontier. Called Pontiac's "Conspiracy" or "Rebellion," because of the Ottawa chief who helped lead it, the uprising threatened for a time to throw the white frontier back toward the Atlantic. The Indians struck in the spring of 1763, and one by one the frontier forts fell. Within a few weeks, along a thousand-mile frontier, only Forts Niagara, Detroit, and Pitt held out. Marching to the relief of Fort Pitt, where Pittsburgh now stands, Col. Henry Bouquet led about 500 men, regulars, and American rangers. At Bushy Run, 25 miles east of his destination, Bouquet encountered and fought a strong force of Indians. On the second day of fighting, August 6, he lured them into the open and in a bitter battle drove them from the field—demonstrating that, properly led, British troops could match the Indians in cunning and surprise. Four days after the victory at Bushy Run, Bouquet relieved Fort Pitt and made the Pennsylvania frontier comparatively safe for the thousands of settlers who streamed into the region in the next few years. Bushy Run halted the advance of the Indians into the middle Colonies and laid the groundwork for a later campaign into the Ohio country that ended the Pontiac rebellion.

Present Appearance. A 162-acre State park includes the principal scenes of action on the battlefield. Of particular interest is the hill on which the British troops planted their "flourbag fort." Here bronze plates reproducing Bouquet's dispatches and a map of the battlefield are located at the base of a huge block of granite. Trees have been planted to show the first positions taken by the British. On a hill to the west of the "flourbag fort" site are the unmarked graves of 50 British soldiers who fell in the action. A museum is located near the "flourbag fort" site, and roadways and foot trails give access to the main features of interest. The park also contains four picnic areas and an arboretum.[51]

39. Chew House (Cliveden), Pennsylvania

Location. Germantown Avenue between Johnson and Cliveden Streets, Germantown.

Ownership and Administration. Private.

Significance. This fine Georgian home is the most important surviving landmark of the hard-fought battle of Germantown, October 4, 1777. In this action Washington's army narrowly missed winning a significant victory over a large contingent of the British Army guarding the northwestern approaches to newly occupied Philadelphia. Although not decisive in its immediate military results, the battle of Germantown had vast political implications. Combined with the victory at Saratoga in the same month, it proved a major influence in the consummation of the French alliance that spelled final victory for the new American Nation.

Following his victory over Washington's army at Brandywine (see pp. 139–140) on September 11, 1777, Gen. Sir William Howe occupied Philadelphia on September 26. He dispersed his forces to cover the city, stationing some 9,000 men in Germantown on the north, 3,000 in New Jersey, and the remainder in Philadelphia and on the supply lines into the city. Washington concluded that the situation was favorable for a blow against the enemy at Germantown, then a small village stretching for 2 miles along the Skippack Road, which ran from Philadelphia to

Reading. The American plan of attack called for a complicated four-column movement, resembling the earlier pincers movement against Trenton but more intricate in timing and maneuver. In the early fighting on the foggy morning of October 4, the Americans drove the redcoats back until six British companies took refuge in the stout stone house of Chief Justice Benjamin Chew, on the outskirts of the village. They

A determined stand by British troops in the Chew House wrecked Washington's plan of attack at Germantown on October 4, 1777. The house had been completed in 1763 by Benjamin Chew, later Chief Justice of the Supreme Court of Pennsylvania. Courtesy, Samuel Chew.

harassed the American advance from this fortress. Units of Washington's forces marched to the sound of the firing at the Chew House, throwing the carefully arranged battle plan into disorder. In the fog and smoke, American troops fired on one another and fled panic stricken from the field. The British counterattack threw them back exhausted and confused, and Washington withdrew about 25 miles to an earlier camp at Pennypacker's Mill.

The battle had been a near thing for the British. But for the fog and, more importantly, the confusion created in the American ranks by the stubborn enemy stand in the Chew House, Germantown might have been a decisive victory for the patriot forces. As it was, despite their defeat, the Americans derived a significant advantage. John Adams, American Commissioner to France, writing to a member of the Continental Congress about the Battles of Saratoga and Germantown, said: "General Gates was the ablest negotiator you had in Europe; and next to him General Washington's attack on the enemy at Germantown. I do not know, indeed, whether this last affair had not more influence upon the European mind than that of Saratoga. Although the attempt was unsuccessful, the military gentlemen in Europe considered it as the most decisive proof that America would finally succeed." [52]

Affirming Adams' interpretation of the significance of Germantown, the British historian, Trevelyan, wrote: "Eminent generals and statesmen of sagacity, in every European court, were profoundly impressed. * * * The French Government, in making up its mind on the question whether the Americans would prove to be efficient allies, was influenced almost as much by the Battle of Germantown as by the surrender of Burgoyne." [53]

Present Appearance. The two-story Chew Mansion was built by Benjamin Chew in 1763 at Cliveden, his country estate. The house was constructed of Germantown stone quarried a short distance from the site. The front wall is built of regular ashlar masonry; the other walls are of stuccoed rubble masonry grooved to resemble ashlar. The belt course, window sills, and lintels are of dressed sandstone. Five huge urns adorn the roof. The house has an imposing entrance hall, brightened by windows of 24 lights and separated from the stair hall by a screen of 4 columns—an unusual feature. Small office rooms open on either side of the entrance hall, with the two main rooms, dining and drawing rooms, at the back. The kitchen and servants' rooms originally were in detached wings at the rear. An early barn, part of which now houses the office of the private owner, stands at the rear of the house. Benjamin Chew's commission as chief justice of Pennsylvania is displayed in the office. The house is not open to the public except on special occasions.[54]

40. Conrad Weiser Home, Pennsylvania

Location. Conrad Weiser Memorial Park, U.S. 422 near Womelsdorf, Berks County.

Conrad Weiser's skill in negotiating with the Indians played an important role in the defeat of the French in North America. His home near Womelsdorf, Pa., is preserved by the State.

Ownership and Administration. Historical and Museum Commission, Commonwealth of Pennsylvania, Harrisburg.

Significance. Conrad Weiser, peacemaker among the Indians, contributed largely to the rapid advance of the 18th-century frontier and thereby to the development of the English Colonies. Although somewhat neglected by historians, his role in Indian affairs was in truth an important one. Emigrating from Germany in 1710, at the age of 14, Weiser lived near Schoharie, New York, where he learned much about the Indians and their language and matured his thinking on the Indian problem in general. In 1729 he moved to Pennsylvania's Tulpehocken Valley where he prospered as a farmer. His appreciation of Indian affairs and knowledge of Indian langauges were probably unequaled in the Colonies, and provincial officers often sought his services as an ambassador to the Six Nations. Weiser's skill and courage were largely responsible for winning the support of the Iroquois for the English. He helped formulate an Indian policy based on recognition of the Iroquois as sovereign over the other Indians of Pennsylvania, but in the process alienated the Delawares and Shawnees. Weiser saw the Indian problem as one common to all the Colonies, not to be solved by the separate efforts of the Provinces. He helped avert war between Virginia and the Iroquois in 1743, and his influence proved instrumental in shifting the emphasis of British Indian policy from New York to

Pennsylvania. Weiser won over the western tribes by the Treaty of Logstown in 1748, thereby extending Pennsylvania's Indian trade to the Mississippi. After the death of one of his influential Indian friends in 1748, Weiser lost his commanding position as a "backwoods diplomat," although until his death he remained one of the best Indian interpreters. Weiser's later career, including a military command in the French and Indian War, lacked the significance of his earlier work, but the Indian alliances he had helped to form were an important factor in England's victory over France in the climactic struggle for North America. Weiser's death on July 13, 1760, closed a long career of valuable service to the developing English Colonies.

Present Appearance. In Conrad Weiser Memorial Park stands the restored two-room house built by Weiser on his Womelsdorf plantation. The graves are nearby of Weiser, his wife and a number of his Indian associates. The house serves as a museum. In addition to the main house, the original Weiser springhouse and other outbuildings are maintained.[55]

41. Forks of the Ohio, Pennsylvania

Location. Point State Park, Pittsburgh.

Ownership and Administration. Department of Forests and Waters, Commonwealth of Pennsylvania, Harrisburg.

Significance. The point of land where the Monongahela and Allegheny Rivers meet to form the Ohio is a site of surpassing significance in the story of American expansion westward from the Appalachian Mountains. From the mid-18th century through the early years of the 19th, the Forks of the Ohio was a strategic key to the Ohio Valley and the vast territory drained by the upper Mississippi. Control of this point was a major objective in the struggle for North America, and men of three nations fought and died struggling for the forks. The bustling town of Pittsburgh arose sheltered by the series of fortifications on the point, the first permanent English settlement west of the Allegheny Mountains. This was a point of entry in the late 18th and early 19th centuries for the waves of settlement pushing into the Ohio and upper Mississippi Valleys, making it an early gateway to the West.

George Washington visited the forks in November 1753, during his mission to Fort Le Boeuf to sound out the intentions of the French and

warn them away from the Ohio country. Washington strongly endorsed
the forks as the best site to command the rivers. In February 1754
workmen of the Ohio Company under Capt. William Trent began building the first outpost at the forks. In April a force of French and Indians
seized the hastily built stockade. They built Fort Duquesne, named in
honor of the Governor General of New France. The rival French and
British claims to the Ohio country, emphasized by the determination of
each power to control the forks, precipitated the final preindependence
struggle, which spread abroad and became the Seven Years' War.

Lt. Col. George Washington, commanding a small force raised to support the new fort at the Forks of the Ohio, learned that the French had
captured the position and pushed through the mountains to establish
a camp at Great Meadows, 11 miles east of present Uniontown. He
surprised and defeated a French scouting party on May 28 near Great
Meadows, firing what some historians have called the first shot of the
French and Indian War. Coulon de Jumonville, commanding the
French scouting party, was killed in the ambush in the glen that now
bears his name. A short time later French troops from Fort Duquesne
laid siege to Washington's command and on July 4, 1754, forced him to
surrender the hastily built Fort Necessity. Fort Duquesne was an objective the following year of Gen. Edward Braddock, whose British regulars
met shattering defeat a few miles east of the Forks of the Ohio. For 3
years longer Fort Duquesne served as a French base for raids on the
English frontier.

In 1758 British and colonial troops under Gen. John Forbes made a
remarkable march through the Pennsylvania wilderness and found
Duquesne destroyed and abandoned by the French because of pressures
elsewhere and the desertion of Indian allies. Col. Hugh Mercer with 200
men was left at the point, now named Pittsburgh, to built a temporary fort
farther up the Monongahela. Work on an ambitious permanent fortification began early in September 1759 and was completed 2 years later.
Pentagonal in outline, the walls of Fort Pitt (named for the then Prime
Minister) were earthen casements and represented a notable engineering
achievement for the time and place. Buildings constructed parallel to
the inside faces of the walls were of frame-and-brick construction.

Fort Pitt invited settlers, mostly Virginians, to follow Braddock's trail
and settle at the adjacent town that now began to take shape. In 1763,
during the Pontiac uprising, Fort Pitt was one of the few frontier out-
posts that held out against the warriors swarming down from the North-

west. A relief column under Col. Henry Bouquet lifted the siege 4
days after decisively defeating the Indians in the Battle of Bushy Run,
August 5–6, 1763. Bouquet built five redoubts as outworks to Fort Pitt,
one of which, a small brick blockhouse, stands today. Fort Pitt deteriorated as the French and Indian threat faded, although the settlement
at the forks remained an important base for traders, backwoodsmen, and
westward-moving settlers. As pioneers moved rapidly into the Northwest
after the Revolution, the forks became the center of a rapidly growing
frontier settlement. A fifth and last fort was built at the forks in the
winter of 1791–92, when war with the Indians in the Old Northwest
flamed anew. This post, LaFayette or Fayette, was built near the banks
of the Allegheny, a quarter of a mile above the site of Fort Pitt, which
had fallen into ruin. This post furnished troops in the Whisky Rebellion
in 1794 and served as a supply and training depot in the War of 1812.
But the military significance of the site was now secondary to its geographical location as the gateway to the trans-Appalachian interior.

Early in the 19th century, by flatboat and wagon, thousands of
American and foreign immigrants passed through Pittsburgh en route
to the old Northwest. The town became an industrial and commercial
center where pioneers could outfit themselves for the trek west.

Present Appearance. A few years ago the point of land at the Forks of
the Ohio lay beneath commercial structures and railroad tracks. Development of the 36-acre Point State Park, however, has removed the
commercial and industrial intrusions, including 15 acres of railroad
tracks. When completed, the park development will have opened the
sites of Forts Duquesne and Pitt. Archeological investigation has uncovered much useful information about Fort Pitt, and a study commissioned by the regional planning commission in 1945 provided the groundwork for developing the State park, including the task of relocating
bridges and traffic arteries. The flag bastion of Fort Pitt has been
restored and the Monongahela bastion will be rebuilt. A museum will
be developed within the Monongahela bastion under the administration
of the Pennsylvania Historical and Museum Commission. The Bouquet
blockhouse will be retained on its original site. Promenades on the
Allegheny and Monongahela riverfronts extend 50 feet beyond existing
harbor lines, and stone bleachers seating 3,000 persons have been erected
along the Allegheny riverfront. In summer the City of Pittsburgh
anchors a barge here, and free concerts and other programs are presented. Point State Park, in the shadow of the skyscrapers of modern

Pittsburgh, when completed, will provide an eloquent interpretation of the origins and growth of this Gateway to the West.[56]

42. Graeme Park, Pennsylvania

Location. Graeme Park, Keith Valley Road, Horsham.

Ownership and Administration. Historical and Museum Commission, Commonwealth of Pennsylvania, Harrisburg.

Significance. This Pennsylvania fieldstone house, located about 25 miles north of central Philadelphia, is one of the most distinguished of

This striking fieldstone house at Graeme Park, Horsham, Pa., is the only surviving building on the country estate of Sir William Keith, Royal Governor of Pennsylvania from 1717 to 1726.

many architectural examples of 18th-century houses in the region. The structure reflects the work of master builders and possesses exceptional value as a type specimen of its period and locale. In addition, the house has been identified traditionally as the home of Sir William Keith, Royal

Governor of the colony from 1717 to 1726, although recent investigation suggests that it was originally constructed as a malt house, part of an industrial settlement planned by Keith for the production of grain. The present house was one of a number of buildings that made up the Graeme Park settlement; none of the others has survived.

About 10 years after Sir William Keith's return to England in 1728, the estate came into the possession of Dr. Thomas Graeme, a prominent Philadelphia physician, husband of the Governor's step-daughter. Graeme bought the property for a country estate and experimented with a variety of farming techniques. Recent research indicates that the present house was made into a dwelling during Dr. Graeme's ownership. Graeme's daughter, Elizabeth, inherited the estate when her father died in 1772. Her husband, Henry Fergusson, was a loyalist who served with British forces during the Revolution. Later owners divided the estate into small parcels of land for sale or rent, and in 1801 Samuel Penrose purchased the small lot on which the present house stands. About 1810 Penrose built a new dwelling, and from this time on the old house was not used as a main dwelling. Work done by owners in the 19th and 20th centuries has been mainly to preserve the property.

Present Appearance. The house is plain and almost severe in exterior design and contains 2½ stories, with a high gambrel roof and two tall chimneys rising from the center deck of the roof. The structure is approximately 60 by 25 feet in size, with walls 2 feet thick of fieldstone carefully laid and fitted. Windows and doors are tall and narrow, set in plain frames that accentuate the austerity of the exterior design.

While the exterior is plainly colonial, the interior paneling, mantels, and door frames are Georgian of an advanced design. The first floor consists of a small entry and stairhall, a square center room, and two flanking rooms. The spacious paneled parlor on the east end of the first floor is notable for its marble-trimmed fireplace and wainscoted walls, which rise 14 feet from floor to ceiling. The second story also consists of three rooms, similar to the first-floor plan although with lower ceilings. The half-story third floor contains one large finished and three small unfinished rooms.

The house was recently donated by its private owners to the Commonwealth of Pennsylvania. Graeme Park is in process of restoration over a 6-year period, involving extensive archeological and historical research to provide the basis for an authentic restoration to protect the outstanding features of the building.[57]

John Bartram built his Philadelphia home in 1731, shown here, with his own hands.   Courtesy, Philadelphia Historical Commission.

43. John Bartram House, Pennsylvania

Location.   54th Street and Eastwick Avenue, Philadelphia.

Ownership and Administration.   City of Philadelphia, administered by Fairmount Park Commission, Philadelphia.

Significance.   The house and gardens of John Bartram stand as a memorial to a pioneer American botanist, and are an eloquent symbol of the rise of scientific inquiry in the English Colonies of the 18th century. John Bartram was America's first native botanist and has been called the greatest natural botanist of his time.   Born in 1699 near Darby, Pa., he acquired a love of nature in the countryside around Philadelphia. His learning was self-taught, and his interests were those of a collector and describer of plants rather than a formal scientist.   He had an extensive correspondence with leading botanists abroad and made a number of important journeys throughout the Colonies observing and collecting plants and noting everything on the colonial scene—wildlife, and the earth itself.   A Quaker by birth and inclination, he was ejected by the Society of Friends probably because his broad knowledge of life and science made difficult his conformation to the strict orthodoxy of the faith.   Many famous figures of the time came to his gardens.

Bartram was appointed botanist to the King in 1765, and important field trips were made in the service of the Crown. Like Franklin and Washington, who were his frequent guests, Bartram was representative of the best elements in the developing Colonies. He was a man of curiosity and keen intellect, equally at home with the great figures of his time and with the slaves whom he freed but who remained with him as paid servants. The gardens, filled by Bartram with rare and exotic plants, were enlarged by his son, William, and after a period of neglect were saved to perpetuate the memory of a notable American of the 18th century.

Present Appearance. John Bartram's house, built with his own hands in 1731, is one of distinctive, even unusual character, preserving the flavor of Bartram and his time. The 2½-story colonial building is of local stone with tall Ionic columns probably added when the house was remodeled some years after its original construction. A recessed porch and window casings of carved stone help give the house its distinctive character. Interior furnishings are of the period of Bartram's significant work.[58]

44. Mount Pleasant, Pennsylvania

Location. Fairmount Park, between East River Drive and Columbia Avenue entrance, Philadelphia.

Ownership and Administration. City of Philadelphia, administered by Philadelphia Museum of Art.

Significance. Situated on a hilltop overlooking the Schuylkill River, Mount Pleasant is the most important of a number of distinctive homes in Philadelphia's Fairmount Park. In the opinion of the architectural historian, Thomas T. Waterman, it is the finest colonial house north of the Mason-Dixon line. Its somewhat pretentious character re-creates vividly the atmosphere of wealth and station enjoyed by the men who helped to make Philadelphia the leading city of the Colonies.

Mount Pleasant has an unhappy historical association with Benedict Arnold, who bought it in 1779, little more than a year before his attempted betrayal of West Point. The house was later confiscated and Arnold's possessions sold publicly. The mansion was leased for a short time to Baron von Steuben and eventually came into the possession of Gen. Jonathan Williams of Boston. It remained in the Williams family until it became the property of the City of Philadelphia in 1868.

Mount Pleasant reflects the wealth and luxury that centered in Philadelphia, the largest city of the colonies. It is located in Fairmount Park, and was built in 1761–62.

Present Appearance. Mount Pleasant is an opulent representation of late Georgian design, constructed of rubble masonry coated with stucco to resemble dressed-stone masonry. The hilltop location, its 6-foot hewn-stone basement, its 12-foot ceilings, and high, hipped roof with balustraded deck, combine to impart a lofty appearance in keeping with the elaborate design. The north and south walls are windowless, relieved only by the brick belt course that extends around the house. Pavilions on the east and west sides frame arched doorways, above which are Palladian windows opening onto each end of the second-floor hall. The first floor consists of a large entrance hall that extends through the house, serving both east and west entrances. The stairway rises from a small separate hall at the southeast corner. The north room on the first floor is a large parlor extending across the end of the house. In the middle of the north wall is a chimney piece almost 8 feet wide, flanked by pedimented doors set, curiously, against the solid wall behind them. The three second-floor chambers are especially notable for their design and workmanship, most evident in the scrolled ornamentation and arched cupboard doors in the great chamber on the southwest corner. The house has been furnished handsomely in period style by the Philadelphia Museum of Art, and is maintained by this institution as an outstanding survivor of 18th-century Philadelphia.[59]

45. Valley Forge, Pennsylvania

Location. Port Kennedy, off Valley Forge Interchange of Pennsylvania Turnpike, Montgomery and Chester Counties.

Ownership and Administration. Valley Forge Park Commission, Commonwealth of Pennsylvania.

Significance. No name in American history conveys more of suffering, sacrifice, and triumph than Valley Forge. Washington's ragged, hungry troops staggered into the camp on December 19, 1777, the wreckage of a defeated army. They endured a bitterly cold and uncomfortable winter, but emerged as a trained army. The military training and discipline imposed at Valley Forge created a force that would meet the enemy on equal terms from then on, and at last defeat him.

Washington's 11,000 troops were mostly unfit for service when he took them into winter quarters at Valley Forge. They had experienced a series of fruitless marches and costly skirmishes, capped by defeat at Brandywine and failure at Germantown. From this camp, named for

General Washington used this house as his headquarters while the army was encamped at Valley Forge.

a small iron mill on Valley Creek which the British had destroyed, the Army could defend itself and also observe the approaches to Philadelphia. Approximately 900 log huts were raised, and fortifications were thrown up to protect the camp and command nearby roads and rivers. The soldiers were not permitted to huddle in their cabins, but were rigorously drilled and disciplined by "Baron" Frederick von Steuben who, even if he magnified his European rank and title, was nevertheless a drillmaster of surpassing skill. When spring came the Army was ready for the field as never before, and at Monmouth on June 28, 1778, it made its debut as a skilled force able to meet and defeat British regulars in open combat.

Present Appearance. Valley Forge State Park, embracing 2,000 acres on both sides of the Schuylkill River, includes extensive remains of the major forts, lines of earthworks, the artillery park, Washington's headquarters house, quarters of other top officers, and the grand parade ground, where Von Steuben rebuilt the Army and where news of the French alliance was announced on May 6, 1778. The Mount Joy observation tower affords a comprehensive view of the campsite and the countryside it was designed to command. A dominant feature of the park is the massive National Memorial Arch bearing on one face the inscription: "Naked and starving as they are, we cannot enough admire the incomparable patience and fidelity of the soldiery—Washington at Valley Forge, February 16, 1778." The Washington Memorial Museum, maintained by the Valley Forge Historical Society, contains thousands of relics, including Washington's field tent. Adjacent to the museum are the striking Washington Memorial Chapel and the Valley Forge Memorial Bell Tower. Reconstructed huts, handsome memorials, monuments, and markers tell the story of the men who wrote at Valley Forge an imperishable chapter in the story of America's struggle for independence.[60]

46. The Brick Market, Rhode Island

Location. Thames Street and Washington Square, Newport.

Ownership and Administration. City of Newport and Preservation Society of Newport County.

Significance. The Brick Market was designed by Newport's Peter Harrison, merchant and shipowner often called America's first professional architect. He designed a number of the town's distinguished

The Brick Market, built in 1762–63 in Newport, R.I., was the last work of architect Peter Harrison. It is today rare as an example of this type of colonial building. Courtesy, John T. Hopf.

buildings, chiefly as a labor of love. The Brick Market was constructed in 1762–63, although its details were not all completed until 1772. The ground floor, originally built with open arcades, was intended for use only as a market house, while the two upper floors were given over to drygoods stores and offices. All rentals and profits derived from the building went to the Newport town treasury to be used for the purchase of grain to supply a public granary for the town. After the Revolution the upper part of the building housed a printing office. In 1793 the upper stories were remodeled as a theater and served this purpose until 1799. In 1842 the building was altered to serve as the townhall. The third floor was removed and the second made into one large room with galleries on three sides. From 1853 until 1900 the old market served as city hall for Newport. As an outstanding example of Harrison's mature work and as one of few remaining colonial business structures, the Brick Market is a notable survivor of colonial America.

Present Appearance. The Brick Market was Harrison's last architectural work, and his design for the structure is one of the country's earliest examples of open arcades surmounted by great pilasters. The model for the design was Inigo Jones' Old Somerset House in London, although Harrison, following the specifications given him, used brick rather than stone construction. Despite this and other modifications, the building is remarkably faithful to its prototype. The exterior of Brick Market was completely restored in 1928 and the interior 2 years later. It now houses the offices of the Preservation Society of Newport County.[61]

47. First Baptist Meeting House, Rhode Island

Location. North Main Street between Waterman and Thomas Streets, Providence.

Ownership and Administration. Church property.

Significance. The First Baptist Meeting House is one of New England's most notable public buildings, both architecturally and historically. Its origins date from the establishment of the first Baptist organization in America, in Providence in 1639. In addition to its religious role, the meetinghouse from its very beginning has been the scene of commencement ceremonies for Brown University.

The First Baptist Meeting House, of Providence, R.I., built in 1774–75, is one of New England's most notable public buildings.

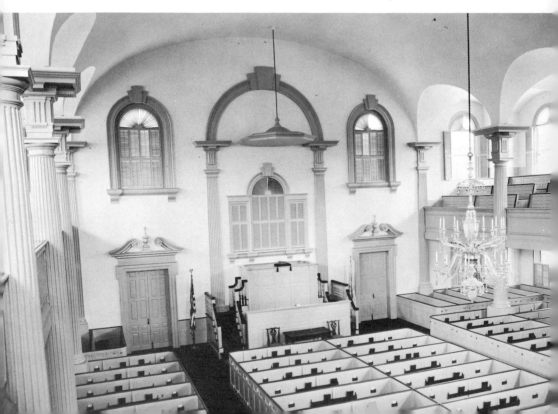

Joseph Brown, well-to-do merchant, amateur architect, and member of a famous Providence family, is credited with the design of the church. He based it largely on the plans of English churches reproduced in his personal copy of Gibbs' *Book of Architecture*. The imposing spire was based on an unexecuted design by James Gibbs for St. Martin's-in-the-Fields, London. The church was dedicated in May 1775, a few weeks after the outbreak of the Revolution, but in design and feeling it belongs to the colonial period and illustrates outstandingly the maturity of native architecture on the eve of the Revolution.

Present Appearance. The church as originally built was 80 feet square, with a door on each side and the main entrance under the spire on the west end. A gabled extension with a pedimented portico on the west end housed the stairs to the tower and spire, which rose 185 feet above the ground. An unusual feature of the body of the church is the set of two tiers of roundheaded windows. The low-pitched roof and the squareness of the structure combine to give the church an aspect of spaciousness and dignity. The interior is trimmed in wood. Galleries run along each side, supported by great fluted Doric columns. Over the five bays on each side are groined vaults that join the shallow vault over the nave. The interior was extended in the 19th century and the original pews, pulpit, and slave gallery are gone, but otherwise the meetinghouse has retained its character to an unusual degree.

In 1956 committees were appointed by the church to study ways and means to restore the building. A gift from John D. Rockefeller, Jr., a Brown University alumnus, made possible a complete rehabilitation and restoration that, it is estimated, will add at least another hundred years to the life and use of the building. The high pulpit was restored along the lines of the original design, and the white paint was replaced by sage, the original interior color. The meetinghouse was rededicated in a series of services in April 1958.[62]

48. Old State House (Old Colony House), Rhode Island

Location. Washington Square, Newport.

Ownership and Administration. State of Rhode Island, administered by the Old State House in New Port, Rhode Island, Inc.

Significance. The Old State House is an outstanding public building of colonial America, possessing both historical and architectural distinction. Designed by Richard Munday, the building was erected in 1739–

41 to house the General Assembly of the Colony of Rhode Island, and it served also as a center for public meetings and religious and social functions.   The death of George II, the succession of George III, and the

The Old State House, erected in Newport in 1739–41, originally housed the General Assembly of Rhode Island Colony.   Courtesy, John T. Hopf.

colony's acceptance of the Declaration of Independence were among the momentous events proclaimed from the second-floor balcony.   During the Revolution the State House served as a hospital for British and later French forces quartered in Newport.   When George Washington came to Newport to visit the newly arrived French Army, a banquet was held in the great hall on the first floor.   The May sessions of the Rhode Island Legislature were held in the Old State House from 1790 until the dedication of the new State House in Providence in 1900.

Present Appearance.   The State House is 2½ stories high, built of red brick resting on a granite masonry basement.   The gabled roof, cut off to form a flat deck at its peak, is surmounted by a two-story octagonal cupola. The dominant feature of the main facade is the center doorway with balcony. The interior consists of a large room (40 by 80 feet) on the first floor with a row of square Doric columns running down the middle, and three rooms on the second floor. The State House was partially restored in 1917 under the direction of Norman M. Isham and is today a public monument.[63]

49. Redwood Library and Athenaeum, Rhode Island

Location.   50 Bellevue Avenue, Newport.

Ownership and Administration.   Redwood Library and Athenaeum, Newport.

Significance.   Redwood Library is important both historically and architecturally. Historically, it is a striking representation of the intellectual development of the American Colonies in the 18th century. Still in use, it is beyond doubt one of the oldest library buildings in continuous use in the United States. Redwood Library was the outgrowth of a philosophical society founded in Newport in 1730, to which Abraham Redwood donated 500 pounds sterling in 1747 for the purchase of books. In all, Redwood's donation bought more than 1,200 volumes, which

The Redwood Library and Athenaeum, Newport, R. I., is one of the Nation's oldest library buildings in continuous use. Designed by Newport's Peter Harrison, it was completed around 1750 to house books purchased through a donation by Abraham Redwood. Courtesy, John T. Hopf.

were purchased in London.   To Redwood's gift, other Newport citizens added 5,000 pounds for construction of a library building on land donated by Henry Collins.   The building was completed about 1750.   The architect was the well-known Peter Harrison, of Newport, and his design for the original part of the building introduced the Palladian style to America.

Present Appearance.   The original structure was based on English adaptations of the Roman Doric temple, with portico and wings.   Unfortunately, the reduced scale of the building greatly impaired the effectiveness of this design.   The siding was of wood, rusticated and painted to resemble stone masonry, making the library a very early example of this treatment in Georgian architecture.   The central library room housed the stacks of books, and small offices were housed in the wings.   The library has been enlarged three times, most recently in 1913.   The original part of the building was restored by Norman M. Isham in 1915 to Peter Harrison's design.[64]

50. Camden Battlefield, South Carolina

Location.   5 miles north of Camden on county road just west of U.S. 521 and 601, Kershaw County.

Ownership and Administration.   2 acres are held by the Hobkirk Hill Chapter, Daughters of the American Revolution; the rest is in private ownership.

Significance.   Although it was the worst of a series of disasters to American forces in the South, the Battle of Camden, August 16, 1780, actually had a beneficial result in that it brought the capable Nathanael Greene to the American command.   Second only to Washington as a skilled tactical commander, Greene then launched a decisive campaign that, even though barren of victories, cleared the southern interior of British troops within a year.

The surrender of Gen. Benjamin Lincoln at Charleston on May 12, 1780, left only one organized American force in the South, and this was wiped out at Waxhaws on May 29.   In July, however, another American army, consisting of Continentals and militia, advanced into South Carolina from the North under Gen. Horatio Gates.   Confident that he outnumbered his opponent, Lord Charles Cornwallis, Gates detached part of his force to aid the partisan leader, Thomas Sumter, in a raid on distant British supply lines.   Gates and Cornwallis collided near Camden on the morning of August 16, 1780.

The battle was of short duration. Gates formed the Continentals under Baron de Kalb (originally Johann or Hans Kalb, son of a peasant) on the right and the militia on the left. As the British advanced, the militia suddenly gave way and streamed from the field in wild flight. The British dashed through in pursuit and soon isolated and surrounded the Continentals. They continued to fight tenaciously until De Kalb was shot down, when the remnants quit the field. Gates failed to rally the beaten army, but managed to reassemble part of it at Hillsborough on August 19. Cornwallis fell back to Winnsboro after Maj. Patrick Ferguson's defeat at Kings Mountain, and Gates moved to Charlotte. There on December 2 he was relieved by Nathanael Greene.

Present Appearance. The battlefield today is little changed from its original appearance. It is a flat area of open fields and pine woods, bordered on the east and west by small streams, with no intrusions on the historic scene. A stone monument erected by the Hobkirk Hill Chapter, Daughters of the American Revolution, marks the approximate site of De Kalb's fall, and a roadside narrative marker completes the interpretive development of the battlefield.[65]

51. Drayton Hall, South Carolina

Location. 12 miles west of Charleston on S.C. 61, Charleston County.
Ownership and Administration. Private.
Significance. John Drayton, a member of the Royal Council, acquired property fronting the west bank of the Ashley River in 1738, where he built Drayton Hall. It has remained in the hands of Drayton's descendants to this day. Drayton Hall, the best surviving example in South Carolina of the colonial plantation house, symbolizes the great wealth and culture that marked the colony in the 18th century. It is architecturally far ahead of the great Virginia houses of the same period.

Present Appearance. A monumental brick structure of two stories over a high basement, Drayton Hall has a double-hipped roof of the type common to many Georgian houses in the South. The west ("land") facade is marked by a two-story portico fronting a recessed central bay. The sheltered porch thus formed is approached by parallel flights of steps. No such feature distinguishes the "river" facade, which employs a classic pediment to emphasize the main axis. Here the approach is by a double flight of steps meeting at the main entrance.

The interior is distinguished by spacious rooms with magnificent

East facade, facing the Ashley River, of Drayton Hall, called "the best surviving example in South Carolina of the colonial plantation house."

paneling and richly ornamented ceilings. Especially impressive are the stair hall, with its double flight of stairs, and the entrance hall, with fireplace after a design by the great British architect, Inigo Jones. The other rooms are almost equally fine.

From the scope of the plan and the advanced architectural details, Drayton Hall appears to be the creation of a professional architect. Yet nothing has been discovered thus far to give a hint of his identity.

No productive use is being made of the 550 acres comprising the plantation. Except for a sizable lawn around the mansion, it has been allowed to revert to a tangled woodland. The house, although apparently structurally sound, stands in need of repair. Brickwork needs repointing in a number of places, steps and other exterior features show some deterioration, and wasp nests are numerous on the walls. The house is rather sparsely furnished with fine antiques, some of which were among the original furnishings. The house has no regular inhabitants, although a caretaker lives nearby.[66]

52. Miles Brewton House, South Carolina

Location.   27 King Street, Charleston.

Ownership and Administration.   Private.

Significance.   The Miles Brewton House was designed by Architect Ezra Waite and built in 1765–69 for a prominent Charleston citizen from whom it takes its name.   It is notable chiefly for its architectural excellence; such historical interest as the house possesses springs directly from its architectural distinction.   Because it was the most splendid townhouse in Charleston, it was occupied as a military headquarters in two wars—during the Revolution by Sir Henry Clinton, and in the last days of the Civil War by Federal officers of the army of occupation.

Present Appearance.   The Miles Brewton House is generally conceded by authorities to be the best example of the "Charleston double house," and one noted architect calls it the "finest town house of the colonial period." [67]   A two-story house of almost square design, it is covered by a sharply ridged, hipped roof, and the main facade is dominated by a two-story portico.   The house is richly ornamented, both inside and out, with a wealth of details. [68]

53. Mulberry Plantation, South Carolina

Location.   30 miles north of Charleston on U.S. 52, beside Cooper River, Berkeley County.

Ownership and Administration.   Private.

Significance.   Besides possessing a considerable degree of architectural interest, Mulberry Plantation illustrates well a number of important facets of 18th-century American history.   It was constructed in 1714 by Thomas Broughton, later a Royal Governor of South Carolina.   Located on the frontier, the house was built over a cellar fort, with firing slits in the foundation walls.   During the Yamassee War, 1715–16, Mulberry Plantation was a fortified stronghold to which a number of neighboring colonists fled for protection.   During the latter days of the American Revolution, when British troops overran the surrounding countryside, the plantation served as headquarters for a cavalry unit.

Present Appearance.   With its ricefields, dikes, and canals still in a good state of preservation, Mulberry is one of the most impressive of the river rice plantations that brought great wealth to the colony in the 18th

A view across the north ricefield of Mulberry Plantation, from high ground near the mansion.

century. Architecturally, the most distinctive features of the mansion are the four "flankers" that extend from the corners of the central section, with hipped roofs, bell-shaped turrets, and iron weather vanes. The house and grounds are in excellent condition. Major interior alterations were made in 1800 and some restoration in the early 20th century, but apparently few major structural changes have been made since the house was built. The two main ricefields still exist, as well as the original dikes and rice canals. Mulberry Plantation is not open to visitors.[69]

54. Robert Brewton House, South Carolina

Location. 71 Church Street, Charleston.
Ownership and Administration. Private.
Significance. The Robert Brewton House, built about 1730 by the prominent Miles Brewton for his son, has survived two wars and two major fires to achieve a unique double distinction. Besides being one of the oldest surviving Charleston houses, it is the earliest accurately dated example of the "single house," an architectural type peculiar to that

city. The "single house" shows traces of West Indian influence and is a fine example of the adaptation of structural design to climatic conditions. As the name suggests, the "single house" is of single-room thickness. It stands with its long axis perpendicular to the street, and along one of the long sides (generally the south or west) runs a piazza, overlooking a small enclosed garden. The entrance is through a gate on the street end of the piazza. Thick walls of brick, covered with white or pastel-tinted stucco, are topped by tile roofs. The piazza, which during the 18th century was of wood and only one story high, evolved during the 19th century into the two-story appendage so familiar in present-day Charleston. This design admirably served its purpose of making the hot South Carolina summers bearable and, coupled with the town's sea breezes and the relative absence of malaria, made Charleston the summertime mecca of the plantation families.

Present Appearance. The Robert Brewton House has undergone little exterior change, except that the piazza has been removed (necessitating a new entrance treatment) and there is no side garden. Three stories high, there are angle quoins, key blocks over the windows, and a wrought-iron balcony on the street front. The mantelpieces and other interior woodwork show fine workmanship. The house is well maintained and in the best of condition. It is not open to visitors.[70]

55. St. Michael's Episcopal Church, South Carolina

Location. 80 Meeting Street, Charleston.

Ownership and Administration. St. Michael's Church Corporation, Charleston.

Significance. Called by Hugh Morrison "one of the great Georgian churches of the Colonies," [71] St. Michael's provides an outstanding illustration of the advance of wealth and culture in South Carolina during the first half of the 18th century. The colonial assembly authorized construction of the edifice in 1751 but, although it was virtually completed within 2 years, it was not dedicated until 1761. The architect is not known, although it may have been the noted Peter Harrison.

Present appearance. The stucco-covered building is of brick, furnished by Zachariah Villeponteux, who was noted for the quality of his product. The exterior features a two-story Roman Doric portico, the first giant portico built on a Georgian church in the colonies, and an unusually solid spire. The latter rises from a square base in a series of diminishing octagons to a terminal spire, the top of which is 185 feet above the street. The interior is marked by a coved ceiling and low side galleries supported by fluted Ionic columns. Waxed and polished cedar woodwork adds to the beauty of the interior.[72]

St. Michael's Episcopal Church of Charleston, S.C., is noted for its early giant portico and unusually solid spire.

56. Long Island of the Holston, Tennessee

Location. South edge of Kingsport in the South Fork of the Holston River, Sullivan County.

Ownership and Administration. Various private and corporate owners.

Significance. Long Island of the Holston was for many years a jealously guarded possession of the Cherokee Indians. It became the scene of momentous events during the early years of exploration and settlement in the Old Southwest, the springboard for the initial settlement of Kentucky and Middle Tennessee.   In its environs was fought the battle that gave those feeble settlements precious time to consolidate their posi-

A view westward along the northern shore of the Long Island of the Holston, which played a prominent part in the early history of the Tennessee country.

tions during the first 2 years of the American Revolution.   Long Island derived strategic importance from its location just east of the junction of the North and South Forks of the Holston.   Nearby was the crossing of the Great Indian Warpath, a major trail to the northeast from central Tennessee.   Thus the island figured significantly in the colonial struggle with the Indians that began in the middle of the 18th century.

Col. William Byrd, leading a colonial expedition into Cherokee country, built Fort Robinson at the river junction in 1761 and introduced white occupation of the area.   When Byrd's force abandoned the fort soon afterward, the Indians resumed possession, although more and more white hunters and traders began passing through en route to the hunting grounds of Kentucky and Tennessee.   Among them was Daniel Boone. In March 1775, while Richard Henderson was still negotiating with the Cherokees for their Kentucky land, he sent Boone with 30 axmen to open the trail that was to gain fame as the Wilderness Road.   Boone's trailmaking began at Long Island on March 10, and 2 weeks later his party reached the Kentucky River, having marked the way that was to lead 200,000 emigrants to Kentucky within the next 20 years.

The Cherokees cast their lot with the British when the Revolution began.   Stung into action by colonial settlement on the east Tennessee land they claimed, the Indians moved to crush the frontiersmen in July 1776.   The defenders of Eaton's Fort, on high ground near Long Island, sallied onto Long Island Flats and, after a bitter fight, drove the Cherokees from the field.   Two months later a punitive expedition against the Indian towns cowed the Cherokees, bringing 2 years of relative peace to the southwestern frontier.   At the Treaty of Long Island, in July 1777, the Indians relinquished their claims to the land occupied by whites in east Tennessee.

Besides being the starting point of Boone's Wilderness Road, Long Island was a jumping-off point for the settlement of central Tennessee. Just before Christmas of 1779, Col. John Donelson lead a flotilla of flatboats from there on the long and hazardous voyage down the Tennessee and up the Cumberland to establish Cumberland Colony, the first permanent white settlement in middle Tennessee.   The importance of Long Island as a terminus and starting point led to the establishment of a boatyard directly across the river from the west end of the island.

Present Appearance.   Long Island is approximately 4 miles long and ½-mile wide.   The eastern third of the island is now taken up with a housing development, known as Long Island, and a fuel-supply yard for the nearby acetate plant of the Tennessee Eastman Co.   The central third, largely undeveloped except for an interplant railroad that crosses the island diagonally, is held by six separate owners.   The western third, virtually undeveloped, is in a single ownership and retains much of its primitive appearance.[73]

57. Greenway Court, Virginia

Location.   1 mile south of White Post, near Va. 277, Clarke County.

Ownership and Administration. Private.

Significance. Greenway Court was for 30 years the home of Lord Thomas Fairfax, the only English peer residing in the Colonies, a friend to young George Washington, and proprietor of a 5-million-acre grant of Virginia lands. Inheriting the proprietary through his mother, daughter of Lord Thomas Culpeper, Fairfax was forced into a long defense of his lands by a formidable political attack that began in 1733 and continued intermittently until after his death in 1781. He took up residence at Greenway Court in 1752, to safeguard his interests, and lived out his years there in comfort, although on a scale far below that enjoyed by the average upper class Virginian. In truth, the estate was never completed. The projected manor house was never built, and Fairfax resided in another house that was planned as a hunting lodge. From 1762 until his death he maintained the land office for his Northern Neck Proprietary at Greenway Court. Washington visited there a number of times, first in 1748 as a member of a surveying party and later in his capacity as a large landed proprietor himself. Lord Dunmore, Royal Governor of Virginia, spent some time at Greenway Court during the Shawnee campaign of 1774, and a number of other prominent Virginians were there at one time or another. Fairfax, a leading citizen of Virginia during the third quarter of the 18th century, had an important influence on the careers of Washington and, indirectly, John Marshall, whose father also did some survey work for the proprietor. The land speculation that centered at Greenway Court for more than a decade was typical of the preoccupation with frontier lands that touched all Virginians in the years just before the American Revolution.

Present Appearance. Of the buildings existing during Fairfax's lifetime, the limestone land office, probably built in 1762, and restored in 1930, still stands and is in fair condition. It is a thick-walled structure 28.4 by 18.4 feet, with a heavy hewnboard door and narrow shuttered windows. The "hunting lodge" has been replaced by a two-story brick farmhouse built in 1828. The property is now occupied by tenants, but appears to be well maintained.[74]

58. Mount Airy, Virginia

Location. 1 mile west of Warsaw, U.S. 360, Richmond County.
Ownership and Administration. Private.
Significance. Mount Airy was built by Col. John Tayloe, 1758–62, as

Mount Airy, Va., is still owned by descendents of the builder, Col. John Tayloe. It is one of the very few 18th-century stone houses in Virginia, and is an ideal full Palladian villa.

designed by the noted Virginia architect, John Ariss. Its significance rests chiefly on architectural distinction. Mount Airy is one of the few stone houses built in Virginia during the 18th century, and represents the first instance in the Colonies of the achievement of the ideal full Palladian villa, with dependent wings connected to the main house by quadrant passages.

Present Appearance. The dark-brown sandstone walls, laid in courses of random heights, are trimmed with light-colored sandstone. The entrance facade features a projecting pavilion of rusticated limestone with a crowning pediment. The south facade, facing the broad valley of the Rappahannock, is similar except that the three entrances are framed by round arches. The entire composition of the facade is copied from a design in James Gibbs' *Book of Architecture.* The interior was destroyed by fire in 1844, and the roof has been remodeled. Mount Airy is still owned by Tayloe descendants. It is not open to visitors.[75]

59. St. John's Episcopal Church, Virginia

Location. East Broad and 24th Streets, Richmond.

Ownership and Administration. The church and southern half of cemetery are owned by the congregation of St. John's Episcopal Church.

The northern half of the cemetery is owned by the City of Richmond.

Significance. In St. John's Church on March 23, 1775, Patrick Henry, spellbinding orator of the Revolution, achieved immortal fame with his "Liberty or Death" speech, which sounded a clarion call for his fellow Virginians. Henry had been in the public eye for a dozen years. His brilliant defense of colonial self-government in the "Parson's Cause" of 1763 attracted widespread attention. Two years later his "Virginia Resolutions," inspired by the Stamp Act, stirred the Colonies and propelled Henry to leadership of the radical party in Virginia. None who heard the speech was likely to forget the concluding words: "Caesar had his Brutus—Charles the first, his Cromwell—and George the third . . . may profit by their example." Henry continued to hold the forefront during the decade of increasing colonial agitation that ended in war. As a delegate to the First Continental Congress in September 1774, he strongly supported the radical measures, and his conduct gave evidence of strong nationalist leanings.

Virginia's Royal Governor, Lord Dunmore, called a meeting of the general assembly for late in November 1774 but prorogued it when he learned of the participation of the Virginia leaders in "The Association" to boycott British goods. Members of the prorogued assembly arranged to meet in Richmond on March 20, 1775. For the meeting place, they chose the largest building in the community, the "New Church" or the "Church on Richmond Hill," as it was variously called. When the convention assembled, most of the leaders of Virginia politics were present. Among the approximately 120 members were George Washington, Thomas Jefferson, Patrick Henry, George Wythe, Benjamin Harrison, Edmund Pendleton, Robert Carter Nicholas, Carter Braxton, George Mason, Richard Henry Lee, Thomas Nelson, Jr., Richard Bland, and Andrew Lewis.

The tone of the convention was conciliatory at first, but Henry soon offered a series of resolutions to put the colony into a state of defense. The resolutions were defended by Lee, Washington, and Jefferson, but the conservative members—Pendleton, Bland, Nicholas, and Harrison—attacked them as rash and provocative. On March 23 Henry rose to defend the resolutions in a short speech, which closed with the following stirring words, as reported later:

> There is no retreat but in submission and slavery! Our chains are forged. Their clanking may be heard on the plains of Boston! The war is inevitable—and let it come!! I repeat it, sir, let it come!!! It is vain, sir, to extenuate the matter. Gentlemen may cry, peace, peace,

but there is no peace. The war is actually begun! The next gale that
sweeps from the north will bring to our ears the clash of resounding
arms! Our brethren are already in the field! Why stand we here idle?
What is it that gentlemen wish? What would they have? Is life so
dear or peace so sweet, as to be purchased at the price of chains and
slavery? Forbid it, Almighty God—I know not what course others
may take; but as for me, give me liberty, or give me death.

The speech swept the convention to Henry's viewpoint, and his resolutions passed. True to his prophecy, news of the outbreak of fighting at
Lexington and Concord came within a short time, and the Colonies were
at war.

The church in which Henry made his speech was built in 1740–41, on
land donated by Col. William Byrd, and remained the only church in
Richmond until 1814. Originally constructed as a simple rectangular
building, 25 feet wide and 40 long, with the long axis running east and
west, the church was enlarged in December 1772. At this time an addition was built on the north side and the interior rearranged so that the
addition became the nave. At the same time, also, a belfry was constructed over the west end of the original church. This was the church
as it existed at the time of Patrick Henry's famous speech.

Present Appearance. St. John's Church has been altered several
times since 1772. In 1830 the nave was enlarged and the interior of
the church rearranged. In the next few years, the original belfry was
taken down and replaced by a tower and bell at the north end. A chancel and vestry room were added to the south end in 1880, giving it the
cross shape it now has. A hurricane blew down the spire in 1896. The
replacement was similar to the original spire of the time of Henry's
speech. In 1799 the City of Richmond added two lots to the church
property, and the church cemetery became a public burying ground.
It was the only public cemetery in Richmond until 1826. Among the
graves are those of George Wythe and Elizabeth Arnold Poe, mother of
Edgar Allan Poe.

The church is attractively maintained and is one of the most noted of
Richmond's historic shrines. In spite of inadequate parking space, visita-
tion averages about 50,000 people a year. The area surrounding St.
John's Church has been designated a historic zone, and plans for its
restoration are being carried out by the Historic Richmond Foundation.
In the few square blocks of the zone are about 70 ante bellum homes, a
number of which have already been restored.[76]

60. Stratford Hall, Virginia

Location. 3 miles north of Lerty on Va. 214, Westmoreland County.

Ownership and Administration. Robert E. Lee Memorial Foundation, Inc., Stratford Hall, Va.

Significance. Stratford Hall, probably best known as the birthplace of Robert E. Lee, is of major importance both historically and architecturally. The list of noted men who were born or lived there reads like a miniature "Who's Who" for Virginia: 4 members of the Governor's council, 12 burgesses, 4 members of the Virginia Convention of 1776, 2 signers of the Declaration of Independence, several Governors of Virginia, members of the Continental Congress, diplomats, and military leaders. Of those born at Stratford Hall, in addition to the great Confederate general, the list includes the signers of the Declaration (Richard Henry and Francis Lightfoot Lee) and three other Revolutionary leaders (William, Arthur, and Thomas Ludwell Lee).

Present Appearance. Architecturally, Stratford Hall is a notable example of early Georgian architecture, yet with many features that make it unique. Its H-plan gives it a kinship with the Capitol building at Williamsburg and Tuckahoe in Goochland County, Va. It is a huge bulk with raised basement, unaccompanied by the usual pilasters and other academic forms. One of its chief distinguishing characteristics is the presence of twin sets of four-chimney stacks on the wings, connected by arches and enclosing balustraded roof decks. The monumental great hall is outstanding for its period. Four original service dependencies flank the mansion. The acreage owned by the administering foundation is only a portion of the original 16,000-acre estate on which Col. Thomas Lee built the house in 1725–30. The Stratford Hall estate, maintained as a historic-house museum and operating 18th-century plantation, is in excellent condition. The formal gardens have been restored, as well as walks, shrubbery, and minor dependencies.[77]

61. Westover, Virginia

Location. On James River 7 miles west of Charles City Courthouse, Charles City County.

Ownership and Administration. Private.

Significance. The present Westover Mansion was built by William

Byrd II in 1730–34 on one of the earliest Virginia plantations, first occupied in 1619. Typical of the tidewater tobacco plantations, Westover was a vast, 1,200-acre estate that barely provided a living for its owner. Typical of his class, Byrd supplemented his income as a tobacco planter with large-scale speculation in western lands.

Westover was built by William Byrd II between 1730 and 1734.

Present Appearance. One of the most famous Georgian houses in the United States, Westover is noted for the quality of its construction and for its architectural completeness. The mansion proper consists of a two-story central section on a high basement, and two attached wings. The east wing is a replacement of the original, which was destroyed during the Civil War. Several dependencies, including the original kitchen, which is reputed to antedate the present house, stand nearby. Notable features of the mansion include formal doorways in Portland stone on both main facades; a steeply pitched hip roof, rising to a sharp ridge instead of a deck; an offcenter main hall, utilizing one of the regularly spaced facade windows as a light source; and a finely detailed interior with full-length paneling and enriched plaster ceilings. Exterior features include three original gates, the distinguished central set probably made by Thomas Robinson, of London; an underground tunnel from the house to the riverbank; formal gardens, containing the grave of William Byrd II; the site of the first Westover Church, about 400 yards west of the house, where a number of prominent Virginians are buried, including the first Benjamin Harrison, of Berkeley, the first William Byrd and his wife, and Capt. William Perry, who died in 1637; and the remains of an old icehouse. The mansion group was restored about 1920 and came into possession of the present family in 1921. The garden and grounds are open to visitors.[78]

62. Wren Building, Virginia

Location. College of William and Mary, Williamsburg.

Ownership and Administration. College of William and Mary, State of Virginia.

Significance. The College of William and Mary was chartered on February 8, 1693, and was the first successful college in Virginia and the second in all the English Colonies. Middle Plantation, later named Williamsburg, was chosen as the site, and the cornerstone was laid in 1695. Designed by Sir Christopher Wren, the college building was completed in its original form in 1702, when two sides of the proposed quadrangle were finished. Accidentally burned in 1705, the building was subsequently rebuilt and a third side of the quadrangle was completed in 1732. The building was damaged by fire again in 1859 and 1862, with consequent alterations in each reconstruction. When John D. Rockefeller, Jr., undertook its restoration in 1927, only two-thirds of the original wall height remained. Timely discovery of "Bodleian Plate" at Oxford University, depicting several important buildings of 18th-century Williamsburg, permitted an authentic restoration of the Wren Building.

Present Appearance. One of the largest buildings erected in the English Colonies up to that time, the Wren Building, was four stories high (including English basement and attic) and 136 feet long. The mature Renaissance design, clearly identified with the 18th century although constructed partly in the 17th, incorporates a formal symmetry, with the central axis accented by round-arch portal, balcony, sharp-pitched gable, and cupola. Balancing the central axis are uniformly spaced windows and narrow dormers. The north wing, completed at the same time as the front portion, contains the "Great Hall"; the south wing, constructed in 1732, is the chapel. Restoration in 1928 was authentic, with the only alterations being additional stairs and other minor details needed to adapt the building to a continuing academic use. Painstaking research was necessary in order to permit authentic replacement, because the interior woodwork had been destroyed completely by fire.[79]

D. Historic Districts Eligible for the Registry of National Historic Landmarks

In several theme studies undertaken by the National Survey of Historic Sites and Buildings, instances were found where a number of historic buildings grouped in proximity, when viewed collectively, formed an outstanding illustration of a past era. Such groups have been designated historic districts and declared eligible for the Registry of National Historic Landmarks. A historic district may or may not contain individual structures which receive on their own merits the landmark designation. The following historic districts illustrate 18th-century English colonial development.

1. Old Deerfield, Massachusetts

Location. Deerfield, off U.S. 5 and Mass. 10, Franklin County.

Ownership and Administration. Homes privately owned; museum and museum houses owned and administered by Heritage Foundation and Pocumtuck Valley Memorial Association; buildings owned by Deerfield Academy.

Significance. Deerfield was the northernmost outpost of the New England frontier at the end of the 17th century. Its name lives in history as a symbol of the hardship endured and the final triumph won by the settlers who challenged the French and Indians of the interior. Negotiations with the Pocumtuck Indians in 1667 opened to white settlement a tract of 8,000 wilderness acres in the Connecticut Valley. The Indians received fourpence an acre for the land, a price that the white men considered very liberal. The first settlers arrived in the spring of 1669, and by 1673 twenty families had broken ground for farms, laid out a village street and set aside house lots much as they exist today. In the latter year the colonists established an independent town whose name soon began to appear on official documents as Deerfield.

The people of Deerfield lived in constant apprehension of Indian attacks. A series of Indian raids in September 1675 brought death to many men and forced the survivors to retreat to the south. Despite this setback, Deerfield was reoccupied and built anew within a few years, stronger than before. As evidence of its new strength, in September 1694 the fortified village rallied and beat off a surprise attack by Indians under French leaders.

Deerfield was still the northernmost colonial outpost on the Connecticut River at the opening of the 18th century. When Queen Anne's War broke out in 1702, the French made haste to ally themselves with the Indians for the purpose of attacking Deerfield. A force of 200 French regulars and nearly 150 Indian warriors swept down on Deerfield at daybreak on February 29, 1704, surprised the sentries and threw open the gate of the stockade that surrounded the village. The struggle raged for 5 hours. More than half the population perished or were seized as prisoners, and nearly half the houses were looted and burned. Only the timely arrival of reinforcements from settlements to the south saved Deerfield from total disaster. The French and Indians withdrew to Canada with more than a hundred prisoners—men, women, and children—many of whom were later released.

Troops took station at Deerfield to prevent a recurrence of this catastrophe, and slowly the settlement was reborn. Occasional minor raids continued to plague the town until the final major attack in 1746, but never again did the town suffer the horror of 1704. Deerfield was well on the way to prosperity as a wheat and cattle center by the middle of the 18th century, and its inhabitants reflected the better times in their comfortable homes and household treasures. This period of dawning refinement and taste is reflected today in many of the 18th-century dwellings of Old Deerfield.

The outbreak of the Revolution brought tension again to Deerfield. Some inhabitants remained aggressively loyal to the King while others embraced the patriot cause with equal ardor. When hostilities opened at Lexington and Concord, Deerfield sent its young men to war and then served as a supply center for American troops operating in the region.

The town won a new reputation as a center of education after the

John Williams House: Williams was the first resident minister of Deerfield, who was captured by Indians and later released. The citizens of Deerfield voted in town meeting, in January 1706, to build a new house for him. This structure serves today as a dormitory for Deerfield Academy.

establishment of Deerfield Academy in 1797. Deerfield largely escaped the currents of progress and growth that rapidly transformed other communities of the young Republic. Spared in great measure from the impact of modern urban and industrial development, Old Deerfield is today a memorable evocation of America's colonial frontier.

Present Appearance. Old Deerfield consists principally of an unusual collection of dwellings dating from the 18th and early 19th centuries together with public buildings extending for a mile along elm-shaded Old Deerfield Street. Among the most notable of these structures, open to the public, are the Frary House, part of which antedates the massacre of 1704; the Sheldon-Hawks House, built in 1734; the Ashley House, dating from the early 18th century; and the Asa Stebbins House, finished in the 1790's. Memorial Hall, built in 1799 for Deerfield Academy, is on Memorial Road just off Old Deerfield Street. The building now serves as a museum housing an outstanding collection of furniture, pewter, household objects, farm implements, and other items relating to early Deerfield and the New England colonial period. Among the museum exhibits is a heavy, nail-studded door identified as being from the original Sheldon Tavern. In the door are holes chopped by the Indians in an effort to break into the fortified house during the fighting of February 29, 1704. Although all the houses are not open to the public, many have been carefully restored to preserve the atmosphere of a village that, while meeting the needs of the modern day, illustrates the charm, craftsmanship, and discrimination of the period when Old Deerfield rose from the ruins of frontier war.[80]

2. Huguenot Street, New Paltz, New York

Location. Huguenot Street, New Paltz, Ulster County, on the Walkill River.

Ownership and Administration. Jean Hasbrouck House (Memorial House) owned by Huguenot Patriotic, Historical and Monumental Society, New Paltz, N.Y. Other houses privately owned.

Significance. Five stone houses clustered along New Paltz' Huguenot Street constitute a remarkable picture of an early 18th-century community. They are: Abraham Hasbrouck House, Louis Bevier House,

The Daniel du Bois House is one of several 18th-century dwellings that make Huguenot Street in New Paltz, N.Y., a vivid link with Huguenot settlement in colonial America. Courtesy, Cortlandt Van Dyke Hubbard.

Daniel du Bois House, Hugo Freer House, and Jean Hasbrouck House (Memorial House). Huguenot settlement, both Walloon and French, was a significant facet of American development in the 17th and 18th centuries, and nowhere is it more graphically illustrated by historic buildings than at New Paltz. Although the original Huguenot settlement of New Paltz dates from the latter part of the 17th century, the five listed houses are of the 18th century, incorporating parts of the earlier wooden houses they replaced.

Although surrounded by the Dutch and friendly with them, the Huguenot settlers of New Paltz resisted intermarriage with their neighbors and for many years preserved their own way of life. For all practical purposes, they were an independent, self-governing body that the Crown and, later, the State of New York, tolerated. In 1785 the State legislature confirmed the ancient grants and petitions and incorporated the town into the State government. The original system of goverment for New Paltz consisted of a council of 12 heads of families. Later descendants of the original dozen continued to govern, exercising judicial power, allocation of land, etc. The plain folk who settled New Paltz did not have the widespread influence on American social and cultural development that can be claimed for the more sophisticated Huguenot communities in Charleston and elsewhere, but nowhere is Huguenot settlement better preserved in terms of extent and integrity of physical remains than on Huguenot Street in New Paltz. Even without its Huguenot associations, the existence of five early 18th-century buildings on one continuously inhabited street would justify recognition of the New Paltz community as an outstanding survivor of colonial America. When the deeper significance is added of Huguenot Street as a haven for European refugees, the New Paltz community may well be unique in terms of its period and historical significance.

Present Appearance. The houses of Huguenot Street have a pronounced Dutch colonial aspect. The Jean Hasbrouck House, built about 1712 by one of the 12 original patentees of the settlement, has been preserved in original form to an unusual degree. Its rough stone walls, topped by high, steep-pitched roof, give it an appearance almost medieval in character. The interior follows the center-hall plan, with two rooms on each side. At the entrance door is an early shed stoop. This house is owned by the Huguenot Patriotic, Historical, and Monumental Society, and is open to the public as a historic-house museum. The Abraham Hasbrouck House, built about 1717, is also relatively unaltered. Its rough-faced stone walls, gabled roof with sloping shed dormers and three chimneys, strongly reflect Dutch colonial design.

The Daniel du Bois House was built about 1775 on the site of an earlier stone fortress, the walls of which may have been incorporated in the later dwelling. The house was enlarged and its interior altered in the 19th century. The center portion of the Bevïer House, home of an original New Paltz patentee, dates from the end of the 17th century, although the house was substantially enlarged about 1735. In addition to the thick stone walls and steep-pitched roof, the Freer House, built early in the 18th century, has clapboard gable windows, solid shutters, and divided door with overhang hood, common in Dutch colonial architecture. In addition to the above houses, the Deyo House may also be mentioned, although portions of the walls of the present house are all that remain of the original structure built by Pierre Deyo, another of the New Paltz patentees. The house was extensively remodeled in the 19th century, and little of its original construction was spared.[81]

3. Elfreth's Alley, Philadelphia, Pennsylvania

Location. North of Arch Street between Front and Second Streets, Philadelphia.

Ownership and Administration. Privately owned houses and four houses owned or leased by the Elfreth's Alley Association.

Significance. The dwellings fronting this narrow street are a unique representation of Philadelphia architecture. Half of those now standing were erected either before the middle of the 18th century or before the opening years of the Revolution, while the other half were constructed in the postcolonial and Federal years.

The alley itself was opened between 1702 and 1704 by mutual agreement between Arthur Wells and John Gilbert, both of whom lived on Front Street. Wells donated 5 feet of land extending from Front to Second Streets on the south side of the intended alley, while Gilbert, who owned the land on the north, donated 10 feet. Because Arthur Wells died shortly after the alley was paid out, it was first known as Gilbert's Alley. Following his death it came to be called Preston's Alley, after Paul Preston, who had married Gilbert's widowed daughter-in-law. Not until about 1750 was it commonly called Elfreth's Alley, for Jeremiah Elfreth, who then lived on Second Street just north of the alley. His first wife was a sister of Paul Preston's wife, and his fifth wife was the widow of a grandson of Arthur Wells. Elfreth had acquired title, through these two wives, to land on both sides of the alley at its Second Street end.

By the time the alley came to be known by Elfreth's name most of the present dwellings on the south side and two on the north side, at the west corner of Bladen's Court, had been built. Of these the two oldest surviving dwellings on the entire alley are Nos. 120 and 122 on the south side. Benjamin Franklin frequently visited the latter house, undoubtedly, because William Maugridge, the tenant from 1728 to 1731, was one of the original members of Franklin's junto.

The house next oldest is probably No. 108, built sometime after 1725 and before 1750 by Thomas Wells, a shipwright and the eldest son of Arthur Wells. Across the street on the north side, the two-story house at the northwest corner of Bladen's Court, No. 117, was probably built about 1734 by William Parker, a young blacksmith; the house next door, No. 119, was built between 1737 and 1747. This house was purchased in 1757 by Matthias Meyer, a German potter from Hilsbach. His daughter Hannah was married here in 1770 to the Reverend John Peter Gabriel Muhlenberg, the "fighting parson" of Revolutionary fame, whose father, Henry Melchior Muhlenberg, patriarch of the Lutheran Church in Pennsylvania, often called on the Meyers when he was in the city.

Next in age are the two houses numbered 130 and 132 across the alley on the south side near Second Street. These were built for income-producing purposes shortly after 1741 by Adam Clampffer, a German shopkeeper who lived nearby on Second Street. He and his heirs rented both properties to a succession of tenants until after the Revolution. By the middle of the 19th century, the narrow little house now No. 134 had replaced the original frame tavern and shop erected long before the Revolution. Sometime between 1753 and 1755 Richard Hall, a house carpenter, built the house numbered 118. Moses Mordecai, one of the original members of Mikveh Israel Congregation, was a tenant here in 1769 and possibly earlier. Jeremiah Elfreth built No. 124 and the original dwelling at No. 126 between 1741 and 1762, when he sold both properties. House No. 126 is being restored and will be used as a permanent museum for the Elfreth's Alley Association.

Down toward Front Street, Nos. 110, 112, and 114 were erected sometime between 1757 and 1762 by Thomas Patterson, another house carpenter. The three-story house at No. 116 represents the postcolonial period. It was built in 1785–86 by the brothers Benjamin and Enoch

Taylor, who were bricklayers and masons. Across the street, No. 137, near Second Street, was built in 1789 by the cabinetmaker Josiah Elfreth, a grandson of Jeremiah Elfreth. The house adjoining on the east, No. 135, is known as the Coach House from the high arched passage that originally led back to stables belonging to Jeremiah Elfreth's house on Second Street. In 1811 the premises were described as "brick stores" owned by a distiller, John Angue, who had purchased the frame shops and the Elfreth dwelling, fronting on Second Street, in 1805. Whether the present house is identical with the brick stores or was erected after 1811 has not been established definitely.

Apparently the first dwelling built on the north side of the alley, erected between 1713 and 1727, occupied the sites of the lots now numbered 129 and 131. The present dwellings on the site, Nos. 129 and 131, presumably were built between 1796 and 1798. At the opposite end of the alley on the same side, the two houses numbered 109 and 111 appear to have been put up by John Pechin, a carpenter, possibly about 1811. On the site of the present No. 109 there had been an earlier dwelling, probably built between 1775 and 1779, which was occupied for 6 months in 1780 by Stephen Girard. The next two houses, Nos. 113 and 115, were probably built between 1805 and 1809 by Ephraim Haines. Haines had purchased the two lots in the autumn of 1805, at which time they included two brick stables. That on No. 113 had been erected in 1763, while the one on No. 115, standing since 1748 when the premises included "a large smith's shop * * * with four good forges, good stable and garden behind the same," was then owned by the blacksmith, William Parker, who was living in No. 117.

Bladen's Court, separating these last two properties, was opened between 1749 and 1753 by Abraham Carlile and Thomas Maule. The latter had recently purchased No. 117 from Parker but lived in Front Street north of the alley and next door to Carlile. Both their Front Street properties extended west this far. Carlile had the dubious distinction of being one of the two loyalist Quakers hanged in 1778. During the British occupation of Philadelphia in 1777, he had served the British as a keeper of the city gates at the north end of the town. A house carpenter and original member of the Carpenters' Company, he may have built the Spinning-Wheel House at the north end of the court, for it stands on what was once his property. The remaining houses in the center of the north side of the alley represent the Federal period of domestic architecture.

Until 1775, the sites of the present Nos. 125 and 127 may have been occupied by the "pothouse and potter's kiln," which were adjuncts of the property in 1741. The land was vacant, however, when Daniel Trotter purchased these two lots and the two to the west in 1793. He built a frame shop on No. 125 and in 1798 a second shop on No. 127. These were purchased by Barney Schumo, a turner, in 1810. Before his death he may have built the present No. 127, because his executors in 1819 sold a "messuage" and lot here. The dwelling now No. 125—the only four-story house on the alley—was not erected until after 1836.

It is obvious that these little houses were not the dwellings of merchant princes or members of the so-called first rank of society, but were occupied by artisans and tradesmen. Many of them stayed here only a year or two, although others lived out their lives on the alley. Only a handful were more than lightly touched by the decisive events of their particular generation; for many, so fleeting was their stay that few recorded evidences of their lives here have survived. Yet the houses themselves have survived, practically unchanged, while the city around them has altered to such an extent that only a vestige of its original character remains, and the alley is a present witness of the past.

Present Appearance. To preserve the alley, the Elfreth's Alley Association was established in 1934 as a nonprofit organization, its membership open to all. The association has acquired title to the two easternmost houses on Bladen's Court: Nos. 1 and 2, better known as the Spinning-Wheel House, and leased for $1 a year each No. 114, where Daniel Trotter lived for 30 years, and No. 124, occupied by the chairmakers Gilbert Gaw and John B. Ackley in the 1790's. The rental income derived from these four properties is used for their maintenance and for the upkeep of the association garden in the rear of Bladen's Court.

Elfreth's Alley Day is held annually on the first Saturday in June. From noon until 5 o'clock various alley residents open their homes to the public, and hostesses garbed in colonial costumes serve lunch and welcome visitors. The income derived from this annual fete day is currently used for restoring No. 126, owned by the Philadelphia Society for the Preservation of Landmarks. At this writing, the exterior of the building has been restored and restoration of the front room on the first floor is partially completed. When finished, the first floor of the restored building will be used as a permanent museum and gift shop and the second floor as a permanent headquarters for the association. On the third floor a small apartment will be occupied by a permanent caretaker, thus permitting the building to be open to visitors all year.

Late in 1957 the association, believing that tradition and legend should be bolstered by fact, agreed to engage a researcher to investigate the history of the alley and its colonial residents. Title searches were made to establish the physical development of the alley and definitive historical and genealogical research begun to determine the background, relationships, and activities of the people who lived on and were associated with Elfreth's Alley.[82]

4. Charleston, South Carolina

Location. Two "old and historic areas," one bounded approximately by Broad, East Bay, East Battery, South Battery, Logan, or Lenwood Streets, and the other by Cumberland, State, Chalmers, and Meeting Streets.

Ownership and Administration. Various ownerships, mostly private.

Significance. When the Oyster Point Peninsula became the seat of government for the Carolina Colony in 1680, its strategic location at the junction of the Ashley and Cooper Rivers promised a bright future for the infant city. The promise was fully borne out in the following century, when Charleston became the largest and wealthiest metropolis south of Philadelphia. This wealth—based on rice, indigo, and furs—together with a cosmopolitan population made Charleston one of the most sophisticated colonial cities.

Nowhere were wealth and culture more graphically exemplified than in architecture. During the 18th century, and even up until the catastrophe of the 1860's, Charlestonians had the means to build on as grand a scale as they liked. At the same time, the peculiar climatic conditions—heat, humidity, and the prevailing sea breezes—encouraged an architectural adaptation that continued to influence construction until comparatively recent times. Peculiarly Charlestonian is the "single house" design, one room in width, with a long side piazza to catch the breeze.

Present Appearance. Despite wars, a series of costly fires, and a major earthquake, much of historic Charleston has survived. Within the 2 "old and historic areas" are about 550 buildings dating from the 18th and the first half of the 19th centuries. St. Michael's Episcopal Church and the Miles Brewton and Robert Brewton Houses are treated elsewhere in this volume, as well as the Col. John Stuart House, the Colonial Powder Magazine, the Daniel Elliott Huger House, the Exchange (Customhouse), the French Protestant Huguenot Church, and the Jacob Motte and William Rhett Houses. The following are also worthy of special notice:

(1) City Hall, 80 Broad Street. Constructed in 1800–1801 as a branch of the Bank of the United States, with design attributed to Gabriel Manigault.

(2) William Blacklock House, 18 Bull Street. Built about 1800 of the noted "Carolina gray" brick. Privately owned.

(3) First Baptist Church, 61 Church Street. Robert Mills designed this impressive Greek Revival building, which was dedicated in 1822.

(4) Heyward House, 87 Church Street. Built about 1770, it was owned by Thomas Heyward, Jr., a signer of the Declaration of Independence. Washington visited there for a time in 1791. Owned by the Charleston Museum.

(5) St. Philip's Episcopal Church, 146 Church Street. Third church used by the congregation, it was begun in 1835 and the steeple, designed by E. B. White, was added in 1848–50.

(6) Old Marine Hospital, 20 Franklin Street. Designed by Robert Mills, it was constructed in 1833. Now headquarters of the Charleston Housing Authority.

(7) College of Charleston, 66 George Street. The central building, designed by William Strickland, was built in 1828–29, with wings and portico by E. B. White in 1850. The library, by George W. Walker, was built in 1854, and the porter's lodge about 1850, by E. B. White.

(8) Simmons-Edwards House, 14 Legare Street. Built about 1800 by Francis Simmons, it is noted for its iron fence and gates. Privately owned.

(9) Nathaniel Russell House, 51 Meeting Street. Built about 1808, it is a notable example of Adam architecture, possibly designed by Russell Warren. Headquarters of the Historic Charleston Foundation.

(10) Branford-Horry House, 59 Meeting Street. Double house built by William Branford about 1751, with portico added by Elias Horry in the 1830's. Privately owned.

(11) South Carolina Society Hall, 72 Meeting Street. Home of a society dating from the colonial period, the building was designed in 1800 by Gabriel Manigault and the portico added in 1825, after a design by Frederick Wesner.

(12) Court House, 77 Meeting Street. Constructed in 1752 as the statehouse, it was rebuilt within the original walls after a fire in 1788 and

has been used as the seat of county government since 1790.

(13) Fireproof Building, 100 Meeting Street. Designed by Robert Mills, it was constructed in 1822–27 and now houses the South Carolina Historical Society.

(14) Joseph Manigault House, 350 Meeting Street. A simplified Adam-style mansion, it was the earliest work of Gabriel Manigault, dating from about 1790. Owned by the Charleston Museum.

(15) Gen. William Washington House, 8 South Battery. Built by Thomas Savage about 1768, it was acquired by Washington in 1785. Privately owned.

(16) William Gibbes House, 64 South Battery. A three-story clapboard house built before 1789 and redecorated in the Adam style in 1794. Privately owned.[83]

5. Williamsburg, Virginia

Location. The restored area, about 130 acres in the center of Williamsburg, is bounded roughly by Francis, Waller, Nicholson, North England, Lafayette, and Nassau Streets.

Ownership and Administration. Property within the restored area, with a few exceptions, is owned by Colonial Williamsburg, Inc.

Significance. Williamsburg was the colonial capital of Virginia, from 1699 to 1780, and was highly important as a political and cultural center. More than 80 surviving colonial buildings would qualify Williamsburg as an important historic community under any conditions, but the remarkable restoration project that has been carried out under the corporation founded and financed by the late John D. Rockefeller, Jr., has made it unique. Since its inception in 1926 the project has involved restoration of the original structures, and reconstruction on the original sites of more than 400 buildings. More than 90 gardens in Williamsburg have been restored in keeping with 18th-century designs, using only plants and flowers known to have been grown here before 1800. Painstaking research has preceded every step of the project, and the excellent interpretive program gives Colonial Williamsburg great value as a living exhibit of the 18th-century way of life. Skilled craftsmen in 18th-century attire are constantly occupied in their respective shops, restored and equipped with authentic tools, producing items of silverware, ironwork, woven fabrics, and other articles of the kind made here in the 18th century.

Life at Williamsburg in the 1700's encompassed not only the common folk but also many of the extraordinary figures of the period. Patrick Henry, Thomas Jefferson, George Washington, George Mason, George Wythe, Edmund Randolph, and other leading patriots served as bur-

The Public Magazine, one of the remaining original structures, stands near the center of Williamsburg, the restored colonial capital of Virginia.

gesses here, debated and resolved the important issues that resulted in many of our democratic concepts, and played important roles in the movement for independence. Through association with places frequented by patriot leaders, as well as by the creation of its unique atmosphere, Colonial Williamsburg fulfills its purpose, that "the future may learn from the past."

Within the town of Williamsburg, but outside the boundaries of the Rockefeller-sponsored project, is the College of William and Mary, the second-oldest institution of higher education in the United States, birthplace of the famous honor society, Phi Beta Kappa. The college contributes to the atmosphere at Williamsburg in several important ways, not only because of its important library and learned faculty, and the efforts of its departments of drama, fine arts, and history in 18th-century studies, but also because of the Wren Building (described separately in this study, pp. 175–176), Brafferton Hall (built in 1723 to house the first permanent Indian school in the Colonies), and the president's house, which was built in 1732 and has been used since then by the chief executives of the college.

The historical character of the area is enriched still further by the fact that Williamsburg is so close to Jamestown, the first permanent English settlement, founded in 1607 and capital of Virginia until 1699. On the other side of Williamsburg and almost as close is Yorktown, scene of the surrender of Lord Cornwallis which assured American independence in the Revolutionary War. (See p. 73.) These historic areas are connected by the Colonial Parkway, which passes through Williamsburg. Colonial Parkway, Yorktown Battlefield, and part of Jamestown Island, are administered together as Colonial National Historical Park, a unit of the National Park System.

Present Appearance. Within the boundaries of Colonial Williamsburg are more than 500 original (restored) and reconstructed buildings. The following are the most important of the original structures:

(1) Public Magazine, Market Square. Built in 1715–16 to hold the public arms and ammunition, its most dramatic moment came on the night of April 20–21, 1775, when the colonial Governor, Lord Dunmore, removed the powder to prevent it from falling into the hands of the colonial militia. Owned by the Association for the Preservation of Virginia Antiquities.

(2) Ludwell-Paradise House, Duke of Gloucester Street. A large brick house built before 1717 by Philip Ludwell II and later occupied by his daughter Lucy, widow of John Paradise.

(3) Old Court House, Duke of Gloucester Street. Built in 1770, it now houses an interesting archeological exhibit.

(4) Bruton Parish Church, Duke of Gloucester Street. Built in 1710–15, with the tower added in 1769, the church was restored in the first decade of the 20th century by the Reverend W. A. R. Goodwin, who later inspired John D. Rockefeller, Jr., to undertake the Williamsburg restoration. Here, as young men, came Presidents Washington, Jefferson, Monroe, and Tyler, as well as many other distinguished Virginia leaders and statesmen.

(5) George Wythe House, Palace Green. Built about 1750 by the amateur architect, Richard Taliaferro, it was left to his son-in-law, George Wythe, 20 years later. One of the leading Virginians of his generation, Wythe taught law to Jefferson, John Marshall, James Monroe, and Henry Clay.

The most notable reconstructed buildings are:

(1) The Capitol, end of Duke of Gloucester Street. Original constructed 1701–5. Reconstructed to the precise specifications of the original, using clay obtained from vacant lots within town for the bricks, handmade and kilned locally.

Once the seat of Government of a vast and powerful colony that stretched to the Mississippi River, the colonial Capitol Building at Williamsburg has been carefully reconstructed to its appearance of the early 1700's. Here met not only the high court and Governor's Council, but also the House of Burgesses, America's first representative legislative assembly. Courtesy, Colonial Williamsburg.

(2) The Governor's Palace, Palace Green. Original constructed 1706–20. The handsome, Georgian structure is flanked by beautifully paneled brick offices and guardrooms. On the grounds are a smoke-house, laundry, wellhead, salthouse, formal gardens, and an orchard, including an artificial canal and a holly maze.

(3) Raleigh Tavern, Duke of Gloucester Street. Original built before 1742. This long, 1½-story frame hostelry ranked next only to the Capitol as a scene of Revolutionary activities.[84]

E. Other Sites Considered

In the process of selecting the comparatively few historic sites of such outstanding character as to merit recognition as Registered National Historic Landmarks, a great many sites were studied, evaluated, and found not to meet the criteria. The sites described below are deemed to possess noteworthy historical values but not to possess "exceptional value" within the meaning of the criteria, within the segment of history discussed here. Such sites may satisfy the criteria as applied to other phases of history, however.

CONNECTICUT

1. Jonathan Trumbull War Office

Location: West Town Street off Conn. 89, Lebanon, New London County.

Tradition identifies Trumbull's "War Office," a simple frame building, as the headquarters from which Gov. Jonathan Trumbull rendered valuable service to the patriot cause by forwarding much-needed supplies to the Continental Army. The structure dates probably from about 1732 and was originally a store—its proprietor Joseph Trumbull, father of Jonathan. The "War Office" formerly stood next to the Trumbull home, but both buildings have been moved and it now rests diagonally across Lebanon Commons from the home. The building was restored in 1891 when it was acquired by the Connecticut Society of the Sons of the American Revolution.

2. Nathan Hale Birthplace

Location: South Street, Coventry, Tolland County.

This house was built in 1776 by the father of Nathan Hale, the "Martyr Spy of the American Revolution." Hale never saw the completed house because he was executed on September 22, 1776, more than a month before the family moved into the structure. The older dwelling, in which Hale was born on June 6, 1755, was pulled down after the building of the new house. According to local tradition, a part of the ell of the present house is a remnant of the original birthplace structure. The house has notable woodwork detail and has been furnished handsomely by the Connecticut Antiquarian and Landmark Society.

3. Newgate Prison and Granby Copper Mines

Location: East Granby, Hartford County.

The mines on Copper Hill at East Granby, often called the Simsbury mines, were reportedly the first copper mines developed in British America. The first company to work the mines was established in 1707. "Granby coppers" were coins in common use for many years after 1737. In 1773 the mine caverns were made the permanent prison for the colony, and Tory prisoners were confined there during the Revolution. In 1790 Newgate became the State prison and served this purpose until 1827. The prison structures, dating mostly from the early 19th century, are largely in ruins although the copper caverns still survive.

DELAWARE

4. Cooch's Bridge

Location: Christiana Creek, 2 miles southeast of Newark and 1 mile east of Del. 896, New Castle County.

About 700 American troops under Gen. William Maxwell ambushed a part of the British Army advancing against Philadelphia and a sharp little battle occurred here on September 3, 1777. The redcoats gradually forced the Continentals back and, when their units became disorganized,

Maxwell's men fled to rejoin the main part of their army.   This was the only Revolutionary War action in Delaware.   Although the Americans lost the skirmish, the British victory had little effect on the campaign against Philadelphia.   Cooch House stands near the bridge and was occupied for a short time by the British general, Cornwallis.   It was built in 1760 and is privately owned.   Maxwell's skirmish is commemorated by a monument at the entrance to the Cooch House grounds.

5. New Castle

> *Location: On the Delaware River 6 miles south of Wilmington, New Castle County.*

New Castle was founded in 1651 by Peter Stuyvesant as the seat of New Netherland government on the South (Delaware) River, the counterpart of New Amsterdam on the Hudson.   It received its present name when seized by the British in 1664, after being called Fort Casimir and New Amstel by the Dutch, and Trinity by the Swedes who held it briefly. William Penn received the colony in 1682, and it was the place where he first set foot in America.   It was the colonial capital and very briefly the State capital of Delaware.

Several important early structures are preserved in New Castle, including the brick State (Court) House, the center portion of which was built early in the 18th century, with subsequent additions over a period of 200 years; the Amstel House, built before 1730, home of the first Governor of Delaware, Nicholas Van Dyke; Immanuel Episcopal Church, built between 1703 and 1710; the Governor Gunning-Bedford House of about 1730; and the Presbyterian Church, built in 1707. New Castle's historic buildings collectively represent a broad span of occupation and will be examined in more detail as a historic district in the study dealing with architecture.

GEORGIA

6. Fort King George and Fort Darien

> *Location: On the Altamaha River 1 mile east of Darien, McIntosh County.*

Fort King George was established in 1721 as one of a chain of frontier forts intended to block the eastward expansion of France and Spain in North America. It consisted of a rude wooden stockade on a low bluff overlooking the Altamaha River. It was burned in 1725, rebuilt in 1726, and abandoned in 1727. Nine years later, however, a colony of Scottish Highlanders built a stockade nearby, called Fort Darien, which was an important defensive bastion in the early years of Georgia. A contingent from Darien was present in 1742 at the Battle of Bloody Marsh, which turned back the last full-scale Spanish attempt to destroy the colony.

Fort King George State Park (12½ acres), administered by the Georgia Historical Commission, includes the sites of both forts. No trace of Fort Darien remains above ground, but the site of Fort King George is marked by the remains of a moat and an earthwork embankment, possibly altered somewhat by 19th-century lumbering operations on the bluff. Archeological excavations have disclosed a military cemetery with about 100 burials, and the site of an earlier Spanish occupation.

7. Kettle Creek Battlefield

Location: 8 miles southwest of Washington, north of Ga. 44, Wilkes County.

Georgia and South Carolina militia under Elijah Clarke, John Dooly, and Andrew Pickens fell upon a Tory force under Col. John Boyd, en route to Augusta. Pickens, the senior officer, concentrated his troops and attacked at breakfast time on February 14, 1779. The surprised Tories recovered and made a momentary advance, but were then driven across Kettle Creek and dispersed after Boyd fell with a mortal wound.

Augusta, just occupied by the British, was evacuated by them a few days after Kettle Creek, but other British forces shortly won a new victory that led to the reoccupation of Augusta. Kettle Creek thus had no decisive effect on the course of the war, but it boosted patriot moral and checked sharply the cause of loyalism in Georgia and South Carolina. The Daughters of the American Revolution own 12 acres of the battlefield. A memorial shaft erected by the Federal Government in 1930 is located on the plot, which otherwise appears much as it did at the time of the battle.

8. New Ebenezer

> *Location: 13 miles north of Rincon, Effingham County, on the*
> *Savannah River near Ga. 275.*

Two hundred Salzburg Lutherans, who came to America to escape religious persecution, settled in 1736 at New Ebenezer after spending 2 years in a temporary colony 6 miles to the west. They built the first church in Georgia, in 1741—replaced in 1769 by the present brick structure. Their gristmill and sawmill were the first in Georgia; their ricemill probably the first in the present United States. Silk culture was their most successful industry, however, and was practiced here long after it was abandoned elsewhere in Georgia. The town was depopulated in 1779 when British troops occupied the area, terrorizing the inhabitants and using the church for a hospital and stable. New Ebenezer never regained its prominence and within half a century had become almost a ghost town.

The site of New Ebenezer today is largely second-growth pine and other small timber, with a few open patches. The only original building still standing is Jerusalem Church (1769), recently renovated. Nearby is a burial ground dating from the late 18th century. Connected to the church by a breezeway is a modern Salzburger Memorial Parish House, built in 1957–58 to house a small museum dealing with the history of the Salzburgers in America.

INDIANA

9. Fort Sackville (George Rogers Clark State Memorial)

> *Location: U.S. 50 near Lincoln Memorial Bridge (Wabash River),*
> *in Vincennes.*

The George Rogers Clark Memorial, a Doric temple surrounded by landscaped grounds, stands on the site of Fort Sackville, the British post captured by Clark in his daring raid from Kaskaskia in February 1779. Clark's operations against the British in the Old Northwest played an important role in opening the territory to American occupation, and the seizure of Sackville was a dramatic and significant episode in the campaign.   Seven large murals depict Clark's life and the events that helped win the Old Northwest for the United States.   A bronze statue of Clark stands in the center of the structure.

KENTUCKY

10. Blue Licks Battlefield

Location: U.S. 68 at crossing of Licking River, near Blue Lick Springs, Nicholas County.

A State park of 100 acres commemorates the battle of August 19, 1782, in which Indians ambushed and badly defeated a pursuing force of Kentuckians.   Often called the "last battle of the Revolution," it was the worst defeat suffered by an American force in Kentucky during the war.   Daniel Boone was one of the Kentucky commanders; his son Israel was slain in the fighting.   Some American dead are buried on the field, and a museum contains a small relief model of the field with points of interest identified.   Most of the battlefield is included in the park area.

11. Fort Boonesborough

Location: 9 miles north of Richmond on U.S. 227, Madison County

Daniel Boone began to construct the stockade, Fort Boonesborough, in April 1775, with his 30 axmen who had just opened the Wilderness Road through Cumberland Gap.   Boonesborough was the scene of the Transylvania Convention in May 1775, the first legislative assembly west of the Appalachians.   The stockade was not completed until Indian hostilities beginning in July 1776 made it necessary.   Among several attacks during the War for Independence, the most notable was a 2-week siege in September 1778.   Boonesborough was the busiest town in the western country after settlement reopened following George Rogers Clark's brilliant campaign of 1778–79.   A rapid decline followed, however, and it soon became a ghost town.

A Daughters of the American Revolution marker is located on the original site of the fort, set off by a stone wall, but no trace remains of the stockade itself.   The Transylvanians of Henderson, Ky., have placed another marker nearby.   The cabins of a resort development cover part of the site.   During winter, the resort is closed and visitor access to the site is prevented.

12. Fort Harrod

> *Location: Pioneer Memorial State Park, Lexington and Warwick Streets, Harrodsburg, Mercer County.*

Followers of James Harrod claimed the distinction of establishing the first permanent settlement in Kentucky, at Harrodsburg in 1775, after a false start in 1774.   Fort Harrod was built in 1777 and was one of three Kentucky stations that held out successfully against Indian attacks during the critical early years of the War for Independence.   George Rogers Clark was at Fort Harrod when he planned his remarkable campaign of 1778–79.

The fort disappeared quickly after its period of usefulness ended, to be marked only by a neglected burial ground.   The citizens of Kentucky undertook in the 1920's to develop the area surrounding the fort site as Pioneer Memorial State Park, and it was dedicated as such in 1934. The fort has been reconstructed at the park, on a slightly reduced scale, consisting of blockhouses and cabins connected by a 12-foot-high log palisade.   The original spring, still flowing, stands within the enclosure. The buildings are furnished with pioneer relics.

13. Locust Grove

> *Location: Blankenbaker Lane, Louisville.*

This house was the home of George Rogers Clark during the last 9 years of his life.   It was built by his brother-in-law, Maj. William Croghan, in 1802–5.   After Clark's death in 1818 he was buried on the property and his body remained there until 1869 when it was moved to Cave Hill Cemetery in Louisville.   A red brick house of architectural distinction, especially noted for its interior paneling, Locust Grove will be treated at greater length in the study dealing with architecture.

MAINE

14. Arnold Trail

Location: Between Augusta and the Canadian border; see below.

Benedict Arnold's expedition in the autumn of 1775 failed in its objective of seizing Quebec, but it had an important result in forcing the division of Lord Howe's army to provide reinforcements for Quebec. Thus Howe could not subjugate the Middle States in 1776, and the British suffered a major setback trying to reunite Howe's army in 1777. Arnold left Fort Western (now Augusta) on September 24, 1775, moved up the Kennebec River about 70 miles, portaged to the Dead River, followed up it to Chain of Ponds near the present Canadian border, and arrived at Quebec early in November with 600 of the 1,100 men with whom he had started. The route can be determined along rivers with considerable accuracy. The sites of numerous portages and campgrounds need fuller study, however, which has been undertaken by the Maine Division of State Parks. The results may provide justification for classifying the Arnold Trail as eligible for the Registry of National Historic Landmarks.

15. Fort George

Location: Heights above Castine, Hancock County.

The Fort George Memorial contains well-preserved earthworks of a fort constructed by the British in 1779 and reoccupied by them during the War of 1812. The site of Castine was an object of imperial rivalry for a century and a half, secured by the British under the treaty ending the Seven Years' War in 1763. The British built strong fortifications in 1779 and in the same year turned back an American attack. The earthwork remains, covering about 3 acres, are now in a State memorial.

16. Fort Halifax

Location: U.S. 201 at Winslow, Kennebec County.

Fort Halifax was established in 1754 as an outpost against Indian attack on a site selected by Gov. William Shirley. The blockhouse, the only such structure remaining in Maine from the Revolutionary period, stands on the north bank of the Sebasticook River and was on the route of Benedict Arnold's march to Quebec in the autumn of 1775. The site and blockhouse constitute a major feature of the Arnold Trail, which extends from Augusta to the Canadian border at Coburn Gore. (See pp. 35–36, 200.) The blockhouse will be considered at greater length in the architectural study.

17. Fort Western

Location: Bowman Street near east end of Kennebec Bridge, Augusta.

Replicas of the original blockhouses and palisades of Fort Western stand on the site of New Plymouth Trading Post (1626), along with the surviving garrison house. Fort Western was established in 1754 for protection against Indians, and consisted of a large garrison house for both officers and men, and two small blockhouses, all surrounded by a timber stockade. The chief historical significance of the post was as the starting point for Benedict Arnold's expedition against Quebec in 1775. (See above.)

MARYLAND

18. Brice House

Location: Prince George and East Streets, Annapolis.

This outstanding Georgian house was begun in 1766 and has been spared major alteration through almost 200 years. The house was constructed entirely of oversize brick on a fieldstone foundation, 186 feet long, and has been attributed by some authorities to William Buckland. The 35 rooms have individual distinguishing characteristics and are notable in combination. The 90-foot chimneys rise above the steep-pitched roof and dominate the neighborhood. Brice House was acquired by a private owner in 1953 and has been restored with great fidelity and care. It will be considered further in the study of architecture.

19. Carroll-Caton House

Location: Lombard and Front Streets, Baltimore.

Charles Carroll of Carrollton shared this home, his daughter's, in his later life. The Revolutionary patriot, signer of the Declaration of Independence, and longtime leader in Maryland affairs was born in Annapolis in 1737 and spent some years abroad studying law. He was an ardent supporter of the independence cause and served as Senator from Maryland in the First Congress under the Constitution. Active also in business affairs, he was considered one of the Nation's wealthiest men when he died in this home in 1832. The house was erected in 1823, a red brick, $3\frac{1}{2}$-story mansion with exceptional interior and exterior trim, on land given Mary and her husband, Richard, by Carroll. It is now a city recreation center.

20. Chase-Lloyd House

Location: 22 Maryland Avenue, Annapolis.

This dwelling, attributed to William Buckland, was begun by Samuel Chase in 1769 and was completed probably about 1774, having been purchased in the meantime by Edward Lloyd IV. No other three-story house was built in Annapolis prior to the War for Independence. The great central hall is particularly distinguished, along with the wealth of ornamental plaster and woodwork in the interior. The last private owner of the house bequeathed it to the Protestant Episcopal Church in 1897 as a home for destitute elderly women, and the two upper floors are still used for this purpose. The first floor is open to the public.

21. Fort Frederick

Location: 5 miles south of town of Clear Spring, Washington County, off U.S. 40.

The Maryland Assembly provided for the construction of this fort in the spring of 1756 because the frontier was dangerously threatened by French and Indian attack following Gen. Edward Braddock's disastrous defeat near present Pittsburgh in 1755. Fort Frederick was a stone quadrangle with corner bastions strengthened by earthen embankments, placed on a plateau near the north bank of the Potomac River. It was designed for a garrison of 200 but could hold 400 if needed.

Fort Frederick was garrisoned until 1763 and may have discouraged Indian attacks, but it played only a minor role in the French and Indian War. Prisoners were confined here during the War for Independence and a garrison was placed here during the Civil War. After a period in private ownership, the State of Maryland acquired it. The walls and other features were reconstructed or restored, based on archeological investigations begun in 1934. The property is now included in Fort Frederick State Park, which includes a museum and recreational facilities.

MASSACHUSETTS

22. The Adams Birthplaces

Locations: 133 and 141 Franklin Street, Quincy.

John Adams lived in the house of his birth (133 Franklin Street) until he was 29 in 1764. His son, John Quincy, was born in the second house in 1767, which was both home and law office to the father although his practice and public career began to keep him more and more in Boston. He acquired title to the first house in 1774, but both houses were occupied by tenants after 1783 while the family was in Europe. John Quincy purchased both houses from his father in 1803 and lived in the second from 1805 to 1807. Both houses were deeded by the Adams heirs to the City of Quincy in 1940, and have been declared eligible for the Registry of National Historic Landmarks in the study of "Political and Military Affairs, 1783–1830." They are of simple saltbox design, in good condition although both have undergone some alteration. The earliest part of the second house probably dates from about 1663, while the John Adams birthplace is believed to have been built about 1681.

23. Hancock-Clarke House

Location: 35 Hancock Street, Lexington.

John Hancock and Sam Adams were staying in this house with the Reverend Jonas Clarke on the eventful night of April 18, 1775. Hancock and Adams were hustled away before the exchange of shots on Lexington Green, a quarter of a mile away, to avoid capture by the approaching British force. The house was built by Hancock's grandfather, and he had spent seven of his boyhood years there. The earlier part of the house was constructed in 1698, the later in 1734. The Lexington Historical Society moved the building in 1896 to a new site across the road from its original location. A brick addition was made in the rear 6 years later to afford protection for valuable possessions of the society.

24. Jason Russell House

Location: 7 Jason Street, Arlington.

Jason Russell, 58 years old and lame, conducted his family to safety on the opening day of the War for Independence, April 19, 1775, and then returned to defend his home. During the British withdrawal from Lexington and Concord toward Boston, a group of minutemen was surprised by a flanking party and took refuge in Russell's house. Russell himself was killed in the doorway by the pursuing British, and 11 of the patriots were killed also. Eight who took refuge in the cellar held out successfully. Bullet holes in the house are evidence of the fighting. A number of objects relating to the first day of the Revolution are displayed. The gray clapboard house, erected about 1680, was occupied until 1890 by Russell descendents. After being turned around and moved back from the road, the house was rescued in 1923 by the Arlington Historical Society and carefully restored.

25. Munroe Tavern

Location: 1332 Massachusetts Avenue, Lexington.

General Earl Percy, commander of the British relief party from Boston which aided the retreating British column being harrassed by minutemen on the Lexington-Concord Road on April 19, 1775, established a temporary headquarters at the Munroe Tavern. The building was also an aid station for British wounded, being located a mile southeast of Lexington Green. The older part of the tavern was built in 1695 and an ell, added sometime after 1770, existed at the time of the Revolution but was later removed. The building is owned and exhibited by the Lexington Historical Society. It is a clapboard structure, surrounded by large trees, containing objects dating from the Revolutionary period.

26. Vassall-Craigie-Longfellow House

Location: 105 Brattle Street, Cambridge.

This colonial mansion was built in 1759 by Col. John Vassall, Jr., and served as George Washington's headquarters for 9 months beginning in July 1775. More significantly, it was the home of Henry Wadsworth Longfellow from 1837 until his death in 1882. The furnishings reflect the period of the poet's residence. The property is owned by the Longfellow House Trust, which was formed in 1913 by members of the Dana and Longfellow families to preserve the structure as an outstanding historical monument and architectural example. It has been declared eligible for Registered National Historic Landmark status under the study of "Literature, Drama, and Music."

NEW HAMPSHIRE

27. General John Stark House

Location: 1070 Canal Street, Manchester.

From 1758 to 1765 this small frame dwelling was the home of the Revolutionary War officer, Gen. John Stark, who won his greatest fame in the Battle of Bennington, August 16, 1777. (See pp. 124–125.) The home is a good example of the farmhouse of the region and contains period furnishings and museum exhibits. It is owned by the Molly Stark Chapter of the Daughters of the American Revolution.

28. General John Sullivan House

Location: Newmarket Road, Durham.

This substantial country house, built in 1716, was John Sullivan's home for more than 10 years before the outbreak of the War for Independence.

Sullivan was a member of the Second Continental Congress, which appointed him brigadier general in June 1775, and he served with distinction under Washington and in independent command. He retired from the Army in 1779, health broken after a punitive campaign against the Iroquois and Tories of Western Pennsylvania and New York, but later served New Hampshire in important posts, including that of Governor from 1786 to 1790. A monument near the house commemorates Sullivan's services to State and Nation. The home is privately owned.

29. John Paul Jones House

Location: Middle and State Streets, Portsmouth.

John Paul Jones lived in this building, then a boardinghouse, from October 4 to November 7, 1782. He was in Portsmouth to supervise the outfitting of the *America,* a ship of the line being constructed for the Continental Navy. It was awarded to France before completion, however, to replace a French ship wrecked off Boston through fault of a local pilot. The house was built in 1758 and became the property of the Portsmouth Historical Society in 1920, which maintains in it an extensive collection of items relating to Portsmouth history.

30. Moffatt-Ladd House

Location: 154 Market Street, Portsmouth.

John Moffatt built this three-story house for his only son, Samuel, in 1763, and then "rescued" the house and lived in it to the age of 94 after creditors forced Samuel to flee from Portsmouth. The structure is square, with pedimented windows and quoins at the corners that lend interest to the somewhat plain facade. The most distinctive features of the house are its large paneled entrance hall and handsome staircase, although the interior is characterized throughout by rich ornamentation. It is leased from the Ladd family, collateral descendents of the builder, and administered by the National Society of the Colonial Dames of America in the State of New Hampshire. It is open to the public. Because its principal significance rests on its architecture, the Moffatt-Ladd House will be evaluated further in the architectural study.

31. Wentworth-Coolidge Mansion (Gov. Benning Wentworth House)

Location: Off U.S. 1A on Little Harbor, 2 miles south of Portsmouth.

The earliest part of this rambling framehouse dates from about 1695. Later additions gave it a total of 40 rooms, but several rooms have been removed and placed elsewhere. The house has considerable architectural interest, reflecting the several periods of its construction. Its historical interest is as the home and headquarters of Benning Wentworth, Royal Governor, 1740–67, an able defender of royal interests. He died here in 1770. The last private owner presented the house to the State of New Hampshire in 1954, and it is maintained for public benefit.

32. Wentworth-Gardner House

Location: Gardner and Mechanic Streets, Portsmouth.

Madame Mark Hunking Wentworth built this exceptional Georgian house in 1760 as a present to her son, Thomas, a younger brother of John Wentworth, last Royal Governor of New Hampshire. The house is two stories high, with hipped roof and rusticated wood facade. The front door has an unusual broken-scroll pediment, and the windows in the lower floor are pedimented. The interior is distinguished by a wealth of paneling and carved woodwork. Many of the fireplaces retain their original Dutch tiles. The house is the property of the Wentworth-Gardner & Tobias Lear Houses Association, and is open to the public. It will receive further treatment in the study of architecture.

NEW JERSEY

33. Boxwood Hall (Boudinot House)

Location: 1073 East Jersey Street, Elizabeth.

Elias Boudinot occupied Boxwood Hall from 1772 to 1795. He was a lawyer, served during the War for Independence as commissary for

American soldiers held by the British, was President of the Continental Congress, a signer of the Treaty of Paris (1783), and later Superintendent of the U.S. Mint in Philadelphia. The house was built about 1750. It had several owners and many alterations after Boudinot moved to Philadelphia. In 1870 the two lateral wings were demolished, the gabled roof removed, two stories superimposed, and a service wing added at the rear. The Boxwood Hall Memorial Association was formed in the late 1930's to save the structure from demolition. It was purchased, turned over to the State, restored through a WPA project, and opened to the public in 1943 as a historic house museum.

34. Fort Mercer

> *Location: 1 mile from town of National Park, on Delaware River at the end of Hessian Avenue, Gloucester County.*

Fort Mercer, at Red Bank, guarded the New Jersey side of a line of underwater obstructions intended to close the Delaware River to British ships bringing supplies to the enemy garrison in Philadelphia. Two thousand Hessians assaulted the fort on October 22, 1777, but the 400 defenders held firm. The attackers lost their commander and 400 men; the besieged fewer than 50. Fort Mifflin, on the Pennsylvania side, was evacuated a few weeks later after a heavy bombardment, however, making Mercer's position untenable. A 20-acre reserved area includes a monument commemorating the action of October 22 and traces of the fort's moat; also the Whitall House, which dates from the same period. The U.S. Government owns the site, which is administered by the Board of Chosen Freeholders. Gloucester County administers the Whitall House except for two rooms in the charge of the Daughters of the American Revolution.

35. Middlebrook Encampment

> *Location: North edge of Bound Brook on Mountain Avenue, Somerset County.*

George Washington's army used the Middlebrook area as a main base and encampment in May–June 1777 and from November 1778 to June 1779. The Continentals covered Philadelphia and balked British operations in New Jersey during the earlier period without risking a major engagement, contributing to General Howe's decision to withdraw from New Jersey. The use of Middlebrook as one of several army camps in winter and spring, 1778–79, is an interesting episode of the war. The Washington Camp Ground Association owns a part of the surviving camp area, a 23-acre tract at the north edge of town, at the foot of First Watchung Mountain. The tract includes a small summer cabin used by Girl Scouts, a speaker's stand, and a memorial flagpole.

36. The Old Barracks

Location: South Willow Street opposite West Front Street, Trenton.

Colonial authorities began the construction of Trenton Barracks in 1758 because of public resentment over the quartering of soldiers in private homes during the French and Indian War. The structure originally had a main section 130 feet long, and two wings, each 58 feet long. Officers' quarters were added later to the north wing. British, Hessian, and Continental soldiers were housed here at various times during the War for Independence—Hessians, for instance, at the time of Washington's surprise attack in December 1776. The building was sold after the war to private owners, and much was demolished later to provide right-of-way for Front Street, but in 1902 the Old Barracks Association was organized to preserve what remained. The property was given to the State in 1917, although the association continued to administer it. The building is maintained with public funds, and various patriotic and historical groups have furnished the rooms partitioned from the original large barracks rooms.

37. "Rockingham" (Berrien House)

Location: Rocky Hill, Somerset County.

General and Mrs. George Washington lived in Berrien House, which is nearly 225 years old now, in 1783 while Continental Congress met at Princeton. Washington wrote his Farewell Address to the Army in a second-floor room. The house changed hands many times after the war until it was purchased and restored by the Washington Headquarters Association of Rocky Hill. Nearby quarrying operations necessitated

removal of the structure to a site about one-quarter mile distant.   In 1935
the property was deeded to the State, and in 1956 the house was moved
again.   At this writing restoration was nearly complete and opening to
the public anticipated soon.

38. Wallace House

Location: 38 Washington Place, Somerville, Somerset County.

General and Mrs. George Washington lived in this house while part of
the Continental Army camped at Middlebrook (see pp. 208–209), about
5 miles to the east.   The owner, William Wallace, had not completed its
construction when the Washingtons moved in.   Sullivan's expedition
against the Iroquois in 1779 was planned here.   The white clapboard
house has had no major alteration over the years.   It was acquired and
furnished by the Revolutionary Memorial Society, and in 1946 was
presented to the State of New Jersey as a historic-house museum.

39. Westminster

Location: 149 Kearny Avenue, Perth Amboy, Middlesex County.

The Proprietory House (Westminster), erected in 1764, was the residence
of the last Royal Governor of New Jersey, Benjamin Franklin's son,
William.   It was also the headquarters of General Howe during the British occupation of Perth Amboy.   Soon after the Revolution the interior
was destroyed by fire, and during most of the 19th century it served under
various ownerships as a resort hotel.   The Presbyterian Board of Relief
for Disabled Ministers and Widows and Orphans of Deceased Ministers
took possession in 1883, naming the structure "Westminster."   Since
1911 it has been a roominghouse and has suffered a number of alterations.
It remains under private ownership.

NEW YORK

40. Conference House (Billopp House)

Location: The foot of Hylan Boulevard, Tottenville, Staten Island.

A British naval officer, Capt. Christopher Billopp, built this two-story, stone house sometime before 1688, and in September 1776 a "peace" conference was held here between Admiral Lord Howe and an American delegation consisting of Benjamin Franklin, John Adams, and Edward Rutledge. Even though it came after the British victory on Long Island, the conference ended without agreement because the patriots insisted on independence and Howe required the withdrawal of the Declaration of Independence. The city of New York acquired the house in 1926 and 3 years later placed it in custody of the Conference House Association under whose auspices it has been restored and furnished in the Revolutionary period.

41. Field of Grounded Arms

> *Location: West bank of Hudson River, Schuylerville, Saratoga County.*

General John Burgoyne's army was stopped by Horatio Gates' American Army at Bemis Heights and retreated northward, to be brought to bay at the settlement of Saratoga, now called Schuylerville. Convinced that his position was hopeless, he surrendered the 6,300 men remaining under his command, who laid down their weapons on the Field of Grounded Arms on October 17, 1777. Most of the original field, 50 to 60 acres on the river plain, has survived as open ground, partly owned privately and the remainder by the Village of Schuylerville for bathing and other recreational purposes.

42. Fort Crown Point (Amherst)

> *Location: N.Y. 8, east of intersection with N.Y. 9N and 22, at west end of Champlain Bridge, Essex County.*

French, British, Americans—all in turn have claimed this strategic point, which juts into Lake Champlain. The French built Fort St. Frederic at Crown Point in 1731 as a base for attacks on the northern British colonies. Gen. Sir Jeffrey Amherst forced them to evacuate the ruined fort in 1759. The new British fort, called Crown Point or Amherst, was located nearby. It was destroyed by fire in 1773 and played a minor role during the War for Independence as an outpost of Fort Ticonderoga, about 12 miles to the south. The stabilized ruins of barracks and earthworks are preserved at Crown Point in an unusual manner. The outlines of the post can be traced easily, and 18th-century colonial warfare is illustrated graphically by the ruins and their setting. Crown Point State Reservation includes the ruins of the French fort, also. Fort St. Frederic has been declared eligible for the Registry of National Historic Landmarks in connection with French exploration and settlement. Fort Crown Point will be evaluated further in the study on architecture, as a superior example of 18th-century military engineering.

43. Fort Johnson

Location: N.Y. 5, in village of Fort Johnson, 3 miles west of Amsterdam, Montgomery County.

Sir William Johnson, Crown Superintendent of Indian Affairs, made Fort Johnson his home and headquarters for more than 10 years, before moving to Johnson Hall. (See pp. 128–130, 213.) It is a two-story square stone mansion with hipped roof, completed in 1749. The interior woodwork is largely original, and furnishings include a number of pieces which belonged to Sir William. His son, John, occupied Fort Johnson when he moved to Johnson Hall, and as a loyalist lost the property during the War for Independence. Fort Johnson is now a museum maintained by the Montgomery Historical Society.

44. Fort Ontario (Fort Oswego)

Location: Oswego, right bank of the Oswego River where it flows into Lake Ontario.

Fort Ontario was a key post in the colonial struggle between England and France, in the American Revolution, and in the War of 1812. It was established in 1755 and deactivated in 1945. Because it threatened the French fur trade, Marquis de Montcalm destroyed the original fort in 1756; it was rebuilt by the British and burned by American troops in 1778; rebuilt again by the British and not surrendered by them until 1796; used as an American supply depot in the War of 1812, to be destroyed by the British in a raid in 1814. The final rebuilding was accomplished between 1839 and 1842, and the buildings remodeled between 1863 and 1872; however, while serving over the years as a military installation, prisoner-of-war camp, and emergency housing unit, many buildings were erected and removed. Fort Ontario is now a State-owned historic site, with a museum on the second floor of the enlisted men's barracks constructed in 1839–42.

Fort Oswego was established in 1726–27 by the British at a site across the Oswego River from the later Fort Ontario, about a quarter mile distant, and was the first direct English encroachment into the lakes region claimed by the French. It was headquarters for English fur agents, competing with the French among the Iroquois. The site is marked by a stone monument surrounded by an iron fence in a commercial and industrial zone.

45. Fort William Henry

> *Location: Lake George Village, U.S. 9 near Lake George Battleground Park.*

Sir William Johnson (see p. 212) established Fort William Henry 2 days after his September 1755 victory on the shore of Lake George over the French and their Indian allies. The site was a valuable military prize, controlling the portage between Lake George and the Hudson River. The French were repulsed easily in March 1757, but succeeded that summer in recapturing the fort after a 6-day assault led by Marquis de Montcalm with nearly 8,000 regular troops, Canadians, and Indians. Montcalm's terms were generous, but his Indian allies could not be controlled. They fell on the occupants of the fort and murdered many. The fort itself was burned and leveled. Recent archeological investigation has uncovered a wealth of 18th-century objects. The New York State Education Department has assisted the Fort William Henry Corp., formed in 1953, in reconstructing the fort. Along with nearby Lake George Battleground, it constitutes an interesting exemplification of 18th-century wilderness warfare.

46. Fraunces Tavern

> *Location: 54 Pearl Street, Manhattan, New York City.*

This is the oldest building in Manhattan, built in 1719 and acquired some years before the War for Independence by William Fraunces, whose tavern became and still is a popular meeting place.   The restaurant on the building's first floor carries on a tradition of 200 years.   It was the scene on December 4, 1783, of Washington's farewell to the officers of the Continental Army.   It was restored in 1907 by the Sons of the American Revolution and serves as their headquarters.   Exhibits, relics, paintings, and furnishings of the period preserve the flavor of Revolutionary times.   It will be considered in more detail in the study of architecture.

47. Herkimer Home

> *Location: South Bank of Mohawk River near Little Falls, on N.Y. 58, Herkimer County.*

This dwelling was the home of Nicholas Herkimer, hero of the Battle of Oriskany.   (See pp. 131–132.)   A comfortable, two-story, brick house, it reflects his solid prosperity as farmer and trader.   Herkimer died 10 days after the battle from the effects of a wound and is buried in a cemetery adjacent to the General Herkimer Monument, on land that was once part of his estate.   The house is owned by the State of New York and administered by the State Education Department.   It contains a number of furnishings that belonged to him.

48. Knox Headquarters

> *Location: 4 miles southeast of Newburgh, on N.Y. 94, Orange County.*

General Henry Knox, distinguished officer and trusted friend of George Washington, made this house his headquarters on several occasions during the War for Independence.   In addition to them, Generals Horatio Gates and Nathanael Greene were seen here.   The earliest part of the building was constructed in 1734 as the hunting lodge of John Ellison; more was added in 1754; and the 2-story-and-attic stone structure was built in 1782 by William Bull.   The house is well furnished with period furniture, and equipped with original woodwork, open fireplaces, and paneling which still serve as models for craftsmen.   The grounds now include only 50 acres, chiefly woodland.   Knox Headquarters is owned by the State of New York and administered by the State Education Department.

49. Newtown Battlefield

> *Location: 6 miles south of Elmira, Chemung County, on N.Y. 17.*

Generals John Sullivan and James Clinton marched through Iroquois country in the summer of 1779, laying waste everything in their path. The only open combat came as the expedition moved along the Chemung River and approached the Indian village of Newtown. Over 1,500 loyalists and Iroquois led by Sir John Johnson and Joseph Brant attempted to ambush the Americans but were routed in a sharp battle on August 29. The defeat at Newtown and the widespread destruction caused by the expedition struck a heavy blow at the Iroquois' waning prestige. The Finger Lakes State Park Commission controls a 300-acre park which includes part of the battle site, on high ground overlooking the Chemung River. Traces are preserved here of the earth fortifications thrown up as the Americans approached. A monument was erected in 1912 to commemorate the battle.

50. New Windsor Cantonment (Temple Hill)

> *Location: Temple Hill Road between Vail's Gate and Newburgh, town of New Windsor, Orange County.*

Six to eight thousand Continental Army veterans encamped here during 1782–83, while negotiations were completed which ended the War for Independence. Temple Hill, with its log "temple," built by the troops for a meeting place, was a central feature, where Washington quelled an attempt by the discontented troops to coerce Congress into settling on the issue of overdue pay. A fieldstone pyramid marks the approximate site of the log structure. The National Temple Association, Inc., owns two tracts totaling 67 acres and has laid plans to reconstruct the temple and other features of 1782–83. A hut, moved to the site some years ago, is identified as an officers' quarters from the period. Washington maintained headquarters in Newburgh at the Hasbrouck House (see pp. 137–138) while his army camped here.

51. Old Fort Niagara

> *Location: N.Y. 18F, mouth of Niagara River, Youngstown, Niagara County.*

This location was strategic because it controlled fur-trade routes from the eastern Great Lakes and afforded an entry to the Northwest frontier. Here are found: a bronze cross honoring Father Pierre Millet and the French garrison who suffered exceedingly here in the winter of 1688; the "stone castle" built by the French in 1726 as a fortified barracks; several other structures dating from the colonial period, and earthworks from the British occupation; a stone platform commemorating the Rush-Bagot Agreement of 1817, which limited armament on the Great Lakes; earthworks and brick casements constructed during the Civil War; and restorations of other Old Fort Niagara buildings, completed in the 1930's, along with interpretive exhibits and dozens of mounted cannon. The Old Fort Niagara Association administers the site under a lease from the Secretary of the Army and under license from the Niagara Frontier State Park Commission. The site has been approved for the Registry of National Historic Landmarks in the study of French exploration and settlement.

52. Schuyler Mansion

Location: Clinton and Catherine Streets, Albany.

Philip Schuyler, later a major general, member of the Second Continental Congress, and U.S. Senator, one of New York's foremost land-owners, built this Georgian mansion in 1762. He was in command of the American Army that fought the delaying action down the Hudson Valley in the summer of 1777, against Burgoyne's invasion. Schuyler's Albany home, once the center of a large estate, was acquired by the State in 1911, restored by 1950, and is administered by the State Education Department. It contains many of Schuyler's personal objects and furnishings. It will be considered in more detail in the study of architecture.

53. Senate House

Location: Clinton Avenue and North Front Street, Kingston, Ulster County.

This stone building dates from 1676 and served as the meeting place for the first session of the New York State Senate, elected under the constitution of April 1777. A British Fleet approached during this session, in September, forcing the delegates to flee to Hurley while the British burned Kingston, leaving only the shell of the Senate House. Rebuilt, it served as a private home until 1888, when the State acquired it as a historic property. It is administered by the State Education Department and furnished with belongings of early settlers of the region. A nearby museum, built in 1927, displays among other items a collection of paintings by the Kingston-born artist, John Vanderlyn.

54. Thomas Paine Cottage

Location: Corner of North and Paine Avenues, New Rochelle.

Thomas Paine, pamphleteer of the War for Independence, lived at several periods in the last years of his stormy life in this two-story frame cottage, built about 1800. He returned to America in 1802 after 15 years in England and revolutionary France. From 1803 to 1806 he lived intermittently at his home in New Rochelle, on the 300-acre farm given him by the State of New York. He moved to New York City in 1806, where he died 3 years later. This New Rochelle house, moved from its original location nearby, serves today as a museum and headquarters of the Huguenot and Historical Association of New Rochelle.

NORTH CAROLINA

55. Alamance Battleground

Location: 8 miles southwest of Burlington on N.C. 62, Alamance County.

The Battle of Alamance took place near the western frontier of North Carolina on May 16, 1771. Gov. William Tryon's militia force defeated overwhelmingly a numerically superior mob of rebellious frontiersmen, climaxing the 7-year socioeconomic-political struggle called the "War of the Regulation." The battle is sometimes viewed as a preliminary engagement of the War for Independence, but it was not that. Instead, it was the most dramatic example of the rising struggle between the frontier West and the conservative East. Conditions common to the American frontier along with local complaints produced the Regulator

Movement and this battle. Alamance Battleground State Historic Site, 40 acres, administered by the State Department of Archives and History, includes the central part of the battlefield. A small visitor center and several field exhibits and markers tell the story of the struggle.

56. Bethabara

Location: Bethabara Road, 2 miles northwest of Winston-Salem, Forsyth County.

Bethabara, or "Oldtown," was the place settled by the Moravian sect that came from Pennsylvania in 1753 to found the Wachovia Colony on land purchased from the proprietor. The town throve at first, but in the latter 1760's Salem, nearby to the southeast, was established as the Moravian "capital" and gradually drew settlers away from Bethabara. Little remains today except the church, built in 1788, and a few houses, of which only two antedate the church. Churchyard markers indicate the sites of the first cabin of Bethabara and the fort (erected 1756). Headstones in the burial ground date from 1754.

57. Brunswick Town

Location: East of N.C. 40, on Cape Fear River just south of Orton Plantation, Brunswick County.

Brunswick was the largest North Carolina port throughout the colonial period. It was important not only commercially but also politically after its establishment in 1726, although Wilmington soon became more powerful politically. Brunswick could claim to be the capital of North Carolina from 1758 to 1770, however, because of the residence here of the Royal Governor. Two important events in the town's history were a 4-day siege by Spanish privateers in 1748 and the "Stamp Act Defiance" in February 1766, a spontaneous uprising in which vessels were released which had violated the Stamp Act and the Governor was placed under virtual house arrest. Brunswick's exposed location led to its abandonment and destruction during the War for Independence. A few families moved back into the area after the war, but it was abandoned completely by 1830.

Until 1958 the site was marked only by the empty walls of St.

Philip's Episcopal Church (built 1740–65), a few exposed foundations covered with underbrush, and the remains of a huge Civil War earthwork, Fort Anderson, overlying a corner of the town. Now established as Brunswick Town State Historic Site on 24 acres of donated land, the area is being excavated, producing many 18th-century artifacts. Trailside exhibits have been set up and the foundations stabilized.

58. Cupola House

Location: 408 South Broad Street, Edenton, Chowan County.

The Cupola House, probably built about 1715, combines features of both colonial and Georgian architectural styles, thus affording an outstanding example of the transition from the one to the other. The second-story overhang (of which no other example survives in the South), beaded clapboards, steeply pitched roof, and great end chimneys are of colonial origin. Georgian features include the octagonal cupola, sliding-sash windows, and notable interior paneling. The house is utilized as the Edenton Public Library.

59. Historic Halifax

Location: Halifax, Halifax County.

The Historical Halifax Restoration Association, Inc., has undertaken the restoration of the historic section of Halifax. The site has been marked of the courthouse in which the "Halifax Resolves" were adopted on April 12, 1776, the first official State action for independence. The Resolves were passed by the Fourth Provincial Congress of North Carolina and sent to Continental Congress where they added impetus to the independence movement. The colonial clerk's office and the gaol, both built in 1758, still survive. Constitutional House, in which the first State constitution was drafted in 1776, has been moved from its original site and restored by the Daughters of the American Revolution.

60. Tryon Palace

Location: Pollack and George Streets, New Bern.

Tryon Palace was one of the finest mansions of its time and place, and has been compared with the Governor's Palace at Williamsburg as a painstaking reconstruction of an important 18th-century building. It was built, 1767–70, to the late Georgian design of John Hawks, an English architect brought to America for this purpose. The two-story central block contained a full basement and attic, and was used for the Governor's residence and assembly meetings; of the two connecting wings, the west was stables and the east the kitchen and Governor's secretary's office. The building passed into colonial control in May 1775, and was the seat of North Carolina's State government until the capital was moved to Raleigh in 1794. Deserted, the palace fell rapidly into ruin. In 1944 Mrs. Maude Moore Latham established a trust fund for its reconstruction, and next year the Tryon Palace Commission was established. The fund has been increased by other gifts including the bequest of Mrs. Latham's entire estate, making possible a comprehensive research project and careful reconstruction of the structure. With buildings furnished and grounds landscaped, Tryon Palace has proved to be the object of great visitor interest.

OHIO

61. Schoenbrunn Village

Location: South edge of New Philadelphia, off U.S. 250 and Ohio 16, Tuscarawas County.

Schoenbrunn Village was founded in 1772 by a group of Moravian missionaries and Indian converts from Pennsylvania, and was the first white settlement in what is now Ohio. The War for Independence spelled the end of the prospering little community of 60 cabins, church, school, and cemetery. The Moravians had of course renounced war and refused to bear arms for either side, and they suffered by raids from both sides. Rev. David Zeisberger, the leader, decided in 1777 to abandon Schoenbrunn and concentrate all the Ohio missions elsewhere. Members of the Moravian Church relocated the forgotten village in the present century by means of a map preserved by the mother church at Bethlehem, Pa. The Ohio State Archaeological and Historical Society acquired the site in 1923 and soon reconstructed a number of buildings on their original sites.

PENNSYLVANIA

62. Fort Augusta

Location: 1 mile north of Sunbury on Pa. 14, Northumberland County.

The log walls of Fort Augusta, constructed in 1756–57 at the confluence of the North and West Branches of the Susquehanna, helped protect the Pennsylvania frontier against French invasion.   During the War for Independence the fort was a base for men and supplies, headquarters of American forces in the upper Susquehanna Valley.   Afterward, its usefulness ended, it fell into ruins, except for the commanding officer's quarters where the former commander, Col. Samuel Hunter, continued to reside after obtaining title to the property.   This structure burned in 1852 and was replaced by the colonel's grandson with the present Hunter Mansion.   In 1920 the Commonwealth of Pennsylvania acquired land, including the well and powder magazine, the only surviving features of the original fort.   Eleven years later the tract was expanded to include the Hunter Mansion, which serves now as a museum.   A carefully researched one-sixth scale model of the fort has been placed in front of the mansion.

63. Fort Mifflin

Location: On Delaware River at foot of Fort Mifflin Road, just east of Philadelphia International Airport, South Philadelphia.

Fort Mifflin preserves much of its character as an example of 18th-century military engineering, despite modifications over the years.   It was begun by the British, just below the mouth of the Schuylkill River, in 1772, to defend river approaches to Philadelphia, and completed by Maj. Gen. Thomas Mifflin after the War for Independence started.   After the British captured Philadelphia in September 1777 their water transportation was blocked by Forts Mifflin and Mercer (see p. 208) and a series of obstructions of the Delaware River.   The forts were attacked in October and November and defended stubbornly.   Mifflin was evacuated and destroyed by the Americans on November 16, Mercer (at Red Bank, N.J.) a few days later. A new Fort Mifflin was started in the 1790's, of stone faced with brick and banked with earth. Further construction and repairs were carried out during the War of 1812, during the 1830's and 1840's, during the Civil War, and during the 1930's. It was used for military storage in World War II. Its transfer to the City of Philadelphia as authorized by Congress in 1956 was pending when this was written.

64. Golden Plough Tavern and Gates House

Location: Market Street and Pershing Avenue, York.

Continental Congress was forced to flee from Philadelphia in September 1777 when the city fell to the British. York, west of the Susquehanna River, became the temporary seat of government, its courthouse the Capitol through the autumn and winter of 1777–78. This building has been lost, but the Golden Plough Tavern and the Gates House are being restored to preserve the story of formative and crucial years of York's past. The former, built probably about 1750, is a Germanic half-timber structure of great architectural interest, possibly the only surviving example of a form of construction once common in this area. The latter is identified as the quarters of Gen. Horatio Gates, who came to York as the victor of Saratoga and President of the Board of War in October 1777. A local organization, Historic York County, is carrying on the restorative work. Both buildings will be considered further in the study of architecture.

RHODE ISLAND

65. General James Mitchell Varnum House

Location: 57 Pierce Street, East Greenwich.

James Mitchell Varnum was a lawyer, Revolutionary general, member of the Continental Congress, director of the Ohio Co., and Federal judge for the Northwest Territory. Colonel of the 1st Rhode Island Infantry in 1775, he served with distinction before Boston and at the Battles of Long Island and White Plains, in command of Forts Mifflin and Mercer (see pp. 208, 221–222), and at Valley Forge. He died in Marietta, Ohio, in

1789. The Varnum House is a handsomely furnished, two-story town-house of the late colonial period. It is owned and administered by the Varnum Continentals.

66. General Nathanael Greene Homestead

Location: 20 Taft Street, Arnold Village, Coventry.

Nathanael Greene built this substantial frame house a few years before the outbreak of the War for Independence, while he was in charge of his family's ironworks in Coventry. He rose rapidly in military rank during the war, proving himself one of Washington's ablest officers and exerting a major influence on the victory in the South after receiving command of that theater in October 1780. The State of Georgia presented him with a plantation for his services, and until his death in 1786 he divided his time between that and the Rhode Island "Homestead." The latter, sometimes called the "Mount Vernon of the North," is a 2½-story structure with gable roof. It is owned by the Nathanael Greene Homestead Association and has been restored and furnished in the period of his residence.

67. Vernon House

Location: Clark and Mary Streets, Newport.

The Vernon House was headquarters for the French general, Count de Rochambeau, while his army was in Newport, July 1780 to June 1781. Washington was a guest here from March 6 to 13 while future operations were planned. The Vernon House was built in 1758, a two-story frame building with hipped roof surrounded by a "captain's walk." It will be given attention in the architectural study.

SOUTH CAROLINA

68. Belleville Plantation and Associated Sites

Location: Along upper Santee River east of the crossing of U.S. 601, Calhoun County.

Colonel William Thomson's Belleville Plantation was occupied by the British in 1780. They built a supply base here and a fortified post over-

689-192 O-64—18

looking the Santee River. Belleville and nearby fortified supply points changed hands several times in the course of fierce partisan warfare in which the South Carolina patriot leaders Thomas Sumter and Francis Marion were prominent. The Battle of Eutaw Springs (see p. 226) brought this seesaw conflict to a climax. Among the historic remains at and near the plantation are earthwork fortifications overlooking the Santee; the Thomson Cemetery, said to contain the remains of troops who died in the area; a camp and hospital site; McCord's Ferry, a strategic crossing of the Camden Road over the river; and Gillon's Retreat, plantation of Alexander Gillon, a commodore of the South Carolina Navy during the War for Independence.

69. Colonel John Stuart House

Location: 106 Tradd Street, Charleston.

John Stuart, recently arrived from Scotland, became Superintendent of Indian Affairs for the Southern District in 1762—the counterpart of Sir William Johnson of the Northern District. He became an influential member of various colonial councils and in 1772, at the height of his career, at a cost of £18,000, he built a fine three-story white frame residence in Charleston. He lived here until the outbreak of the War for Independence when he fled to British Florida where he continued to manage British-Indian relations in the South until his death in 1779. The Stuart House is surmounted by a hip roof with a captain's walk. The house is privately owned and has been remodeled in the original style.

70. Colonel William Rhett House

Location: 54 Hasell Street, Charleston.

William Rhett came to South Carolina in 1698 and soon achieved high rank as a colonial leader. He commanded the flotilla that repulsed a Franco-Spanish attack on Charleston in 1706 and led the expedition that captured Stede Bonnet, a notorious pirate. He acquired a plantation outside the fortified walls of the town and, by 1716, had completed the present house. Wade Hampton, famed Confederate cavalry leader, was born here. The exterior of the house has been altered greatly since it was built. The original entrance was probably on the west. Some-time after Hasell Street was built the south side was made into the entrance, and two-story piazzas were added on east and west. The house has been restored and is privately owned.

71. Colonial Powder Magazine

Location: 21 Cumberland Street, Charleston.

The powder magazine was erected, several years after it was authorized in 1703, near the northwest bastion of the city's fortifications. It held the public powder supply for the rest of the colonial period, and shortly before the fall of Charleston in 1780 the powder was removed and successfully concealed in The Exchange. The Powder Magazine is owned by the Colonial Dames and used as a public museum. The low, single-story structure is of unusually small brick covered with stucco. A massive arch supports the central portion of the heavy tile roof.

72. Daniel Elliott Huger House

Location: 34 Meeting Street, Charleston.

Lord William Campbell, South Carolina's last Royal Governor, lived in this house in 1775. Shortly after the Revolution it came into the posses-sion of the Huger (pronounced "U–Gee") family, members of which still own it. Hugers have been prominent in South Carolina for genera-tions. The Huger House is a good example of the unique Charleston "double house." A flight of stone steps leads from the street to the elevated first floor, through which runs a large center hall, to the back door that opens onto a garden. The three-story piazza on the south side is a recent addition. The Huger House is in excellent condition, a showplace of the historic area of Charleston.

73. The Exchange (Custom House)

Location: East Bay and Broad Streets, Charleston.

The Exchange was built 1767–71, following adoption of the Townshend Acts which were designed to tighten the system for collecting customs duties. Confiscated tea was stored here in 1774, and the Provincial

Congress met here in the same year. The Exchange was used as a military prison when the British captured Charleston during the War for Independence. The Federal Government purchased the property in 1818 for use as a customhouse and post office. It was damaged badly by the Federal bombardment of the city during the Civil War, and in 1913 the Daughters of the American Revolution acquired it for museum purposes. The elaborate building has undergone extensive modification over the years. The classic portico facing the Cooper River has been removed, leaving the secondary facade on Bay Street as the main entrance and the riverfront setting destroyed by land reclamation. The cupola and monumental urns are gone from the attic parapet and the spacious arcades have been walled in. The building still presents a solid, imposing appearance, however, and could be restored at least partially.

74. Eutaw Springs Battlefield

> *Location: 3 miles east of Eutawville, Orangeburg County, on S.C. 6.*

Eutaw Springs was the last major engagement of the War for Independence in South Carolina. Here, on September 8, 1781, Gen. Nathanael Greene's Continentals shattered Col. Archibald Stuart's British command. This led to the British evacuation of Orangeburg, leaving the American Army in undisputed possession of the interior of South Carolina. The battlefield is now a State park.

75. French Protestant Huguenot Church

> *Location: 136 Church Street, Charleston.*

Huguenots fled from France after the revocation of the Edict of Nantes in 1685, many coming to the larger cities of the English Colonies and especially to South Carolina. The sizable Huguenot population of Charleston gave the city a distinctly French flavor by the early 18th century. The first Huguenot congregation had been formed in Charleston in 1680, and they erected a church soon afterward. The present handsome Gothic structure, third on the site, was constructed in 1845. For years it was the only Huguenot church in the United States, but it no longer has an active congregation. Badly damaged by an earthquake in

1886 and a tornado in 1938, it has been restored and appears to be in excellent condition. The neatly kept church plot includes a small burial ground which, together with the church, is open to visitors.

76. Jacob Motte House

> *Location: 69 Church Street, Charleston.*

Richard Capers built this brick "double house" about 1745 which later was the home of Col. Jacob Motte, longtime public treasurer of the colony. Through his 19 children he became father-in-law to a number of notable individuals, including Mrs. Rebecca Motte, Thomas Lynch, and William Moultrie. The house was damaged by shellfire during the Civil War and has been altered inside somewhat. Adam-style mantelpieces were installed and the two upstairs front rooms were combined into a single drawing room about 1780. The house is privately owned.

77. Star Fort and Village of Ninety Six

> *Location: 2½ miles south of present Ninety Six, Greenwood County, on S.C. 246.*

Ninety Six began as a trading post in 1730 and continued during the colonial period as an important trading center and seat of justice for much of upcountry South Carolina. The sizable village was fortified during the Cherokee outbreak of 1759–60, and was predominantly Tory as the Revolution came on. Patriot forces were besieged at Ninety Six for 3 days inconclusively in November 1775, but in December the Tories were defeated and dispersed. The British captured Charleston in 1780 and, later in the year, established an outpost and built the Star Fort at Ninety Six. The fort was an earthwork with eight salient and eight reentrant angles, enclosing about one-half an acre northeast of the village. Gen. Nathanael Greene's American force invested and assaulted the fort unsuccessfully in May–June 1781 but withdrew as British reinforcements approached. The British evacuated the fort, however, relinquishing their foothold in inland South Carolina.

The Star Fort outlines are still readily discernible as earthwork embankments 4 or 5 feet high. Scattered brick fragments mark the location of the town, which was burned by the British, later rebuilt, but lost its court in 1800 and declined in importance. Some identifiable remains include the knoll on which the 1775 siege occurred and on which stood the British stockade fort of 1781, the ravine in which flowed the stream supplying water to the garrison, the jail site, the old Charleston Road, and, some distance from the village site, the site of the 1759 fortification. A stone monument stands on S.C. 246 at the junction of a dirt road leading to the fort. At this writing the Greenwood County Historical Society is negotiating for the property and laying plans for developing the site.

TENNESSEE

78. Bean Cabin Site (lost site)

Location: 6 miles north of Johnson City, Washington County, 1½ miles east of U.S. 23.

William Bean initiated permanent settlement in eastern Tennessee when he arrived from Virginia in 1769 and built a rude cabin on Boone's Creek near its junction with the Watauga River. He was joined soon by others from Virginia to form a tiny community, the nucleus of the Watauga settlements. Bean's son, Russell, the first child born to permanent white settlers in Tennessee, was born in the cabin. The site has been inundated by Boone's Lake but a monument stands on the lakeshore above the site.

79. Fort Loudoun

Location: 1 mile east of U.S. 411 at the crossing of the Little Tennessee River, Monroe County.

Fort Loudoun existed for only 4 critical years of the French and Indian War, 1756–60. The southwestern outpost was built for the benefit and at the request of the Overhill Cherokee, but they forced the surrender of the garrison in August 1760. The Indians' later massacre of many of the departing whites created new strains for the future. The earthwork fort was diamond-shaped with log palisades inside a honeylocust hedge, including a blacksmith shop, guardhouse, barracks, magazine, officers' quarters, and storehouses. A partial reconstruction has been accomplished, based on archeological work, sponsored by the Fort Loudoun Association which was formed in 1933 when private owners donated about 6 acres of the site to the State of Tennessee.

80. Sycamore Shoals and (lost site) Fort Watauga

Location: 2 miles west of Elizabethton, on the Watauga River, Carter County.

Sycamore Shoals was chosen as the administrative center of the Watauga settlements under the leadership of James Robertson. The valley was first leased and then (1775) purchased from the Cherokee, and Fort Watauga erected. The Indians attacked the fort unsuccessfully in 1776. The frontiersmen gathered at Sycamore Shoals in 1780 and marched into South Carolina where they dealt the Tory leader, Patrick Ferguson, a crushing defeat at Kings Mountain. The traditional site of Fort Watauga is on a low ridge beside Tenn. 67, about one-half mile southwest of the lower end of Sycamore Shoals. A concrete and stone marker has been placed nearby, by the Daughters of the American Revolution. The site is in a developed residential area.

VERMONT

81. Hubbardton Battlefield

Location: Near Hubbardton, 18 miles northwest of Rutland, Rutland County.

Colonels Seth Warner and Ebenezer Francis, in charge of the rearguard of the American force retreating after the fall of Fort Ticonderoga, remained overnight at Hubbardton without taking proper security measures for their encampment. The British attacked very early the next morning, July 7, 1777, and brought on a short but very severe fight. The Americans scattered with instructions to reassemble at Manchester. Francis was killed. The British advance was delayed, but the cost was exorbitant. This was the only battle of the War for Independence fought on Vermont soil. The site is included in a 50-acre State park.

VIRGINIA

82. Berkeley Plantation

Location: 7 miles west of Charles City, south of Va. 5, Charles City County.

Harrison's Landing, a part of the Berkeley Hundred grant of 1619, was the site of the first Thanksgiving service in America, December 4, 1619; of an Indian massacre in 1622; and of Civil War Gen. George B. McClellan's army supply base in the Seven Days' Battle campaign. One of the early owners of Berkeley Plantation was Giles Bland, who was executed for complicity in Bacon's Rebellion. Benjamin Harrison, the third of this name in Virginia, next acquired the property. His son, Benjamin IV, began building the present mansion (later to be General McClellan's headquarters) in 1726. Benjamin V was a Governor of Virginia and a signer of the Declaration of Independence; Benjamin VI installed the handsome interior woodwork; his brother, William Henry, who went to Ohio, became famous as soldier and politician and, as President, revisited Berkeley Plantation as did William Henry's grandson-President, Benjamin. The mansion is a plain early Georgian building of brick, two stories, with a massive roof, two tall chimneys, and six widely spaced dormers. The interior features notable woodwork and plaster-tinted walls. Flanking the house are two dependencies, altered to two stories about 1800. The plantation, acquired by the present owner's father about 50 years ago, was restored beginning in 1937 and is open to the public.

83. Carter's Grove Plantation

Location: 6 miles southeast of Williamsburg, James City County, on U.S. 60.

This Georgian mansion was built by Carter Burwell in 1750–53 to the design probably of Richard Taliaferro. David Minitree, of Williamsburg, was the contractor-builder. The interior paneling was expertly restored in 1927–29 and certain alterations were made, including an 11-

foot elevation of the rooftree, the addition of dormers, and reconstruction of the dependencies. Carter's Grove is privately owned and not normally open to visitors.

84. Castle Hill

Location: 2 miles north of Cismont, Albemarle County, on Va. 231.

In 1765, Dr. Thomas Walker built the original 1½-story framehouse at Castle Hill, 15 years after his discovery of Cumberland Gap. He owned about 17,000 acres of surrounding land. The present main house was built about 1840 by William Cabell Rives, U.S. Senator and Minister to France under President Andrew Jackson, who married one of Walker's granddaughters. The earlier structure is joined to the rear of the later brick building by a short passageway. The property is privately owned.

85. Christ Church

Location: 3 miles south of Kilmarnock on Va. 3, Lancaster County.

Christ Church is an outstanding example of its particular architectural style and period, and is unusually well preserved. It combines typical early Georgian features with several which are unique, and is valuable also for the integrity of its interior furnishings. Robert "King" Carter, leading Virginia enterpreneur of his generation, built the present Christ Church at his own expense in 1732. His tomb and those of other members of the Carter family are here. The Foundation for Historic Christ Church, Inc., was established in 1958 and has laid careful plans for restoration and preservation of the church and its surroundings. The 1-acre church tract and 12 surrounding acres are owned by Christ Church Parish, Irvington, Va. The church is recognized as a Registered National Historic Landmark under the architectural category in the National Survey of Historic Sites and Buildings.

86. Gadsby's Tavern

Location: 132 Royal Street, Alexandria.

The older portion of this brick building, known for years as City Tavern, was built about 1752 and used intermittently by Washington as military headquarters during the French and Indian War. A taller brick addition was built onto the two-story tavern in the last decade of the 18th century. Washington reviewed the Alexandria militia from the tavern steps in November 1799, one of his last public appearances; and a quarter century later a reception was held here for Lafayette during his triumphal tour of the United States. The tavern has been restored and is open to visitors.

87. George Wythe House

Location: Palace Green, in Williamsburg.

George Wythe pursued here the brilliant career that gave him a permanent niche in American legal history: member of the House of Burgesses, mayor of Williamsburg, Revolutionary statesman, and first professor of law in an American college. The house was built for Wythe in 1755 by his father-in-law, the noted Virginia architect, Richard Taliaferro, and he lived here until 1790. It is a simple, rectangular brick house with hip roof, based on William Salmon's *Palladio Londinensis* (1734), and is one of the exhibit homes of Colonial Williamsburg, which as a historic district is eligible for the Registry of National Historic Landmarks.

88. Germanna

Location: Va. 3, at the crossing of the Rapidan River, Orange County.

Alexander Spotswood (1676–1740) bought 85,000 acres in Spotsylvania County, of which the Germanna tract was the first, while he was Lieutenant Governor and actual executive head of the Virginia government. In this capacity, between 1710 and 1722, he carried out his famous Blue Ridge expedition and promoted many reforms and improvements. He established a colony of German immigrants on the Germanna tract in 1714, partly for frontier defense but mainly to operate his newly developed ironworks. Germanna was the seat of Spotsylvania County from 1720 to 1732. Spotswood erected a palatial home and, after the Germans moved away, continued the ironworks with slave labor. In his later years he served as Deputy Postmaster General for the Colonies.

The site of Germanna now is mostly open fields with intervening thickets of second-growth timber. Traces of the terraces of Spotswood's mansion are still discernible. The Memorial Foundation of the Germanna Colonies in Virginia owns about 270 acres, and the rest of the original tract is in various private ownerships.

89. Hanover Courthouse

Location: 18 miles north of Richmond, Hanover County, on U.S. 301.

Patrick Henry came to prominence when he successfully pleaded the Parsons' Cause in Hanover Courthouse in 1763. Still used as a courthouse, the building is a one-story, T-shaped brick structure with an arcaded piazza across the front. The small, contemporary clerk's office, and other appurtenances typical of a small Virginia courthouse group are nearby. Henry lived across the road at Hanover Tavern for some time after his father-in-law acquired the building in 1760, and Lord Cornwallis stayed there briefly during the Yorktown campaign. The tavern is a rambling, two-story frame building over a high basement, built in stages beginning in 1723. It is now used by the Barksdale Theater.

90. Mount Vernon

Location: 7 miles south of Alexandria, on the Potomac River, Fairfax County.

More than a million Americans visit Mount Vernon each year, making it with the White House one of the best-known residential houses in the United States. Washington inherited Mount Vernon upon the death of his half-brother in 1752, and it remained his home until his death in 1799. Both he and his wife Martha are buried on the grounds.

Official duties kept Washington away from his home for long periods, but by 1787 he succeeded in completing his program for enlarging the house and developing the grounds in accordance with a plan he drafted before the War for Independence, the plan which has been adhered to painstakingly by the present owner, the Mount Vernon Ladies' Association of the Union. The original 8,000-acre plantation was divided into five farms, four of which were subdivided after Washington's death so that only the 500-acre Mansion House Farm remains as an entity. The association acquired title to Mount Vernon in 1858 from Washington's great-grandnephew.

House, outbuildings, and grounds, where a large number of original Washington possessions may be seen, are well maintained and open to visitors every day of the year. Mount Vernon is classified as a Registered National Historic Landmark in the study spanning the years 1783–1830.

91. Pohick Church

Location: 12 miles south of Alexandria, Fairfax County, on U.S. 1.

George Washington, as a vestryman of Truro Parish, was instrumental in choosing the location for the "new" Pohick Church in 1772. He attended services here while residing at Mount Vernon, until the beginning of the War for Independence. The building is typical of the late Georgian parish church of Virginia, having a simple rectangular plan with no tower, resembling Christ Church in Alexandria. It has a low-pitched hip roof with modillioned cornice, and was constructed of brick with sandstone angle quoins and door trim. The symmetrical facades show an unusual feature—rectilinear windows on the first floor and arched windows on the second. Badly damaged during the Civil War, the church has been restored and is used for regular services.

92. Scotchtown

Location: 1 mile north of Negro Foot, Hanover County, on Va. 685.

Scotchtown was the home of Patrick Henry from 1771 to about 1777, and later of Dolley Payne, the future Mrs. James Madison. Henry lived here and was a member of the general assembly in March 1775 when he spoke the words, "Give me liberty or give me death," at an assembly session in Richmond. He left from Scotchtown for Philadelphia to serve in the First and Second Continental Congresses and, as Governor of Virginia, he met at Scotchtown with George Rogers Clark to discuss Clark's proposed campaign against British posts west of the Appalachians. The house was built probably about 1719 and has particularly noteworthy paneling. It is 93 feet long and 35 wide. The main floor is bisected by a large central hall running the width of the structure. Each end is divided into four rooms, with one chimney serving each group of rooms. The Association for the Preservation of Virginia Antiquities acquired the house in 1958, has finished most of the structural restoration work, and is concentrating now on furnishings and landscaping.

93. Shirley Plantation

> *Location: 17 miles southeast of Richmond, Charles City County, on Va. 5.*

Shirley Plantation was one of the earliest Virginia tobacco plantations, originally settled in 1613 and producing for export by 1616. Col. Edward Hill II acquired the property in 1660, and his descendants own it still. Edward Hill III built the present house perhaps as early as 1723. His great-granddaughter, Ann Hill Carter, was Robert E. Lee's mother. More than 200 slaves lived at the plantation in the early 1800's, when it was part of a complex of about 170,000 acres. The house is Georgian, with two-story porticos on both main facades; a double-hipped roof with a single pineapple finial; gabled dormers on all four sides of the roof; and a square, three-story, brick central bulk with deep, denticulated cornice. The interior contains an unusually large entrance hall, a hanging stair rising three flights, full paneling in several rooms, and mantels, overmantels, and ornate broken pediments over interior doorways. The house has all original furnishings, and portraits of prominent members of the Carter family. About eight of the original dependencies remain. Shirley Plantation is open daily to visitors, although it is still an agricultural operation and a private home.

94. Springdale (Hite's Fort)

> *Location: 2 miles north of Stephens City, Frederick County, on U.S. 11.*

Jost Hite, an Alsatian, came to America in 1710 and settled in Pennsylvania before obtaining contracts in 1731 for 140,000 acres in the Shenandoah Valley. Next year he settled 16 families on Opequon Creek, south of present Winchester, thus initiating the westward movement of German settlers from Pennsylvania, an important aspect of late colonial development. Springdale is a two-story structure of gray stone, built by John

Hite in 1753. It is in good condition, privately owned, and not open to visitors. A short distance south of the house are some crumbling, unstabilized stone walls believed to be the remains of Hite's Fort, built by Jost Hite soon after he arrived in Virginia.

95. Tuckahoe Plantation

> *Location: 7 miles west of Richmond, Goochland County, on Va. 650.*

Thomas Jefferson spent 7 of the first 9 years of his life and began his schooling at Tuckahoe, home of his cousins, the Randolphs. Through his mother, nee Jane Randolph, Jefferson inherited a firm standing in Virginia society, and at Tuckahoe the intellectual curiosity was aroused that remained with him all his life. The house was constructed between 1712 and 1730, with its present H-plan achieved through the construction of a T-shaped addition onto the earlier central-hall house. There are elaborately carved interior woodwork of pine and black walnut, a delicate stairway, and small formal entrance porches on the land and river facades. A number of original outbuildings survive, including the schoolhouse in which Jefferson studied. The plantation is privately owned.

WEST VIRGINIA

96. Point Pleasant Battlefield

> *Location: City of Point Pleasant, at junction of Ohio and Kanawha Rivers, Mason County.*

Early in 1774 Dr. John Connolly occupied Fort Pitt in the name of Virginia and began to encourage nearby frontiersmen to aggression against the Indians, thereby bringing on "Lord Dunmore's War." Col. Andrew Lewis, with about 1,100 men from southwestern Virginia, marched up the Kanawha to Point Pleasant where Chief Cornstalk with a large force of Shawnee attacked him early in the morning of October 10, 1774. The Indians withdrew in the late afternoon, after heavy fighting which produced severe casualties: 50 Virginians killed, 100 wounded.   The Shawnee were thereafter unable to halt the settlement of Kentucky or to destroy the weak Kentucky stations during the crucial early years of the War for Independence.   Tu-Endie-Wei State Park, a 2-acre reservation, includes part of the battlefield as well as the graves of Col. Charles Lewis, Chief Cornstalk, and "Mad Ann" Bailey, a noted frontierswoman, and an 84-foot granite shaft commemorating the battle. Mansion House, built in 1796 as a tavern, is maintained as a historic-house museum.   The rest of the battlefield is covered by the city of Point Pleasant.

F. Sites Also Noted

The historic sites listed in this group were noted in the course of the survey but were considered to be of less importance in this phase of history than those already given.

CONNECTICUT

Eels-Stowe House, Milford
Ethan Allen Birthplace, Litchfield
Fort Griswold, Groton
Mystic Seaport, Old Mystic

Nathan Hale School, East Haddam
Nathan Hale School, New London
Pardee-Morris House, New Haven
Putnam Cottage, Greenwich

FLORIDA

Fort George, Pensacola

Fort Tonyn, Nassau County

GEORGIA

Hardwick, Bryan County

Spring Hill Redoubt Site, Savannah

KENTUCKY

Boonesborough Site, Madison County

Bryan's Station Site, Fayette County
Fort Harrod, Harrodsburg

MAINE

Fort George, Castine
Fort Pownall, Stockton Springs

"Montpelier," General Henry Knox House (Replica), Thomaston

MARYLAND

Cresap's Fort, Oldtown
Fort Cumberland, Cumberland
"The Hermitage" and Hollings-
worth Tavern, Elkton

Old State House, Annapolis
Smallwood's R e t r e a t, Mason
Springs

MASSACHUSETTS

Cushing House, Quincy
Mission House, Stockbridge

Quincy Homestead, Quincy

MISSISSIPPI

Fort Rosalie, Natchez

NEW HAMPSHIRE

Cincinnati Hall, Exeter
Fort Constitution, New Castle

Governor Meshech Weare House,
Hampton Falls

NEW JERSEY

Cannonball House, Springfield
Hankinson Mansion, Freehold
Hulse House and Village Inn, Eng-
lishtown
Indian King Tavern, Haddonfield

"Morven," Governor's Mansion,
Princeton
Pluckemin (Village)
Steuben House, North Hackensack

NEW YORK

Bush Homestead, Port Chester
Constitution Island, Hudson River
off West Point
Elijah Miller House and "Washing-
ton Headquarters House," White
Plains
Fort Ann, Washington County
Fort Brewerton, Brewerton
Fort Crailo, Rensselaer
Fort Edward, Washington County

Fort Frey, Palatine Bridge
Indian Castle Church, Fort Plain
Lake George Battleground, Lake
George
Old Stone Fort, Schoharie
Raynham Hall, Oyster Bay, Long
Island
"76 House," Tappan
Ten Broeck Mansion, Albany

PENNSYLVANIA

Charles Thomson Home, Lower Marion Township
The Cloisters, Ephrata
Fort Augusta, Sunbury
Fort Le Boeuf, Waterford
Fort Ligonier, Ligonier

Fort Zeller, Lebanon County
General Greene Inn, Buckingham
Main Magazine, Carlisle
Market Square Presbyterian Church, Germantown

SOUTH CAROLINA

Blackstock Battlefield, Union County
Fort Dorchester, Dorchester County
Fort Johnson, Charleston
Fort Moultrie, Mount Pleasant

Musgrove's Mill Battlefield, Union County
St. Helena Episcopal Church, Beaufort
Tamassee (Andrew Pickens Home), Oconee County

VERMONT

Battle Monument, Bennington
Crown Point Military Road, Springfield to Chimney Point

Ethan Allen Park, Burlington
Old Constitution House, Windsor

VIRGINIA

Bellefont, Staunton
Chiswell Lead Mines, Wythe County
Claremont, Surry County
Draper's Meadows, Blacksburg
Elsing Green, King and Queen County
Fort Chiswell, Wythe County
Fort Egypt, Page County
Green Spring Battlefield, Toano

John Paul Jones House, Fredericksburg
Manakintown, Powhatan County
Matthew Jones House, Fort Eustis
Monticello, Albemarle County
Soldier's Rest (Daniel Morgan Home), Berryville
Tubal Furnace, Spotsylvania County

WEST VIRGINIA

Harewood, Jefferson County
Logan Massacre Site, Ohio Count
Prato Rio (Charles Lee Home), Jefferson County

Traveler's Rest (Horatio Gates Home), Jefferson County

SUGGESTED READING

1. The English Colonies, 1700–1775

ADAMS, JAMES TRUSLOW. *Provincial Society, 1690–1763.* Vol. III of *A History of American Life,* ed. by Arthur M. Schlesinger and Dixon R. Fox. New York: Macmillan, 1927. One of a series attempting to portray the history of America in social terms, this volume focuses on colonial society while minimizing the political and military aspects of colonial history.

ANDREWS, CHARLES M. *The Colonial Period of American History.* 4 vols. New Haven: Yale University Press, 1934–38. A detailed and scholarly study of the American Colonies, written from the "English end," *i.e.,* considering the Colonies integral parts of the British imperial system rather than as embryo States. An advanced work, useful for its examination of the interrelationship between the Colonies and the mother country.

ANDREWS, CHARLES M. *The Colonial Background of the American Revolution.* New Haven: Yale University Press, 1931. Andrews here analyzes the forces and events that produced the Revolution. As in his later and larger work, listed above, he treats all the American Colonies, not just the 13 that revolted.

BRIDENBAUGH, CARL. *Cities in the Wilderness: The First Century of Urban Life in America, 1625–1742.* 2d ed. New York: Alfred Knopf, 1955. *Cities in Revolt: Urban Life in America, 1743–1776.* New York: Alfred Knopf, 1955. Through the medium of five representative cities, Bridenbaugh surveys the cultural, political, economic and social life of urban colonial America, and concludes that the influence of towns upon colonial development has been greatly underrated by historians.

[241

CHANNING, EDWARD. *A History of the United States.* 6 vols. New York: Macmillan, 1932–36. Vols. 1 and 2. One of the standard authorities, Channing was nevertheless a rather discursive historian. The information and interpretation are there, but are sometimes difficult to locate.

GIPSON, LAWRENCE H. *The British Empire Before the American Revolution.* 11 vols. Caldwell, Idaho, and New York, 1936– . A monumental project, of which 10 volumes have been completed, this study is especially valuable for its discussion of the Anglo-French struggle for the North American Continent.

GREENE, EVARTS BOUTELL. *The Revolutionary Generation, 1763–1790.* Vol. 4 of *A History of American Life,* ed. by A. M. Schlesinger and D. R. Fox. New York: Macmillan, 1943. Like Adams' *Provincial Society,* this volume accents social and economic aspects of American history.

MORGAN, EDMUND S. AND HELEN M. *The Stamp Act Congress: Prologue to Revolution.* Chapel Hill: University of North Carolina Press, 1953. This book stands as the best study of the subject.

MORRISON, HUGH. *Early American Architecture, from the First Colonial Settlements to the National Period.* New York: Oxford University Press, 1952. Morrison creditably performs a rigidly defined task: to write "a comprehensive account in one volume of architecture in the American colonies from St. Augustine in 1565 to San Francisco in 1848." This book, profusely illustrated, is invaluable for the study of 18th-century colonial architecture.

OSGOOD, HERBERT L. *The American Colonies in the Eighteenth Century.* 4 vols. New York: Columbia University Press, 1924. As in his earlier study of the Colonies in the 17th century, Osgood focuses on political and institutional history and on the "intercolonial" wars.

PARKMAN, FRANCIS. *History of the Conspiracy of Pontiac.* Boston, 1851, and many subsequent editions. This classic work surpassed everything previously written on Pontiac's War and all writers since 1851 have drawn on Parkman. The book is outstanding not only for its wealth of accurate detail but also for its literary quality.

SAVELLE, MAX. *The Foundations of American Civilization: A History of Colonial America.* New York: Henry Holt and Co., c. 1942. In this college textbook, Savelle undertakes a comprehensive discussion of the colonial period and the beginnings of the United States. Although it contains a few minor errors, it is a lucid discussion of a complicated subject.

2. *The American Revolution, 1775–1783*

ABERNETHY, THOMAS P. *Western Lands and the American Revolution.* New York: Appleton-Century for the Institute for Research in the Social Sciences, University of Virginia, 1937. Basic study of the western land policies of the Colonies during the Revolution and of the political consequences of the westward movement.

ALDEN, JOHN R. *The American Revolution, 1775–1783,* in *"The New American Nation Series,"* New York: Harper and Bros., 1954. This work is especially valuable for its treatment of the military aspects of the Revolution. It also discusses quite fully the British and European situations of the period and gives a briefer treatment of the colonial home front. An excellent one-volume treatment of the entire Revolutionary episode.

ALLEN, GARDNER W. *A Naval History of the American Revolution.* 2 vols. Boston: Houghton Mifflin, 1913. Detailed narrative, based on exhaustive archival research, of the operations of all Continental warships.

BEMIS, SAMUEL FLAGG. *The Diplomacy of the American Revolution.* New York: Appleton-Century, 1935. Basic study of American foreign policy during the war, this book has as a central theme the progressive involvement of the United States in European diplomacy as a result of the alliance with France.

BURNETT, EDMUND C. *The Continental Congress.* New York: Macmillan, 1941. Burnett details the activities of the Continental Congress and assesses its role in the conduct of the war, and in laying the foundation for the governmental forms that sprang from it.

FREEMAN, DOUGLAS SOUTHALL. *George Washington: A Biography.* 7 vols. New York: Charles Scribner's Sons, 1948–57 (Vol. 7 by John A. Carroll and Mary W. Ashworth). The definitive biography of the great American leader, produced by painstaking research into all available sources by one of the most gifted of military historians. The fourth and fifth volumes deal exclusively with Washington's career during the War for Independence.

GIPSON, LAWRENCE H. *The Coming of the Revolution, 1763–1775,* in *"The New American Nation Series."* New York: Harper and Bros., 1954. Gipson here traces the clash between British efforts to tighten imperial administration and the colonial effort to achieve greater autonomy.

MONTROSS, LYNN. *Rag, Tag and Bobtail: The Story of the Continental Army, 1775–1783.* New York: Harper and Bros., c. 1952. A fine study of the military phases of the war, notable for thorough research and the quality of the numerous maps. The author is an admirer of Horatio Gates and considers that Benedict Arnold's pre-treason services to the American cause have been overrated.

SCHEER, GEORGE F., and HUGH F. RANKIN. *Rebels and Redcoats.* Cleveland and New York: World Publishing Co., c. 1957. Described by the authors as "a mosaic that tells a developing story," this is an absorbing history of the war told largely in the words of participants. Much of the value and interest of the narrative is due to skillful editing and the informative narration that links the excerpts.

VAN TYNE, CLAUDE H. *The Causes of the War of Independence: Being the First Volume of a History of the Founding of the American Republic.* Boston: Houghton Mifflin, 1922. *The War of Independence, American Phase: Being the Second Volume of a History of the Founding of the American Republic.* Boston: Houghton Mifflin, 1929. In the first volume, the author surveys the forces that produced the Revolution, and in the second he carries the war to the entry of the French, where death interrupted his labor.

WARD, CHRISTOPHER. *The War of the Revolution,* ed. by John R. Alden. 2 vols. New York: Macmillan, 1952. Ward had nearly completed his history of land operations in the Revolution when he died in 1943, and it was finished by Alden. The book excells in narrative description of battles and movements.

NOTES

1. Max Savelle, *The Foundations of American Civilization* (New York, 1942), p. 644.

2. Edward Channing, *A History of the United States* (6 vols. New York, 1905–29), II, 411.

3. One result of this tide of immigration was the passage by Parliament of an act in 1740 providing for naturalization of foreign Protestants in the American Colonies. This law, which required 7 years' residence and certain oaths (or affirmations), formed the basis of the first naturalization act of the United States. *Ibid.,* II, 414–15.

4. Hugh Morrison, *Early American Architecture* (New York, 1952), p. 291.

5. Imperial and colonial authorities attempted to give the appearance of legality to all their dealings with the frontier problem, particularly with regard to the acquisition of Indian land. A succession of treaties negotiated by colonial and imperial authorities delivered to the whites vast tracts of Indian territory extending from southwestern New York to Tennessee. Whether the Indians who disposed of this land had clear title was of little concern to the land companies and the colonial administrators, who worked closely with, and sometimes for, the speculators. The fiction of honorable negotiation was upheld, although neither Indians nor whites had illusions about the justice or legality of the treaties.

6. The significance of Clark's campaigns in the winning of the Northwest is controversial. As some histories have pointed out, much that he won was later lost, and postwar diplomatic negotiations did not recognize Clark's operations as a successful conquest. Nevertheless, Clark kept alive American claims to the Northwest and protected the new frontier in its most critical period. See John Bakeless, *Background to Glory: The Life of George Rogers Clark* (New York, 1957).

7. Webb House, Conn.: Henry Steele Commager and Richard B. Morris, *The Spirit of 'Seventy-Six: The Story of the American Revolution as Told by Participants* (2 vols. Indianapolis, 1958), II; Historic American Buildings Survey (hereafter HABS), one photograph, 1938; Henry P. Johnston, *The Yorktown Campaign and the Surrender of Cornwallis,* 1781 (New York, 1881), reprinted June 1958; Benson J. Lossing, *The Pictorial Field-Book of the Revolution* (2 vols. New York, 1859), I; "Webb House Built in 1752, Wethersfield, Connecticut": pamphlet published by Connecticut Society of the Colonial Dames of America (n.p., n.d.).

8. Paul L. Ford, "The Writings of John Dickinson," *Historical Society of Pennsylvania Memoirs,* XIV (1895), preface.

9. C. J. Stille, "The Life and Times of John Dickinson, 1732–1808," *ibid.,* XIII (1891), 236–37.

10. John Dickinson House, Del.: Roy E. Appleman, "The John Dickinson House, Kent County, Delaware," MS. report, National Park Service, Oct. 31, 1950; Jeannette Eckman, *Delaware, A Guide to the First State,* American Guide Series (Rev. ed. New York, 1955); Ford, "Writings of John Dickinson"; Stille, "Life and Times of John Dickinson"; Moses C. Tyler, *The Literary History of the American Revolution, 1763–1783* (2 vols. New York, 1897), I; Memorandum of Daniel J. Breslin, Architect, National Park Service, to Regional Director, Region One, National Park Service, Dec. 19, 1952; "The Home of John Dickinson, 'Penman of the Revolution,' " Information Leaflet (n.p, n.d.); HABS, one photograph, 1936.

11. Gundelo *Philadelphia,* D.C.: L. F. Hagglund, "A Page from the Past: The Story of the Continental Gundelo *Philadelphia* on Lake Champlain—1776–1949," pamphlet (Lake George, N.Y., 1949); Alfred T. Mahan, *Major Operations of the Navies in the War of American Independence* (Boston, 1913); R. G. Skerrett, "Another Revolutionary War Vessel Recovered," *Compressed Air Magazine,* vol. 41, no. 7 (July 1936), 5072–75.

12. Lady Pepperrell House, Maine: John Meade Howells, *The Architectural Heritage of the Piscataqua* (New York, 1937); Morrison, *Early American Architecture.*

13. Morrison, *Early American Architecture,* p. 400.

14. Hammond-Harwood House, Md.: *ibid.;* Rosamond Randall Beirne and Edith Rossiter Beran, *The Hammons-Harwood House and Its Owners* (Annapolis, 1954); Deering Davis, *Annapolis Houses, 1700–1775* (n.p., 1947); HABS, seven photographs, 1936–37.

15. Whitehall, Md.: Morrison, *Early American Architecture;* Thomas T. Waterman, *Dwellings of Colonial America* (Chapel Hill, 1950); HABS, six photographs, 1936.

16. Buckman Tavern, Mass.: *Interim Report of the Boston National Historic Sites Commission Pertaining to the Lexington-Concord Battle Road,*

House Docs., 86th Cong., 1st sess., no. 57 (Washington, 1959).

17. Bunker Hill Monument, Mass.: J. R. Alden, *The American Revolution, 1775–1783* (New York, 1954) ; *Final Report of the Boston National Historic Sites Commission to the Congress of the United States* (June 16, 1960) (hereafter *Boston NHSC Report*); Christopher Ward, *The War of the Revolution* (2 vols. New York, 1952), I.

18. Christ Church, Mass.: *Boston NHSC Report;* HABS, eight sheets and four photographs, 1934; George F. Marlowe, *Churches of Old New England* (New York, 1947) ; Morrison, *Early American Architecture;* Edward F. Rines, *Old Historic Churches of America* (New York, 1936).

19. Faneuil Hall, Mass.: *Boston NHSC Report;* HABS, three sheets and six photographs, 1935 and 1937; Morrison, *Early American Architecture;* Rogers W. Young, "Preliminary Survey of Historic Sites in Boston," MS. report, National Park Service, July 17, 1951.

20. M. H. Northend, *Historic Homes of New England* (Boston, 1914), p. 229.

21. Isaac Royall House, Mass.: *Boston NHSC Report;* Fiske Kimball, *Domestic Architecture of the American Colonies and of the Early Republic* (New York, 1922) ; HABS, five photocopies; Morrison, *Early American Architecture;* Northend, *Historic Homes of New England.*

22. Jeremiah Lee Mansion, Mass.: Kimball, *Domestic Architecture;* "Lee Mansion, Marblehead, Massachusetts" (pamphlet, n.p., n.d.) ; Morrison, *Early American Architecture;* Northend, *Historic Homes of New England.*

23. Morrison, *Early American Architecture,* p. 452.

24. King's Chapel, Mass.: *Boston NHSC Report;* Carl Bridenbaugh, *Peter Harrison, First American Architect* (Chapel Hill, 1949) ; Morrison, *Early American Architecture.*

25. Lexington Green, Mass.: *Interim Report of Boston NHSC.*

26. Massachusetts Hall, Mass.: Samuel E. Morison, *Three Centuries of Harvard, 1636–1936* (Cambridge, 1936) ; Edwin W. Small, Boston NHSC survey card, Aug. 17, 1956. The quotation is from Morrison, *Early American Architecture,* p. 463.

27. Old North Church, Mass.: Alden, *American Revolution;* Esther Forbes, *Paul Revere and the World He Lived In* (Boston, 1942) ; *Boston NHSC Report;* HABS, two photographs, 1941; Morrison, *Early American Architecture;* Edwin W. Small, "Old North Church," MS. report, National Park Service, Dec. 19, 1940.

28. Old South Meeting House, Mass.: *Boston NHSC Report;* John C. Miller, *Origins of the American Revolution* (New York, 1943) ; Morrison, *Early American Architecture.*

29. Paul Revere House, Mass.: *Boston NHSC Report;* Forbes, *Paul*

Revere; HABS, one photograph, 1941; Morrison, *Early American Architecture.*

30. Second Boston Town House, Mass.: *Boston NHSC Report;* Charles F. Read, "The Old State House and Its Predecessor, the First Town House," *Proceedings of the Bostonian Society,* 1908.

31. Shirley-Eustis House, Mass.: *Boston NHSC Report;* Morrison, *Early American Architecture.*

32. Wright's Tavern, Mass.: *Interim Report of Boston NHSC.*

33. Macpheadris-Warner House, N.H.: Howells, *Architectural Heritage of the Piscataqua;* Morrison, *Early American Architecture;* Northend, *Historic Homes of New England;* "The Warner House, Portsmouth, New Hampshire," leaflet (n.p., n.d.).

34. Monmouth Battlefield, N.J.: Douglas S. Freeman, *George Washington,* vol. 5, *Victory with the Aid of France* (New York, 1952); Leonard Lundin, *Cockpit of the Revolution: The War for Independence in New Jersey* (Princeton, 1940); W. S. Stryker, *The Battle of Monmouth* (Princeton, 1927).

35. Nassau Hall, N.J.: HABS, two photographs, 1936; Morrison, *Early American Architecture;* Princeton University Department of Public Information, "Facts About Princeton," 1957–58; Henry L. Savage (ed.), *Nassau Hall, 1756–1956* (Princeton, 1956).

36. Princeton Battlefield, N.J.: Alfred H. Bill, *The Campaign of Princeton, 1776–1777* (Princeton, 1948); Alden T. Cottrell, "The Trenton Battle Monument and Washington's Campaign, December 26, 1776, to January 3, 1777," pamphlet (New Jersey Department of Conservation and Economic Development, Trenton, 1951); Lossing, *Field-Book,* II; Lundin, *Cockpit of the Revolution;* Ward, *War of the Revolution,* I.

37. Washington Crossing, N.J. and Pa.: Bill, *Campaign of Princeton;* George Athan Billias, *General John Glover and His Marblehead Mariners* (New York, 1960); Cottrell, "Trenton Battle Monument"; "Washington Crossing State Park," leaflet (Pennsylvania Department of Forests and Waters, n.p., n.d.); Lundin, *Cockpit of the Revolution;* Ward, *War of the Revolution,* I.

38. Bennington Battlefield, N.Y.: "Historic Sites of New York State," pamphlet (New York State Education Department, n.p., n.d.); Edward J. Lowell, *The Hessian and Other German Auxiliaries of Great Britain in the Revolutionary War* (New York, 1884); Howard P. Moore, *The Life of General John Stark* (New York, 1949); Hoffman Nickerson, *The Turning Point of the Revolution* (Boston, 1928).

39. Fort Stanwix, N.Y.: "Historic Sites of New York State"; Nickerson, *Turning Point; The American Revolution in New York: Its Political, Social and Economic Significance,* New York State Division of Archives and His-

tory (Albany, 1926) ; Melvin J. Weig and Charles S. Marshall, "Historic Sites Connected with the Siege of Fort Stanwix and the Battle of Oriskany," MS. report, National Park Service, Aug. 15, 1938.

40. Fort Ticonderoga, N.Y.. S. H. P. Pell (ed.), *Fort Ticonderoga: A Short History* (1951) ; *Guide Book to Fort Ticonderoga* (n.p., n.d.) ; Nickerson, *Turning Point;* Francis Parkman, *Montcalm and Wolfe* (2 vols. Boston, 1893), ch. 32.

41. Johnson Hall, N.Y.: Melvin J. Weig, "Johnson Hall, New York," MS. report, National Park Service, Oct. 1, 1937; HABS, 16 photographs, 1936 and 1940; Arthur Pound and Richard Day, *Johnson of the Mohawks* (New York, 1930).

42. Morris-Jumel Mansion, N.Y.: Lossing, *Field-Book,* II ; Morrison, *Early American Architecture;* John Kent Tilton, "Roger Morris-Jumel Mansion Built in 1765: Washington Headquarters in New York," pamphlet (New York, n.d.) ; Ward, *War of the Revolution,* I.

43. Oriskany Battlefield, N.Y.: Same references as 39.

44. St. Paul's Chapel, N.Y.: Aymar Embury, *Early American Churches* (New York, 1914) ; HABS, 37 photographs, 1937; Morrison, *Early American Architecture;* Rines, *Old Historic Churches of America.*

45. George F. Scheer and Hugh F. Rankin, *Rebels and Redcoats* (Cleveland, 1957), p. 364.

46. Stony Point Battlefield, N.Y.: Henry P. Johnston, *The Storming of Stony Point* (New York, 1900) ; Scheer and Rankin, *Rebels and Redcoats;* Ward, *War of the Revolution,* I.

47. Mahan, *Navies in the War of American Independence,* p. 25.

48. Valcour Bay, N.Y.: Richard M. Ketchum (ed.), *The American Heritage Book of the Revolution* (New York, 1958), pp. 132–33, has a contemporary map of the action and a watercolor sketch of the battle; Hagglund, "Page from the Past"; Lossing, *Field-Book, I* ; Mahan, *Navies in the War of American Independence;* letter from William G. Tyrrell, Historian, New York State Education Department, to National Park Service, Region Five, April 14, 1960.

49. Washington's Headquarters, N.Y.: Freeman, *Washington,* V; E. Irvine Haines, "When Washington Sealed the Republic," *New York Times Magazine,* March 19, 1933; "Historic Sites of New York State"; HABS, 26 photographs and 3 sheets, 1940; Melvin J. Weig, "Historic Sites and Buildings of the Colonial-Revolutionary Period Located in and Around Newburgh, New York," MS. report, National Park Service, Feb. 25, 1937.

50. Brandywine Battlefield, Pa.: "The Brandywine Story, 1777–1952," published by Brandywine Battlefield Park Commission (n.p., 1952) ; Willard M. Wallace, *Appeal to Arms—A Military History of the American Revolution* (New York, 1951) ; Melvin J. Weig, Historic Sites Survey report, 1938.

51. Bushy Run Battlefield, Pa.: "Brief History of Battle of Bushy Run, 1763," pamphlet issued by Bushy Run Battlefield Historical Park Commission (n.p., n.d.) ; Ray A. Billington, *Westward Expansion: A History of the American Frontier* (New York, 1949) ; Howard H. Peckham, *Pontiac and the Indian Uprising* (Princeton, 1947).

52. Orville T. Murphy, "The Battle of Germantown and the Franco-American Alliance of 1778," *Pennsylvania Magazine of History and Biography,* vol. 82 (January 1958), 63–64.

53. George O. Trevelyan, *The American Revolution,* III (London, ca. 1910), 249, quoted in Ward, *War of the Revolution,* I, 371.

54. Chew House, Pa.: Alden, *American Revolution;* Morrison, *Early American Architecture;* Murphy, "Battle of Germantown."

55. Conrad Weiser House, Pa.: Carl Bridenbaugh, "Johann Conrad Weiser," *Dictionary of American Biography,* XIX (New York, 1936), 614–615; *Conrad Weiser Park,* pamphlet issued by Commonwealth of Pennsylvania (Harrisburg, 1956) ; J. S. Walton, *Conrad Weiser and the Indian Policy of Colonial Pennsylvania* (Philadelphia, 1900).

56. Forks of the Ohio, Pa.: John P. Cowan, "Fort Pitt, Pittsburgh, Pennsylvania," MS. report, National Park Service, 1937; letter from John J. Grove, Coordinator, Point State Park, Pittsburgh, Pa., to Region Five, National Park Service, Dec. 28, 1961; Alfred P. James and Charles M. Stotz, *Drums in the Forest* (Pittsburgh, 1958) ; "Part One of the Report of the Point Park Commission" (Mimeo. Pittsburgh 1943) ; "Report on Forests and Waters: Land and People," brochure of Pennsylvania Department of Forests and Waters (n.p., 1958).

57. Graeme Park, Pa.: Harold D. Eberlein and Horace M. Lippincott, *The Colonial Homes of Philadelphia and Its Neighbourhood* (Philadelphia, 1912) ; Morrison, *Early American Architecture;* Nancy V. Wosstroff, "Graeme Park, an 18th Century Country Estate in Horsham, Pennsylvania," MS. thesis, University of Delaware, June 1958.

58. John Bartram House, Pa.: Emily Read Cheston, *John Bartram, 1699–1777, His Garden and His House* (2d ed. N.p., 1953) ; Brooke Hindle, *The Pursuit of Science in Revolutionary America, 1735–1789* (Chapel Hill, 1956).

59. Mount Pleasant, Pa.: Eberlein and Lippincott, *Colonial Homes of Philadelphia;* Luther P. Eisenhart (ed.), "Historical Philadelphia from the Founding until the Early 19th Century," *Transactions of the American Philosophical Society,* vol. 43 (1953) ; HABS, 6 photographs, 1938–39, 31 sheets, 1940; Morrison, *Early American Architecture.*

60. Valley Forge, Pa.: Alden, *American Revolution;* Roy E. Appleman, "Historical Report, Valley Forge Proposed National Park," MS. report,

National Park Service, n.d., HABS, seven photographs, 1937; Harry E. Wildes, *Valley Forge* (New York, 1938).

61. Brick Market, R.I.: Bridenbaugh, *Peter Harrison;* Antoinette F. Downing and Vincent J. Scully, Jr., *The Architectural Heritage of Newport, Rhode Island, 1640–1915* (Cambridge, 1952) ; HABS, one photo, 1937; Morrison, *Early American Architecture.*

62. First Baptist Meeting House, R.I.: *Brown Alumni Monthly,* vol. 58 (May, 1958) ; Embury, *Early American Churches;* Marlowe, *Churches of Old New England;* Morrison, *Early American Architecture;* Rines, *Old Historic Churches of America;* HABS, 28 photographs, ca. 1900, 1937, 1939, and including copies of drawings of 1774 and 1789.

63. Old State House, R.I.: Downing and Scully, *Architectural Heritage of Newport;* John H. Green, *The Building of the Old Colony House at Newport, Rhode Island* (Newport, 1941) ; Morrison, *Early American Architecture;* Roderick Terry, "History of the Old Colony House at Newport," *Newport Historical Society Bulletin,* No. 63 (October, 1927).

64. Redwood Library, R.I.: Bridenbaugh, *Peter Harrison;* Downing and Scully, *Architectural Heritage of Newport;* HABS, three photographs, 1937; Morrison, *Early American Architecture.*

65. Camden Battlefied, S.C.: H. L. Landers, *The Battle of Camden, South Carolina, August 16, 1780,* House Docs., 71st Cong., 1st sess., no. 12 (1929) ; Thomas J. Kirkland and Robert M. Kennedy, *Historic Camden* (2 vols. Columbia, 1905 and 1926), I.

66. Drayton Hall, S.C.: Morrison, *Early American Architecture;* Samuel G. Stoney, *Plantations of the Carolina Low Country* (Charleston, 1938) ; Elise Lathrop, *Historic Houses of Early America* (New York, 1936).

67. Waterman, *Dwellings of Colonial America,* pp. 81–85.

68. Miles Brewton House, S.C.: Morrison, *Early American Architecture;* Waterman, *Dwellings of Colonial America;* Beatrice St. Julien Ravenel, *Architects of Charleston* (Charleston, 1945) ; Albert Simons and Samuel Lapham, *Charleston, South Carolina* (Washington, 1927) ; HABS, six photographs 1938–40.

69. Mulberry Plantation, S.C.: Stoney, *Plantations of the Carolina Low Country;* Edward McCrady, *The History of South Carolina, 1670–1783* (4 vols. New York, 1897–1902) ; Morrison, *Early American Architecture;* Waterman, *Dwellings of Colonial America.*

70. Robert Brewton House, S.C.: Samuel G. Stoney, *This is Charleston* (Charleston, 1944) ; Junior League of Charleston, Inc., *Our Charleston, 1700–1860* (n.p., n.d.) ; Morrison, *Early American Architecture;* Ralston B. Lattimore, Historic Sites Survey card, July 10, 1937.

71. Morrison, *Early American Architecture,* p. 408.

72. St. Michael's Episcopal Church, S.C.; Stoney, *This is Charleston;* Morrison, *Early American Architecture;* HABS, three photographs, 1939–40.

73. Long Island, Tenn.: Billington, *Westward Expansion;* Archibald Henderson (ed.), "The Treaty of Long Island on the Holston, July, 1777," *North Carolina Historical Review,* VIII (1931) ; Samuel C. Williams, *Dawn of Tennessee Valley and Tennessee History* (Johnson City, 1937) ; Williams, *Tennessee During the Revolutionary War* (Nashville, 1944) ; Williams, "Fort Robinson on the Holston," *East Tennessee Historical Society Publications,* no. 4 (1932).

74. Greenway Court, Va.: Charles W. Porter, III, "Greenway Court— Home of Lord Fairfax," MS. report, National Park Service, June 3, 1936; HABS, six photographs, 1936–39; Leonidas Dodson, "The Fairfax Proprietary," *Dictionary of American History,* II, 240.

75. Mount Airy, Va.: Thomas T. Waterman, *The Mansions of Virginia, 1706–1776* (Chapel Hill, 1946) ; HABS, 17 photographs, 1934–39; Edith T. Sale, *Manors of Virginia in Colonial Times* (Philadelphia, 1909) ; Morrison, *Early American Architecture.*

76. St. John's Episcopal Church, Va.: Roy E. Appleman, "National Historic Site Survey Report on St. John's Episcopal Church, Richmond, Virginia," MS. report, National Park Service, Oct. 4, 1946; HABS, 11 sheets and 7 photographs 1934–35; Joseph S. Moore, *History of Henrico Parish and Old St. John's Church, Richmond, Virginia, 1611–1904* (Richmond, 1904).

77. Stratford Hall, Va.: Edmund J. Lee, *Lee of Virginia, 1642–1892* (Philadelphia, 1895) ; F. W. Alexander, *Stratford Hall and the Lees Connected with its History* (Oak Grove, 1912) ; E. M. Armes, *Stratford on the Potomac* (1928) ; Morrison, *Early American Architecture;* Waterman, *Mansions of Virginia;* Charles W. Porter, III, Historic Sites Survey card, Sept. 12, 1936; HABS, 45 photographs, 1932–40.

78. Westover, Va.: Morrison, *Early American Architecture;* Waterman, *Mansions of Virginia;* Sale, *Manors of Virginia;* Sale, *Interiors of Virginia Houses of Colonial Times* (Richmond, 1927) ; HABS, eight photographs, 1939.

79. Wren Building, Va.: *The Restoration of Colonial Williamsburg in Virginia* (New York, 1935) ; Morrison, *Early American Architecture;* HABS, four photographs 1937–39.

80. Old Deerfield, Mass.: Samuel Chamberlain and Henry N. Flynt, *Frontier of Freedom: The Soul and Substance of America Portrayed in One Extraordinary Village, Old Deerfield, Mass.* (Rev. ed. New York, 1957) ; Francis Parkman, *A Half-Century of Conflict,* pt. 6 of *France and England in North America* (2 vols. New York, 1915), I.

81. Huguenot Street, N.Y.: Harold D. Eberlein and Cortlandt van Dyke Hubbard, *Historic Houses of the Hudson Valley* (New York, 1942); HABS—Bevier-Elting House (11 sheets, 1934; 3 photographs, 1910, 1937, 1940), Freer House (8 sheets, 1934; 4 photographs, 1934, 1940), Jean Hasbrouck House (15 sheets, 1940; 20 photographs, 1937, 1940), Abraham Hasbrouck House (2 photographs, 1940); Morrison, *Early American Architecture.*

82. Elfreth's Alley, Pa.: Site descriptions from Hannah Benner Roach, "Elfreth's Alley, Philadelphia, Pennsylvania," MS. report, National Park Service, Region Five, 1961. Only recently has Elfreth's Alley received intensive historical research, although its architectural significance has long been recognized. Little of a definitive nature has been published on the alley, and the description given here is condensed from an authoritative summary generously supplied by the author, who is historian for the Elfreth's Alley Association.

83. Charleston, S.C.: Stoney, *This is Charleston;* Simons and Lapham, *Charleston;* Morrison, *Early American Architecture.*

84. Williamsburg, Va.: Colonial Williamsburg, Inc., *Colonial Williamsburg Official Guidebook* (Williamsburg, 1957); Morrison, *Early American Architecture; Colonial Williamsburg: The President's Report, 1960* (Williamsburg, 1961).

CRITERIA FOR SELECTION
OF HISTORIC SITES
OF EXCEPTIONAL VALUE

1. Structures or sites at which occurred events that have made an outstanding contribution to, and are identified prominently with, or which best represent, the broad cultural, political, economic, military, or social history of the Nation and from which the visitor may grasp the larger patterns of our American heritage.

2. Structures or sites associated importantly with the lives of outstanding historic personages.

3. Structures or sites associated significantly with an important event that best represents some great idea or ideal of the American people.

4. Structures that embody the distinguishing characteristics of an architectural type specimen, exceptionally valuable for a study of a period style or method of construction; or a notable structure representing the work of a master builder, designer, or architect.

5. Archeological sites that have produced information of major scientific importance by revealing new cultures, or by shedding light upon periods of occupation over large areas of the United States. Such sites are those that have produced, or that may reasonably be expected to produce, data affecting theories, concepts, and ideas to a major degree.

6. Every historic and archeological site and structure should have integrity—that is, there should not be doubt as to whether it is the original site or structure and, in the case of a structure, that it represents original materials and workmanship. Intangible elements of feeling and association, although difficult to describe, may be factors in weighing the integrity of a site or structure.

7. Structures or sites that are primarily of significance in the field of religion or to religious bodies but are not of national importance in other fields of the history of the United States, such as political, military, or architectural history, will not be eligible for consideration.

8. Structures or sites of recent historical importance relating to events or persons within 50 years will not as a rule be eligible for consideration.

COLLABORATORS FOR VOLUME VI

Survey Historians (National Park Service)

FRANK B. SARLES, Jr. : COORDINATING HISTORIAN
CHARLES E. SHEDD, Jr. : CONTRIBUTING HISTORIAN
JOHN PORTER BLOOM : PUBLICATIONS EDITOR
ROBERT M. UTLEY : CO-EDITOR

Reviewing Staff (National Park Service)

Herbert E. Kahler, Chief, Division of History and Archeology
Charles W. Porter, III, Chief Historian, Branch of History
John O. Littleton, Chief, National Survey of Historic Sites and Buildings
Roy E. Appleman, Staff Historian, Branch of History
J. Walter Coleman, Staff Historian, Branch of History
Harold L. Peterson, Staff Historian, Branch of History
John W. Walker, Staff Archeologist, National Survey of Historic Sites and
    Buildings
Rogers W. Young, Staff Historian, Branch of History

Consulting Committee (1960)

Richard Howland, Smithsonian Institution (*Chairman*)
J. O. Brew, Peabody Museum of Archaeology and Ethnology
Eric Gugler, American Scenic and Historical Preservation Society
Frederick Johnson, Robert S. Peabody Foundation for Archaeology, Phillips
    Academy
Waldo G. Leland, American Council of Learned Societies
Earl H. Reed, American Institute of Architects

[255

S. K. Stevens, Pennsylvania Historical and Museum Commission
Louis B. Wright, Folger Shakespeare Library

Advisory Board on National Parks, Historic Sites, Buildings, and Monuments
(1960)

Frank E. Masland, Jr., Carlisle, Pa. (*Chairman*)
Harold P. Fabian, Utah State Park and Recreation Commission (*Vice Chairman*)
Edward B. Danson, Museum of Northern Arizona (*Secretary*)
E. Raymond Hall, University of Kansas
John A. Krout, Columbia University
John B. Oakes, New York City
Sigurd F. Olson, Ely, Minn.
Earl H. Reed, American Institute of Architects
Fred Smith, Newark, N.J.
Robert G. Sproul, Berkeley, Calif.
Carl I. Wheat, Menlo Park, Calif.

ACKNOWLEDGMENTS

The work of the National Survey of Historic Sites and Buildings profits from the experience and knowledge of many persons and organizations. Efforts are made to solicit the considered opinion of as many qualified people as possible in reaching final selection of the most significant sites. Assistance in the preparation of this volume from the following is gratefully acknowledged:

Frank Barnes, Regional Historian, National Park Service, Philadelphia, Pa.

James W. Holland, Regional Historian, National Park Service, Richmond, Va.

William T. Alderson, former Executive Secretary, Tennessee Historical Commission, Nashville.

George W. Anderson, Tennessee Eastman Corp., Kingsport, Tenn.

Mrs. Olga G. Atkins, Supervisor of Historic Sites, Trenton, N.J.

Samuel M. Bemiss, Virginia Historical Society, Richmond.

Mrs. E. S. Boyd, Augusta, Ga.

Mrs. Mary G. Bryan, Director, Department of Archives and History, Atlanta, Ga.

James T. Bryson, Councilman, Washington, Ga.

Mrs. Helen D. Bullock, Historian, National Trust for Historic Preservation, Washington, D.C.

Orwin M. Bullock, Jr., American Institute of Architects, Williamsburg, Va.

Mrs. Joseph R. Caldwell, Athens, Ill.

Roderick H. Cantey, Kershaw County Historical Society, Camden, S.C.

Miss Gertrude S. Carraway, Director, Tryon Palace Restoration, New Bern, N.C.

Robert D. Christie, Director, Historical Society of Western Pennsylvania, Pittsburgh.

Mrs. Frank Cogan, Executive Secretary, Antiquarian and Landmarks Society, Inc., of Connecticut, Hartford.

Albert B. Corey (deceased), State Historian, Division of Archives and History, Albany, N.Y.

Albert S. Davis, Jr., Trustee, Washington Campground Association, Somerville, N.J.

Leon deValinger, Jr., State Archivist, Public Archives Commission, Dover, Del.

Mrs. John C. Digges, White Post, Va.

Harold J. Dyer, Director of State Parks, Augusta, Maine.

J. H. Easterby (deceased), Director, South Carolina Archives Department, Columbia.

Mrs. S. Henry Edmunds, Executive Secretary, Historic Charleston Foundation, Charleston, S.C.

Lawrence J. Flynn, Director, Vacation/Travel Promotion, Massachusetts Department of Commerce, Boston.

Henry N. Flynt, President, Heritage Foundation and Pocumtuck Valley Memorial Association, Deerfield, Mass.

James W. Foster, Director, Maryland Historical Society, Baltimore.

Malcolm Gilman, State President, the New Jersey Society, Sons of the American Revolution, Red Bank.

Ralph P. Grant, Kingsport, Tenn.

C. E. Gregory, former Director, Georgia Historical Commission, Atlanta.

John J. Grove, Coordinator, Point State Park, Pittsburgh, Pa.

L. F. Hagglund, Middlebury, Vt.

Dr. & Mrs. Richard Hanckel, Charleston, S.C.

Elmore Hane, Columbia, S.C.

H. Hobart Holley, Quincy Historical Society, Quincy, Mass.

Richard H. Howland, former Executive Director, National Trust for Historic Preservation, Washington, D.C.

Mr. and Mrs. G. E. Hoyt, Oakley, S.C.

Mrs. Daniel Elliott Huger, Charleston, S.C.

Miss Bessie Lewis, Pine Harbor, Townsend, Ga.

Marshall T. Mays, President, Greenwood County Historical Society, Greenwood, S.C.

Miss Helen G. McCormick, Director, Gibbes Art Gallery, Charleston, S.C.

Kyle McCormick, Director, Department of Archives and History, Charleston, W. Va.

Kermit McKeever, Assistant Director, West Virginia Conservation Commission, Charleston.

Frederick D. Nichols, University of Virginia, Charlottesville.

Vrest Orton, Chairman, Vermont Historic Sites, Weston.

Leonard J. Panaggio, Rhode Island Development Council, Providence.

Earl R. Poorbaugh, Director, Maryland Department of Information, Baltimore.

Mrs. Hannah B. Roach, Historian, Elfreth's Alley Asociation, Philadelphia, Pa.

Lloyd D. Schaeffer, Alexandria, Va.

Rev. Charles J. Shealy, former Pastor, Ebenezer Lutheran Parish, Rincon, Ga.

Anthony Slosek, Curator, Oswego County Historical Society, Oswego, N.Y.

Edwin W. Small, Superintendent, Minute Man National Historical Park, Boston, Mass.; formerly Executive Secretary, Boston National Historic Sites Commission.

S. K. Stevens, Executive Director, Pennsylvania Historical and Museum Commisison, Harrisburg.

Mr. and Mrs. F. G. Stewart, Kernstown, Va.

Mrs. Amos Struble, Westchester County Historical Society, White Plains, N.Y.

Lawrence Stuart, Director of State Parks, Augusta, Maine.

J. Truman Swing, Secretary, Brandywine Battlefield Park Commission, Wynnewood, Pa.

William S. Tarlton, Historic Sites Superintendent, Department of Archives and History, Raleigh, N.C.

Russell Tobey, Director of Recreation, New Hampshire Forestry and Recreation Department, Concord.

Arthur L. Townsend, Haddonfield, N.J.

William G. Tyrell, Historian, Division of Archives and History, New York State Education Department, Albany.

Mrs. Graham D. Wilcox, Curator, Stockbridge Library Association, Stockbridge, Mass.

Col. Cooper D. Winn, Jr., Robert E. Lee Memorial Foundation, Inc., former Resident Superintendent of Stratford Hall, Va.

Richard G. Wood, Director, Vermont Historical Society, Montpelier.

LIST OF ILLUSTRATIONS

Index

[263

U.S. GOVERNMENT PRINTING OFFICE : 1964   O—689–192

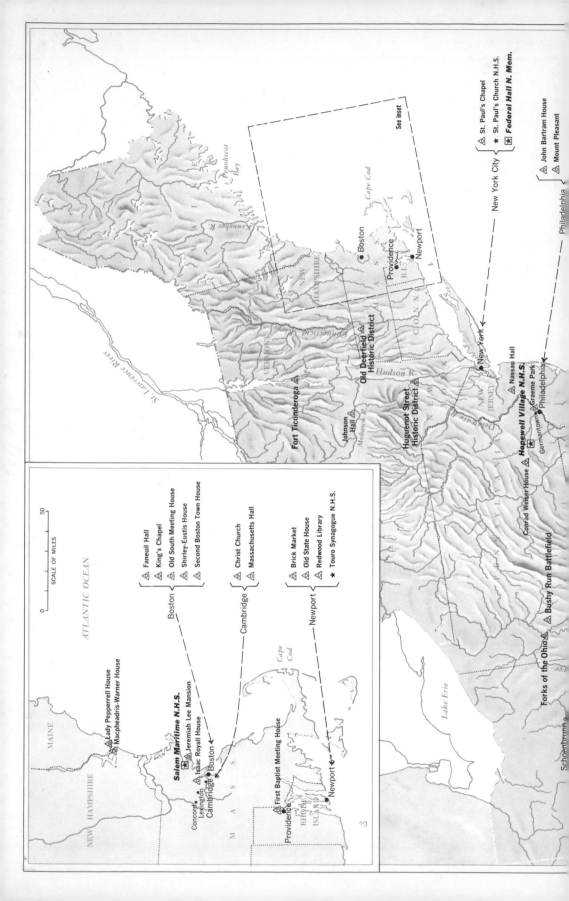